Frontispiece. Aerial view of Cressing Temple

Cressing Temple.
A Templar and Hospitaller
Manor in Essex

edited by
D. D. Andrews

Essex County Council
Planning

Dedication

This volume is dedicated to Cecil Hewett, whose work at Cressing Temple was central to his pioneering re-interpretation of timber-framed buildings; and to the memory of Mike Wadhams, who made a significant contribution to the study of Essex timber buildings.

Editor's note

The papers presented here were given at a conference held at Cressing Temple in September 1992. Many people helped to make that a successful and enjoyable day, but especial thanks are due to Lyndall Rosewarne, Roy Martin, Tim Robey, Margery Sayers, Brenda and Elphin Watkin, and to Dr R. Brunskill

This volume represents an interim statement of what is known about the site and its buildings. Inevitably, where research is on-going and problems remain unresolved, there are some internal inconsistencies and contradictions, and new discoveries have necessitated revisions to the original conclusions reached in some of the papers. In preparing the texts for the press, I should like to gratefully acknowledge the help of Pat Ryan, Adrian Gibson, Carole Smith, Terry Staplehurst, and the staff of the Planning Department typing pool.

David Andrews

ISBN no. 185281084X
© Essex County Council 1993
P. O. Milton Bsc ARICS MRTPI
County Planner,
County Hall,
Chelmsford
CM1 1LF.

Printed by ESSEX *Print* & GRAPHICS, part of Essex County Council

PREFACE

It gives me great pleasure to commend these papers about Cressing Temple. They originate from a conference held at Cressing in September 1992 and cover many features of the buildings and their surroundings. They reflect a rich recorded history stretching back over 900 years. The two great barns are of exceptional interest and importance, all the more so for having been built by the Knights Templar.

The County Council is privileged to own Cressing Temple not only because of its historical importance but because of the opportunities which the Council's ownership opens up for the people of Essex. Much has already been done to give the public access to this important site. The buildings have been repaired and a historic garden is being created, exhibitions are staged, and the site provides the setting for a wide range of events. More remains to be done and the publication of these papers is a step towards this, because to appreciate Cressing fully it is necessary to know something of its history and development. The papers in this volume show how much has been learnt in the past five years, and there is something of interest for everybody. The story of Cressing will continue to unfold, and this can only increase people's enjoyment and appreciation of a site which is of significance not only to the County but to the nation as a whole.

Kathleen M. Nolan

Mrs Kathleen Nolan
Chairman, Essex County Council

Contents

List of Figures

List of Plates

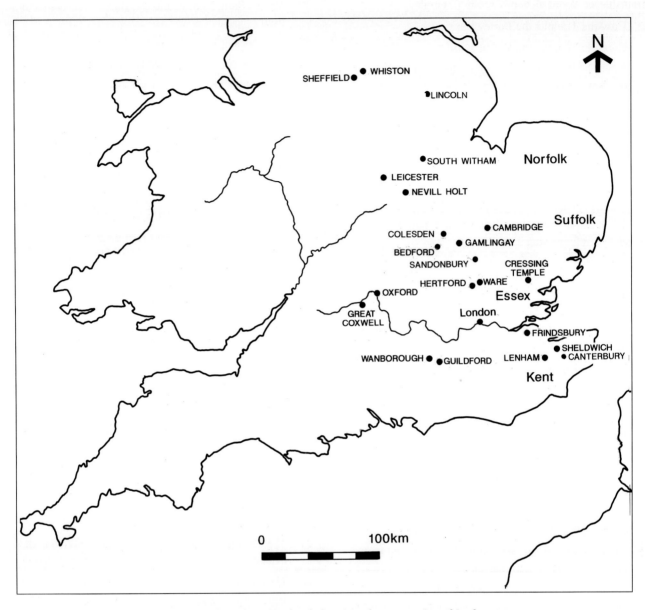

Fig. 1 Map of southern England showing places mentioned in the text

Introduction

by Vic Gray

Plate 1 Cressing Temple, the Barley Barn (photo: P. Rogers)

In the early days of 1987 Essex County Council became aware that Cressing Temple was being offered up for sale by the then owner, Mr A. L. Cullen. It was a site known already to many officers and members. Anyone who had been there recognised the charm of the setting and the magnificence of the buildings. Those who interested themselves in matters architectural, archaeological and historical knew that its attraction was more than aesthetic; that the barns had a significance far beyond the sense of respect and awe which they evoke in anyone who enters them for the first time; and that the site and its buildings would, given the chance, speak much about themselves and their place in the history and changing life of the Essex countryside over the last 800 years.

I wish now that it had been possible to chart more carefully the steps by which a twinkle in the eye - the possibility of acquiring the site for the people of Essex - was gradually translated into a campaign, then a consensus and finally into action. There are many who deserve mention, either for the vigour with which they pursued the goal or for the courage with which they agreed to the purchase of the site. For it *was* courage that was involved. The County Council

had never taken on anything quite like this before. It was, of course, the owner of historic buildings taken on in the course of inheriting or developing specific services and used as functional elements in its operations. It had also shown enlightened policies towards the rescue and preservation of threatened buildings: it had acquired wind- and watermills to ensure that they did not disappear completely as features in our landscape. It had established the Revolving Fund to restore and put back into use and private ownership buildings of historic worth. But Cressing Temple was on a different scale, not only of size but of commitment.

The deed of purchase for Cressing Temple was signed on 29 September 1987. The cost was substantially offset by grants from the National Heritage Memorial Fund, the European Community, and English Heritage. The first of these confines its grants to objects of national pre-eminence and the fact that the site was quickly and without question accepted as being of national importance was a considerable encouragement. Still more, the European Community grant lent tangible weight to the assertion which the architectural historians had made from the beginning that the

5

barns were important not just in English terms but in a wider European context. In the event, taking these grants into account, the site cost the ratepayers of Essex (as they then were) roughly the same as a three-bedroomed house in Chelmsford. No sooner had the ink dried on the deeds than the first priorities were set for the site. Predictably a detailed assessment of the condition and needs of the buildings was seen as a starting point. But if man proposes - even if officers of Essex County Council propose - God disposes. Two weeks after acquisition, on the night of 16 October 1987, the Great Hurricane struck. As if to remind the County Council of the commitment it had taken on, it lifted a horrifyingly substantial number of the tiles from the roofs of the barns.

In the event, and although it seemed an unlikely outcome on the morning after the Great Wind, this proved to be a benign influence on the shape of the programme of works which was already emerging for the site. The task of

overhauling and putting into shape the two barn roofs with their 160,000 tiles was to have been phased over 10 years. Now it had to be done forthwith and, once completed, it meant that the site's crowning glory was put in good order for the foreseeable future. Subsequent gales have failed to impress the roofs and contented themselves with throwing the cartlodge into the adjacent pond, though this has now been restored for a second time.

But if the weather has refused to be left out of the agenda for the site, planning for the future use of Cressing Temple has followed a systematic and deliberate pattern. To make the site available to the people of Essex, there were some basic pieces of infrastructure which needed to be put into place. A car-park was created outside the area of the Scheduled Ancient Monument site, at the southern end of the adjoining Dovehouse Field. Toilets were built into the buildings adjoining the Granary. Durable paths have been laid; lighting installed. Beneath the ground elec-

Fig. 2 Map of Essex showing places mentioned in the text

Plate 2   Cressing Temple, the Wheat Barn (photo: J. Hunter)

tricity has been carried to the various parts of the site. Mains water has been brought to Cressing for the first time, freeing the well, which has fed the farm's needs from medieval times, to serve the newly laid-out historic garden.

Such unglamorous details are essential if the plans for the future are to move forward on solid foundations. Those plans remain today in essence substantially as they were conceived at the time of the acquisition. Behind them there lie a number of firm statements of intent, as important in their own way as the attractions which are gradually being introduced or developed on site. They were set out by the former Chairman of the County Council, Mr Paul White, in what was called the Cressing Charter - at a time before it became impossible to walk down the street without being hit on the head by a charter. The commitments were as follows:

1. To use Cressing as a focus for the County's heritage.
2. To preserve, demonstrate and explain the skills and crafts that went into the creation of the buildings, garden and landscape.
3. To use the opportunities for learning and research offered by the site to enable present and future generations to be aware of the County's history and their personal relationship to it.
4. To make the buildings and grounds available for public use and enjoyment.

These strike me as not a bad set of guidelines for the owner of any historic site, based as they are on respect for the character and history of what has been inherited and on using that character and history as the starting point for future use. I am sure we can all think of places which would have done well to heed such self-imposed disciplines, for, once they have been breached, there is rarely a way back. In the years since 1987 the over-riding commitment to acknowledge and respect the character of the site has consistently been borne in mind by those who have charge of the use of Cressing Temple. Inappropriate uses have been discouraged and where, after the event, there have been misgivings, re-assessments have quickly taken place to ensure that the spirit of the place is not damaged. Certainly there have been occasions when sheer weight of numbers has been a problem but gradually a body of case law has emerged and provided guidelines for the future.

The goal for Cressing is to preserve its character undamaged and to develop within the complex sympathetic features which will add to the pleasure of visitors without detracting from its quiet gravitas. Already an introductory display on the archaeology of the site has been staged in the Granary. The first floor of this building has been refurbished and put into commission, initially for an exhibition, and thereafter as a lecture and meeting room. Work will begin soon on the planting of a medieval garden within the walled garden.

The barns must, of course, remain first and foremost spaces in which to breathe the atmosphere of Cressing's past and to appreciate the skills of their builders. Nothing within must detract from this. But already the Barley Barn is a popular venue for all manner of events, from barn dances to baroque bands, from plant sales to playhouse. The Cressing Temple Festival of Early Music and Drama looks set to become a much valued feature of the county calendar. Within the Wheat Barn will be developed an exhibition to describe the site and its history - from the time of the Templars to its recent history as part of the Essex seed industry. The exhibition will also embrace the challenging task of interpreting the intricacies and skills of the barns' structure, relating them to the wider context of timber-framed buildings in eastern England.

And how should we profile him or her, our future visitor to Cressing Temple? Already it is clear that there is not one, but a multiplicity of profiles, from the Sunday afternoon picknicker to the foreign tourist. Cressing is, after all, almost exactly halfway between Harwich and London and only ten minutes off the A12 with its regular traffic of visitors from northern Europe. And it is less than half an hour from Stansted Airport with daily flights from the USA. I have had the pleasure of welcoming American visitors to Cressing and watching their growing disbelief and awe at the time-spans contained in these timbers - almost unimaginable by the standards of Milwaukee or Biloxi.

Then there are the specific enthusiasts. To those with an interest in timber-framed building, Cressing will always be a place of pilgrimage. The opportunity has already been seized to use Cressing as a centre to which lovers and owners of historic buildings can come to learn more - and not just the principles and practices of the medieval builder but the hard practical modern skills of the restorer and maintainer: the making of wattle and daub, and the intricacies of thatching.

There are also those with an interest in the medieval military orders, the Templars and the Hospitallers. We must remember that these were pan-European organisations and are still of interest throughout Europe. Indeed the Hospitallers survive today, their history unbroken. There is much that could be built on here. Is it too much to imagine Cressing as one day part of a Templar or Hospitaller Trail, linked to other estates, castles and churches from England south to the Mediterranean and east to the strongholds of Cyprus and the Levant? To this may be added the garden enthusiast who will be able to watch, across the years, the moulding of a historic garden from first new planting to the mature reconstruction of the Paradise Garden of the Middle Ages.

One important group which has received considerable attention are the schoolchildren of Essex. A detailed appraisal of the educational potential of the site, compiled within the County Education Department, has highlighted a wide range of topics which could be illustrated from the site. Links with the National History Curriculum throughout Key Stages 1 to 3 (6-14 year olds) have been identified and particular attention drawn to the Core Study Unit for 11 to 14 year olds on "Medieval Realms: Britain 1066 to 1500", for which Cressing is ideal teaching material. But the report also pointed out that the opportunities were not confined to history. Maths, science, technology, art, drama, geography were just some of the areas which could be explored on site visits.

Turning now to this Conference and its place in the scheme of things, it is five years since Cressing Temple was acquired. I have outlined the developments which have taken place over that period in setting in place the physical infrastructure for the future. But there has been vigorous development too in what we could call the infrastructure of knowledge. Just as the site can only effectively be opened to larger numbers of visitors when all car-parks, toilets, services are in place; so too the history and meaning of Cressing can only properly be presented and explained to the public when the facts themselves have been carefully assembled and analysed. This has been as much the labour of the last five years as the piping and wiring and digging.

The skills that have been brought to bear have, for me, highlighted as no other project has done, the range of specialist skills which the County Council embraces and the tremendous advantage of interplay and co-operation between them. Archaeologists, building historians, documentary researchers, garden and landscape specialists have all had a part to play.

This conference is a staging point, a stocktaking of what so far it has been possible to learn about Cressing Temple. It is clear that there is a great way to go yet, that in many areas we are but scratching the surface. But it will also be a timely and, I feel sure, an encouraging reminder to those who have been involved, just how far down the road we have come. Almost everyone contributing today has other jobs to do, other preoccupations and demands to be answered, and at times it must have felt that Cressing was all too often squeezed into the odd corner of the day. Equally, there has frequently been the problem that the programme of research has been dictated by the immediate exigencies of the site. This is particularly true of the archaeological programme, where some of the most tantalising questions must remain unaddressed, let alone unanswered, while excavation has followed, like a shadow, the diggers of service trenches and the would-be planters of gardens.

As with archaeology, so with the other disciplines: one revelation opens the door upon another roomful of questions. Or, to put it most positively, one bridge crossed leads to new fields to be explored. The detailed examination of the building structures, for example, both timber and brick, has so far, quite properly, been inward-looking, geared towards understanding the site itself, its sequences and changes. But as that phase draws closer to its conclusion, the focus can begin to shift, the camera draws back and we can begin to look at the ways in which these buildings relate to and help explain others, both locally and nationally. The barns are exceptional in both their age and their size, but only by taking the next step along the road of

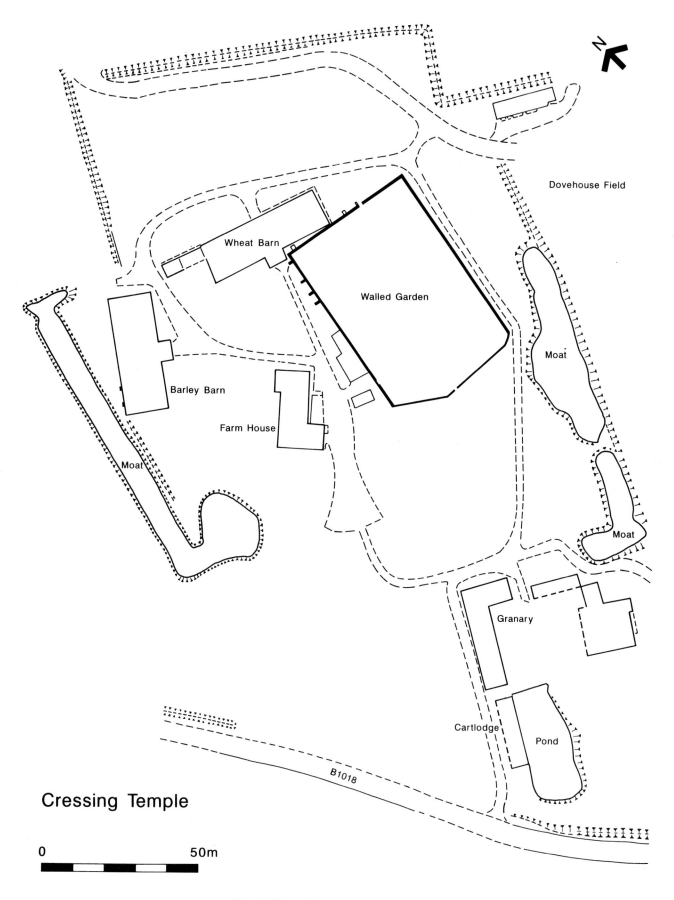

Dovehouse Field

Wheat Barn

Walled Garden

Moat

Barley Barn

Moat

Farm House

Moat

Granary

Cartlodge

Pond

B1018

Cressing Temple

0   50m

Fig. 3 Plan of Cressing Temple today

research and comparing them to other comparable if less magnificent buildings, will their full potential to teach and enlighten be realised.

Similarly, as work progresses on the historical documents about the estate and its history, we begin to glimpse the opportunity afforded to us to look at how the site relates historically to its surrounding landscape - both economically as a Templar manor in the Essex heartlands of the Middle Ages, and physically as a farmstead among other farmsteads, part of and apart from the nearby village community. So far no Essex village has been subjected to the detailed study of developing human settlement within the landscape which Cressing may offer us, having come as far as we have down the road to researching and understanding.

Human activity at Cressing Temple can be traced back at least 3000 years. The Templars came here eight and a half centuries ago. The Essex participants in the Peasants Revolt sacked the site six hundred years ago. Five years is a mere blinking of the eye in the story of Cressing Temple. Yet they have been eventful years. Hurricane and drought have made their mark on the scene. To these barns have come two members of the Royal family, three government ministers, and a leader of the Opposition.

The significance of the site on a national and an international scale has been acknowledged. Meanwhile, quietly and efficiently, the contributors to this conference with their colleagues and associates have, through their excavations, analysis and surveys, together created an underpinning for Cressing Temple, an underpinning of research which will allow the exploration to continue and the meaning of this intriguing and many faceted site to be unfolded for everyone.

Cressing Temple:
Its History From Documentary Sources
by P. M. Ryan

Introduction

In addition to archaeological excavation and the investigation of the standing buildings at Cressing Temple, the research programme includes the study of the surviving historical documents connected with the site. The purpose of this is to establish the history of the owners (Appendix 1), the buildings, the estate management and agricultural practice at what was formerly a major Templar property. The manor was transferred to the Hospitallers on the suppression of the Templars, and then became a major part of the estate of one of the New Men of the 16th century on the dissolution of the monasteries. Documents from both the medieval and post-medieval periods have been located in the Public Record Office, the British Library, the Essex Record Office and the Leicestershire Record Office. Transcriptions of a number of the medieval documents have already been published (cf. Lees 1935, Gervers 1982).

The founding of the Order of the Knights Templars

During the second decade of the 12th century, Hugh of Payens and Godfrey of St Omer, a vassal of the great Crusading house of Boulogne, founded a religious society of knights to protect pilgrims making the journey to the Holy Land. In 1118 these knights were granted quarters in the Temple of Solomon, the palace of Baldwin II, king of Jerusalem. Ten years later, the Pope recognized the new Order as the Brotherhood of the Poor Knights of the Temple of Solomon in Jerusalem, more commonly known as the Templars.

Although the warrior-monks took personal vows of poverty, chastity and obedience, the Order soon acquired great wealth. It is estimated that they held 7000 manors throughout Europe, including fifty major establishments in England. The prime purpose of these estates was to provide revenue to finance their activities which, as they became involved in the Crusades, soon extended beyond their original purpose. Their vast European network of property led to the development of an organisation for the safe keeping and transfer of money, a service soon extended to people outside the Order (Perkins 1910a, 225).

The establishment of the preceptory of Cressing

It is uncertain when the Order was first established in England, but it may have been about 1128 when a number of Templars visited this country. Although the English headquarters was set up on the site of the Old Temple in Holborn, London, the earliest grant of land for which a date has been established was that of the manor of Cressing by Queen Matilda, the wife of Stephen and heiress of the

house of Boulogne in 1137 (Lees 1935, 145-6). In 1146-8, Stephen added the manor and the half-hundred of Witham to the estate. Further land in the adjoining parish of Rivenhall was donated by Matilda's countrymen, Faramus of Boulogne and Gilbert Fitz Mabel. Several landowners made additional gifts of property in the neighbourhood (Lees 1935, 149). The headquarters or preceptory of this estate was located at Cressing.

About 1185 an inquiry into the English possessions of the Order was carried out (Lees 1935). The returns for Witham and Cressing were combined. Stephen was named as the donor of the whole estate. It was described as being 'of five hides, one part of which is demesne land and the other rented to the men'. There is evidence in the Domesday Survey that the size of a hide in Essex was 120 acres, but as the total acreage of the men's holdings amounted to more than 851½ acres, that is over seven hides by this reckoning, it is possible that the hide referred to may have been larger (VCH Essex, I, 333 *et seq.*). Lees (1935, lxxx) suggests that the five hides may have been the geldable or taxable acreage of the estate, whilst the actual acreages of the men's holdings were given.

The medieval manor of Cressing Temple

Later documents give the acreage of the demesne land of the manor as being between 1000 to 1300 acres (Appendix 2). According to an extent of 1309, the Templars' demesne totalled 1,287 acres (Gervers 1982, 54-56). The acreage of the farms listed in a particular of the manor in 1656 amounted to 1,213 acres (ERO D/DAc 96 and 101; Appendix 3). In the mid-19th century, 1,310 acres of land were described in the tithe commutation surveys of Cressing, White Notley, Rivenhall and Witham as having belonged to the Templars and therefore tithe free when in the hands of the owners (ERO D/CT 109, 290, 257 and 405).

More than half of this land was concentrated in one block centred on the manor house site of Cressing Temple and extending into the adjoining parishes of Witham, White Notley and Rivenhall. Another large block lay in the northernmost parts of Cressing and Rivenhall. 'Kingswood' is included in the name of several of these fields suggesting that this was the site of the medieval woodland of the manor. Kingswood and Stablerswood were restored to the Templars in 1293 (Gervers 1982, 3; Appendix 4). They had been taken into the King's hands because 'they had been newly wasted by the sale made therein by Robert de Turville, the late master of the Order'. The third largest block of land lay close to Bulford Mill, possibly the site of the manorial watermill. The remainder was in small blocks of one or two fields scattered throughout the parish (Fig. 6).

Some idea of the medieval organisation of the Cressing

estate can be had from the surviving documents. The demesne land supplied the Order with provisions and income from the sale of crops and livestock. The remainder of the manor was held by two types of tenants - the 'free tenants' and the 'customary tenants'.

The 'free tenants' paid money rents although those with the largest free holdings were also obliged to do 'boon-works' at ploughing and harvest time. In 1185, these holdings ranged in size from the largest, which consisted of 'two virgates, a field called Ravenstock and a meadow', to the smallest with only a house. The smaller holdings tended to be those of artisans or tradesmen, including a mason, a thatcher, a smith, a skinner, a shepherd and a baker.

The 'customary tenants', the majority of whom in 1185 had holdings of ten acres, paid less in money rents but more in labour services. They were required to work on the demesne land for three days every week from the beginning of August to the end of September, and two days every week during the rest of the year. In addition, they had boonwork obligations during the ploughing and harvesting seasons, and carrying services to Maldon every Saturday, and to London twice a year.

Whilst the 1185 inquisition combines the Cressing and Witham returns, a mid-13th century rental lists the Cressing, Witham and Rivenhall parts of the estate separately (PRO DL 43/14/1). Thirty 'free tenants' and about sixteen 'customary tenants' had holdings in Cressing. According to this document, three 'dayworks', that is the labour services required weekly of a 'customary tenant' at harvest time, amounted to reaping an acre of peas and beans or spreading manure on an acre of land. Driving the pigs from Cressing to the Templars' property at West Hanningfield or back counted as one daywork.

The 13th century was a period of economic expansion and many estate owners developed new towns. The Templars recognized the commercial potential of that part of their estate through which the main London to Colchester road passed. They obtained a grant for a weekly market from King John in 1212, and laid out the plots of their new town of Wulvesford along that road in the area now known as Newland Street in Witham (Gervers 1982, 6). It has been suggested that this not only provided additional income from the rents and market tolls but also a new market for their agricultural produce (Britnell 1968, 18). The subsection of the mid-13th century rental in which the new development is listed is easily identified for the majority of holdings are half acre plots with a smaller number of double plots of one acre and a few larger plots (PRO DL 43/14/1). Many of the tenants names indicate a craft or trade occupation e.g. John the taylor, Henry the baker, Constance the glover, John Pottesmonger, Adam Saltster, Hugo the merchant, Reginald the butcher, Geoffrey the sawyer and Geoffrey the cooper.

The suppression of the Templars in 1312

In the late 13th century the popularity of the Templars waned and they fell out of favour with some of the most influential European heads of state. Their extensive privileges and immunities fostered jealousy and ill-feeling amongst both the ecclesiastical and secular authorities (Perkins 1910a, 209-230). Their money-lending activities, notorious pride and secrecy did little to increase their popularity. Philip IV of France and Pope Clement V were amongst the leaders in the campaign for their suppression. Philip was deeply in debt to the Order and their refusal to admit him to their membership must also have done little to improve his feelings towards them. In 1307, he ordered the arrest and examination under torture of all the Templars in France in order to obtain incriminating admissions. They were accused of blasphemy, idolatry, heresy, devil worship and witchcraft. Edward II arrested the English Templars in the following January. Although he forbade the use of torture in the inquisition which followed, he confiscated their estates and used their assets to pay off his own debts. The Templars' enemies were finally successful in their attempts to discredit the Order, and in 1312 Pope Clement ordered its dissolution and decreed that the Templar estates should be handed over to the the Knights of the Order of St John the Baptist of Jerusalem, commonly known as the Hospitallers.

The confiscation and eventual transfer of the Templars' property to the Hospitallers generated a considerable amount of documentation. An extent or statement of the assets and obligations of the Templars' Cressing and Witham estate dated 1309 is included in the Hospitallers' Cartulary (BL Cotton MS. Nero E VI, see Gervers 1982, 54). It lists the assets at Cressing as the capital mansion house and associated buildings, two gardens, a dovecot and a chapel with a cemetery for the burial of the brothers in the manor close. A watermill and a windmill also belonged to the manor. The land, 1287 acres in all, included 1,115 acres described as 'profitable land' (terra lucrabili), 16 acres of meadow, 52 acres of pasture and 104 acres of wood, from which 10 acres of underwood could be cut and sold every year. The cash rents and the value of the labour services are also given. The total income was estimated at £43 16s 9d. The outgoings, £14 14s 0d, included various obligations, amongst which were the upkeep of three chaplains who said masses for the souls of benefactors, the provision of lamps and candles in the Cressing chapel, and the cost of bread and wheat given to 'all the poor people who came to Cressing Temple on three days every week.'

Little is known about the size of the Templar household at Cressing at the time. In 1308, there were only 144 Templars in the British Isles. It has been estimated that approximately twenty were knights, sixteen priests and the remainder were serving brothers or sergeants, common men engaged in the agricultural administration and work of the estates (Perkins 1910b, 255). In his study of the Templars' wealth in England, Perkins suggested that the English branch of the Order was valuable chiefly for the revenue it produced and that the majority of the estates were equipped in the same manner as the ordinary manorial household.

An inventory taken in 1313 in connection with the confiscation points to the household at Cressing having been relatively modest, although the farming operation was quite

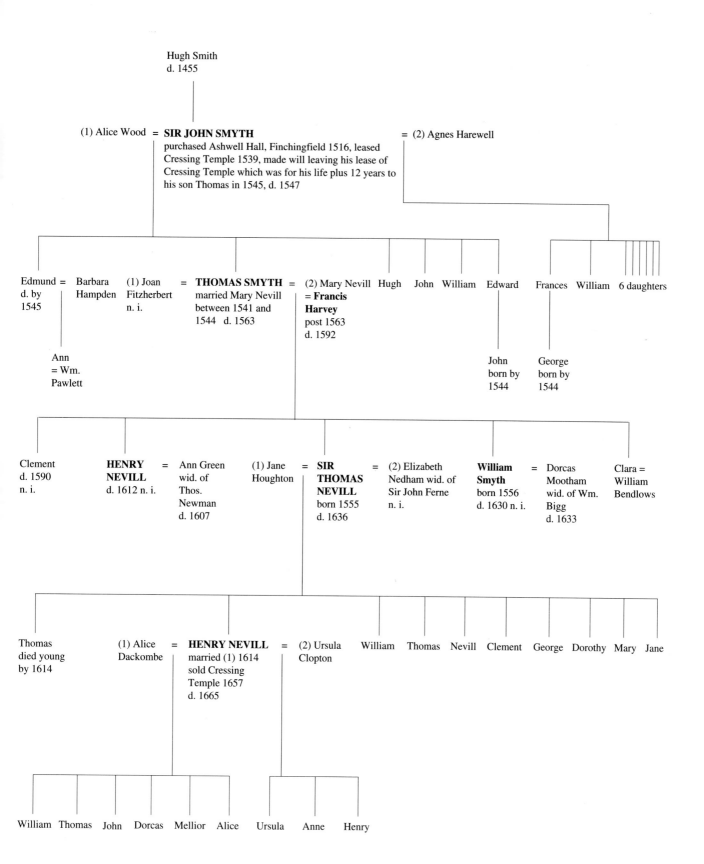

Hugh Smith
d. 1455

(1) Alice Wood = **SIR JOHN SMYTH**
purchased Ashwell Hall, Finchingfield 1516, leased
Cressing Temple 1539, made will leaving his lease of
Cressing Temple which was for his life plus 12 years to
his son Thomas in 1545, d. 1547

= (2) Agnes Harewell

Edmund =
d. by
1545

Barbara
Hampden

(1) Joan
Fitzherbert
n. i.

= **THOMAS SMYTH**
married Mary Nevill
between 1541 and
1544 d. 1563

= (2) Mary Nevill
= **Francis
Harvey**
post 1563
d. 1592

Hugh   John   William   Edward

Frances   William   6 daughters

Ann
= Wm.
Pawlett

John
born by
1544

George
born by
1544

Clement
d. 1590
n. i.

**HENRY
NEVILL**
d. 1612 n. i.

= Ann Green
wid. of
Thos.
Newman
d. 1607

(1) Jane
Houghton

= **SIR
THOMAS
NEVILL**
born 1555
d. 1636

= (2) Elizabeth
Nedham wid. of
Sir John Ferne
n. i.

**William
Smyth**
born 1556
d. 1630 n. i.

= Dorcas
Mootham
wid. of Wm.
Bigg
d. 1633

Clara =
William
Bendlows

Thomas
died young
by 1614

(1) Alice
Dackombe

= **HENRY NEVILL**
married (1) 1614
sold Cressing
Temple 1657
d. 1665

= (2) Ursula
Clopton

William   Thomas   Nevill   Clement   George   Dorothy   Mary   Jane

William   Thomas   John   Dorcas   Mellior   Alice   Ursula   Anne   Henry

Those indicated in capitals were owners of Cressing Temple [Those shown bold described as 'of Cressing Temple']

*Fig. 4 Family tree of the Smyth/Nevills of Cressing Temple, Essex,
and Nevill Holt, Leicestershire*

Plate 3 Nevill Holt Hall, Leicestershire, formerly the seat of the Nevill family (photo: J. Ryan)

substantial (PRO E 154/1/11). It is possible that the royal keepers may have sold or used some of the goods left on the site, although evidence from other locations does not indicate an extravagant life style (Perkins 1910b, 254). The contents of the chapel included several vestments and service books, a legend or history of the saints, and another of the Templars. Altar vessels and furnishings were of brass and pewter. Rooms listed in the inventory appear to be no different to those of other manor houses of the period. They included two chambers, one described as at the chapel end, the hall furnished with two tables, two forms, a ewer and a bell, a pantry, a buttery, a kitchen, and a larder. The bakehouse contained equipment for baking bread, whilst the contents of the brewhouse consisted of two coppers, eight large tubs and ten others, a lead cistern and four casks. The dairy was equipped for making butter and cheese. There was a cider mill and press. A number of old carts, ploughs, harnesses and a variety of implements and tools were found in the smithy. Timber and 3,000 tiles, valued at £2, were found in a storehouse. The granary was empty except for some old lumber. The great barns are not mentioned, but as the inventory was made in May they were probably empty. (Only rooms and buildings which contain items to be appraised are included in inventories.)

The livestock included twenty-five bullocks, eighteen oxen used as draught animals, nine cows, four heifers and five calves. The sheep, which provided not only meat and wool but were milked for the production of cheese, totalled 572 animals of various ages and sexes. One boar, three sows, seventeen other pigs and thirty six piglets, six old geese, eight goslings, one rooster, six hens, two peacocks

Plate 4 Monument in Witham church to Mrs Mary Harvey,wife of Francis Harvey JP, formerly widow of Thomas Smyth Esq of Cressing Temple, and only daughter of Sir Thomas Nevill of Nevill Holt, Leicestershire, who died in 1592 (photo: J. Ryan)

and seven peahens, the only indication of possible high living at Cressing, and a hive of bees completed the list.

The arable land totalled 601 acres, of which 252 acres were sown with wheat, 16 acres with beans, 80 with peas, 25 with dredgecorn and 175 with oats. 53 acres lay fallow.

Witham was a smaller establishment. However its livestock included one cart horse and nineteen young horses, in addition to a small herd of cattle and a flock of 239 assorted sheep.

The Hospitallers at Cressing

The Hospitallers, founded in the mid-11th century, were the oldest of the military orders. Their vows required them to put their healing duties before their military duties. They wore black habits with the familiar white cross associated today with the St. John's Ambulance Brigade.

It was only with considerable difficulty that the Hospitallers obtained possession of the Templar lands, and in some instances they were unsuccessful. However, according to Philip de Thame's report on the resources of the Knights Hospitallers in England in 1338, their Cressing estate included 800 acres of arable land and pasture for 32 cattle and 600 sheep (Larking and Kemble, 1968, 108-90). The deductions for food and clothing suggest that at that time the household consisted of a brother warden and his companion, both of whom were chaplains, three other chaplains, a steward, a baker, a cook, a cellarer, two lads

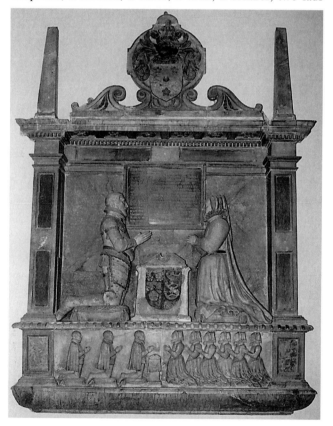

Plate 5 Monument in Tolleshunt D'Arcy church to Sir Thomas D'Arcy of Tolleshunt D'Arcy, who died in 1593, and his wife Camilla who later married Francis Harvey of Cressing Temple (photo: D. Andrews)

and two pages.

The Peasants' Revolt

The third quarter of the 14th century was a period of considerable unrest, which as a result of a substantial increase in the already unpopular poll tax, culminated in the Peasants' Revolt in 1381. The Master of the Hospitallers, Sir Robert Hales, was Treasurer of England and therefore a prime target for the anger of the people. A contemporary account in the *Anonimalle Chronicle* describes events at Cressing Temple on 10th June where he had 'a fine and pleasant manor ... which he had ordered to be filled with victuals and other necessities for the holding of his general Chapter, so it was well supplied with wines and suitably stocked for such an important lord and his brethren, and at this time the commons arrived at the manor, ate the food, drank three casks of good wine and threw the building to the ground, then burning it to the serious damage and loss of the said Master' (Dobson 1970, 125).

The Smyths at Cressing Temple

John Edmondes, gentleman, was leasing the manor house of Cressing Temple by the third decade of the 16th century. He was a wealthy man, assessed on £150 of goods, an exceptionally high sum, in the Lay Subsidy Return of 1523 (PRO E179/168/174). In 1532 he bequeathed the remainder of his lease to his son John of the Middle Temple (PRO PROB 11/24). No evidence has been found which establishes whether he was the first to lease the property from the Hospitallers.

Sir John Smyth, a Baron of the Exchequer of Henry VIII, obtained the lease in 1539. According to his will proved in 1547, he left both his household goods in Cressing Temple and his lease of the property, which was for the term of his own life and twelve years afterwards, to his son, Thomas (LRO DE 91/53). In 1541, a year after the suppression of the Hospitallers, Cressing Temple had been granted to Sir William Huse (Morant 1768, II 113). It is uncertain when the Smyths became the owners. Thomas Smyth, the son of John, married Mary, only daughter of Sir Thomas Nevill of Nevill Holt in Leicestershire (Plate 3). He died in 1563 and his widow subsequently married Francis Harvey, who, on his wife's memorial in Witham church described himself as 'one of the honorable band of Gentlemen Pensioners to the Queen's most Excellent Majesty' who with his wife had 'kept house in worshipful estate and credit at Cressing Temple in the County of Essex the space of XXVII years' (Plate 4). He took a prominent part in local affairs acting as a Justice of the Peace for many years. Francis appears to have retained occupation of Cressing Temple although he married Camilla, the widow of Sir Thomas D'Arcy of Tolleshunt D'Arcy in Essex, a year or two after Mary's death in 1592 (Emmison 1978, 210; Plate 5). He died in 1604.

After the death in 1590 of Mary's natural half brother, Humphrey Blunt, her eldest surviving son, Henry, assumed the name of Nevill in order to fulfil the inheritance conditions of his maternal grandfather's will. This has been the

Plate 6 Monument in Cressing church to Ann, wife of Henry Smyth (also Nevill) of Cressing Temple, who died in 1607 (photo: J. Ryan)

source of considerable confusion as many members of the family continued to use the name Smyth. Henry's wife Anne died in 1607 and is buried in Cressing Church (Plate 6). He took up residence in the family seat at Nevill Holt in Leicestershire, and in 1612 commenced proceedings to settle Cressing Temple on his youngest brother, William, for life. Henry died before the business was completed and his next brother and heir, Thomas, finalised the settlement (LRO DE 221/6/2/7).

In 1626 William Smyth was given permission by the bishop of London to continue holding services in 'a Chappell or Oratorie belonging unto his Manner or dwelling house of Cressing Temple in length about tenne yards and in breadth six yards and more'(GLRO DL/C 342, f20l). William died in 1630 and his wife Dorcas three years later. Sir Thomas Nevill was succeeded by his son Henry in 1636 (Plate 7).

The Nevills and the Civil War

Being Roman Catholics, the Nevills supported the Royalists in the Civil War. Henry Nevill was taken prisoner in the early stages of the struggle. Two of his sons, William and Thomas, were officers in the King's army (Broughton 1985, 26).

In March 1645, Henry was fined £6,000 and threatened with confiscation of his estates in the case of non-payment. He appears to have found the necessary money, but ten years later, in 1656, sought permission to sell his Essex property in order to pay his debts which included two mortgages on Cressing Temple, one with Hugh Audley, Esq., of

the Inner Temple for £10,000 and another with the Lady Judith Carey and Anne Carey for £2,000 (Cal State Papers, Committee for Composition 1643-46, 863; idem 1654- 59, 3262; LRO DG5 594).

The sale of Cressing Temple in 1657

A document in the Essex Record Office headed 'Particular of Cressing Temple' and dated 1656, was probably drawn up in connection with the proposed sale (ERO D/DAc 96; Appendix 3). It commences with 'the Temple farm with a good dwelling house, 2 great barns, stables malthouses corne chambers and all other conveniences in the occupation of Samuel Ellis', and then lists the fields in the vicinity of the manor house. A second document written on the same type of paper and in the same hand, although endorsed White Notley in a different hand, contains particulars of the remainder of the Nevills' Cressing estate (ERO D/DAc 101). It concludes with 'Besides all this the Mannor House with the gardens and orchards, dovehouses and fishponds and all conveniences belonging to it not mentioned before in the particular'. The similarities and internal evidence in the two documents indicate they are parts of one 'Particular'. It establishes that in addition to the manor house there was also a farm house at Cressing Temple by the mid-l7th century.

In 1657 James Winstanley, Edward Sedgewick and George Tuke entered into an agreement to purchase the

Plate 7 Monument in Nevill Holt church to Sir Thomas Nevill, son of Mary Nevill and Thomas Smyth, who died in 1636 (photo: J. Ryan)

property for £21,000. The timber was to be cut, the estate sold as soon as possible, the mortgages paid off and the resultant profit or loss shared amongst the partners (LRO DG5 594). George Tuke was to take up residence in the mansion in order to facilitate the business of selling the property. His relative, John Evelyn, the diarist, visited him there during Christmas and New Year 1659 and recorded the fact that although there was a chapel in the house they were unable to attend services because of the incumbent's death (Bray 1907, 335).

The partners had to break up the estate in order to sell it (LRO DG5 596, 606, 599, 607, 610 and 632). It is uncertain how Sir Thomas Davies acquired part of the property, including the mansion house. He was a godson and one of the residuary legatees of Hugh Audley. It may be that the partners failed to complete the repayment of the mortgage or he may have purchased it directly from the partners or from an intermediate purchaser(Appendix 1).

It is possible that a second particular endorsed 'CressingTemple 1669' may have had some connection with the transfer of the property (ERO D/DAc 97). It begins with 'The Great House with yards, gardens and orchards and 30 acres of pasture'. Details of 'a large farm house with 410 acres of rich land let to Samuel Ellis' in addition to several smaller farms are included. The document concludes with 'a brewhouse and a dairy, two dovehouses well stocked, a very fine malting office, granaried above quit through, and faire stables, and a coach house above one hundred foot in length and granaried above quit through'. The barns are not mentioned, probably because they were included in Samuel Ellis's lease.

There is no entry for the Great House in the Hearth Tax return for 1662, perhaps because it was unoccupied. Some indication of its size is suggested in the lists for 1671 and 1673 when Sir Thomas Davies was assessed on twenty and eighteen hearths respectively (ERO Q/RTh 1, 5 and 7). Relatively few of the larger houses of the Hearth Tax period have survived, and most of the survivors have undergone considerable alterations. Rochford Hall, listed as having thirty-two hearths, Ingatestone Hall with thirty, and Horham Hall near Thaxted with twenty-six, have all been reduced in size. Spains Hall, Finchingfield, with twenty hearths, Dynes Hall, Great Maplestead, with eighteen, and Layer Marney Towers with nineteen, have had some additions.

The 18th century to the present day

No evidence has been found in conection with the demolition of the Great House. Morant, the Essex historian, writing in the 1760s, reported that Sir Thomas's eldest son, Thomas, shot himself at Cressing Temple (Morant 1768, II, 114). Herman Olmius, a wealthy Dutch merchant who resided in the parish of St Peter's le Poor, London, was building up an estate in this part of Essex in the early years of the 18th century and bought Cressing Temple from Thomas Davies' brothers in 1703.

A map of 1794 shows the barns, the present farmhouse, the walled garden, the cartlodge and the present Granary,

but there is no sign of the Great House (Plate 8).

Throughout the 18th and 19th centuries Cressing Temple was owned by descendants of Herman Olmius but was leased to tenants (ERO D/P 30/3/6, Q/RPl passim). The Grimwoods, a substantial farming family, rented the farm from 1758 to 1842. Jeffrey Grimwood, who died in 1842, purchased a number of small farms and cottages in the neighbourhood. The details of his will suggest he was a wealthy man (ERO D/DO T39O; D/DO B21/7-ll; D/DBw M189).

In 1882 Cressing Temple became the property of Mrs Ford (ERO A 6815). After her death it was sold to Mr F J Cullen, a prominent Essex seedsman, in 1913. During the Cullens' period of ownership, much of the land was used for growing seeds. On the retirement of Mr A Cullen the property was sold, and the house, farmyard and adjoining Dovehouse Field were purchased by the Essex County Council in 1987.

Discussion

Harvey (1991) has recently drawn attention to the problems in using documentary sources for the history of landscape. Similar problems have been encountered in this study of the history of Cressing Temple.

Omissions in the record can encourage us to leap to conclusions which may not be correct. Cressing is one of the few parishes in Essex for which there appears to be no Domesday entry. The largest Witham manor, which was in the king's hand in 1086, was rated as being five hides. The inquest into the Templars' lands of 1185 rates the combined manors of Witham and Cressing also as five hides, thus suggesting that Cressing was included in the Witham entry in 1086.

Anomalies in documents can lead to confusion. Such a problem arises in connection with the parish church of Cressing. Matilda's grant in 1137 included the *ecclesia eiusdem vill*, or church of the vill, and Stephen confirmed the grant of the manor with the advowson of the church of the manor in 1152-54. Despite this no church is mentioned in the Witham/Cressing entry of the 1185 Inquest. Stephen's grant of the manor of Witham to the Templars in 1146-1148 specifically excluded the church of Witham and its appurtenances because it had been given to the canons of St Martin le Grand.

A 14th century copy of an ordinance dated 1223 records that as a result of a dispute between the Dean and the Canons of St Martin le Grand, vicars with responsibility for the church at Witham and for the chapel at Cressing would, in future, be appointed by the Bishop of London (LRO DE 221/10/3/6). On the dorse of this document is a memorandum of the founding of the chapel of Cressing by Elphelinus atte Gore and his wife Lovelok, but no date is given. Another document dated 1312 refers to the 'chancel of the church or chapel of Cressing'*(cancellum capello seu ecclesia)* (LRO DE 221/10/3/5).

In his guide to Witham parish church, Henderson (1986) quotes Westminster Abbey Muniments in recounting how the inhabitants of Cressing in Witham appealed to

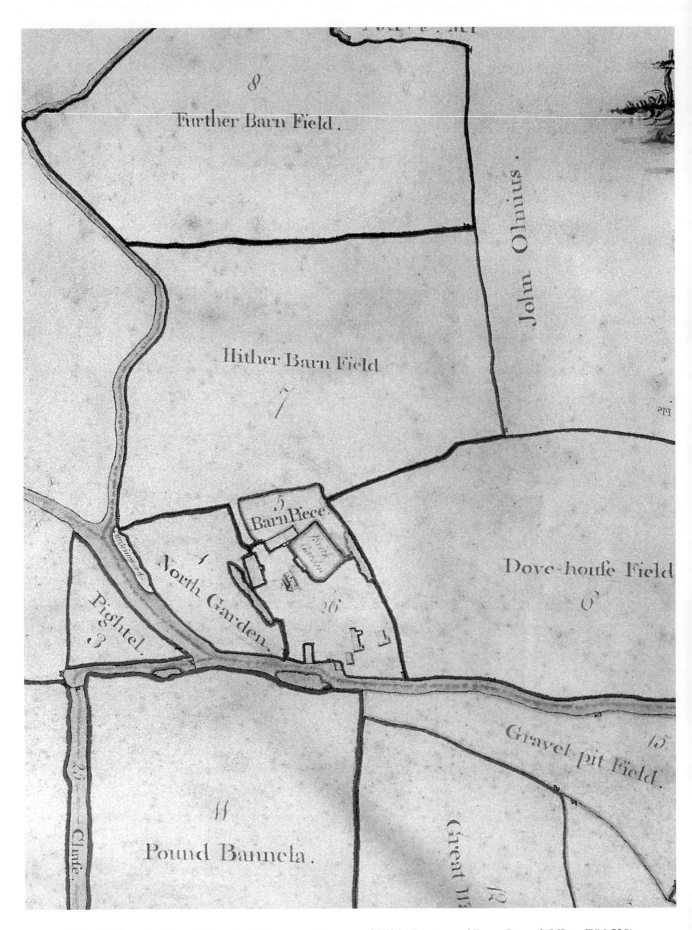

Plate 8   Cressing Temple farmstead from an estate map of 1794 (Courtesy of Essex Record Office; T/M 529)

the Archbishop of Canterbury in 1448 to provide a vicar for Cressing because Sir Thomas Smyth, vicar of Witham, had refused to provide them with the services of the Church. Their children were dying unbaptised and their inhabitants dying unshriven. About 1480 the Dean of St Martins came to an agreement with the parishioners in connection with repairing the church at Cressing (LRO DE 221/10/3/14).

As to records connected with the chapel at Cressing Temple, two years after Matilda's initial grant, a papal bull permitted the Templars to have their own chapels and burial grounds. The 1309 inquiry into the Templars' possessions at Cressing, whilst including 'a chapel dedicated to the Blessed Virgin Mary with a cemetery for the burial of the brothers', expressly states that they had no ecclesiastical benefice.

Was there a mistake in the documentation when Matilda made her grant to the Templars, reference being made to a church which did not exist? Alternatively, did the Templars convert the original church of Cressing into their own private chapel, prompting Elphelinus and Lovelock to found a chapel? To these important questions regarding the churches at Cressing there are as yet no clear answers.

Technical terms can cause problems. What did the appraisers mean by 'profitable' *(lucrabili)* land' in the 1309 extent? Because the total acreage of land in the 1309 extent is approximately similar to that in the 17th century particular of the manor of Cressing and the land listed as Templar land in the tithe awards, it has been assumed that it was the demesne land which was either worked by the Templars or leased.

What is the significance of an item in the inquisition *post mortem* dated 1286 of Bartholomew de Brianzun which records his holding the manor of Kersyng (Cressing) of the Knights of the Temple by service of 51s 6d annually (Cal Inq Post Mortem Edw I, II, 378)? In *c.*1258, the total rent of just one of the free tenants, William de Standon, amounted to 50s 7d, and the annual value of assets of the Cressing estate in 1309 was £43 16s 9d minus expenses of £14 4s 0d (PRO DL 43/14/1; Gervers 1982, 54).

The simple matter of land measurements can lead to false comparisons. It should not be taken for granted that those of one period are the same as those of another. A perch of 17½ feet is referred to in one Cressing document.

Witham, Cressing and Rivenhall were recorded separately in some documents, and were combined in others, so making comparisons difficult.

The original purpose of a document must also be considered. The 1313 inventory is probably a fairly accurate record but it must be remembered that it was made four years after the Templars were arrested. Philip de Thame's report of 1338 is obviously an approximation.

The documentation connected with the sale of the estate by the Nevills and its eventual acquisition by Sir Thomas Davies presents a number of difficulties. First, it is incomplete. Secondly, in the case of draft documents it is not always possible to be certain that the transaction did take place. Thirdly, some of the transactions may have been legal devices rather than actual transactions.

Despite these difficulties, it has been possible to build up an account of the Templars' estate at Cressing and to trace the subsequent owners and many of the tenants up until the present day (Appendix 1).

The principal purpose of estates such as Cressing was to provide income from the money rents of the free tenants and from the sale of produce from the demesne land, which was cultivated during the medieval period, in part at least, by the labour services of the customary tenants. Inventories made at the time of the fall of the Templars suggest that although the agricultural economy was biassed towards arable farming with wheat, oats, peas and beans being the chief crops, animal husbandry also played an important part for a sizeable flock of sheep, some cattle, pigs and poultry were included in the list of livestock. The establishment was self-sufficient with a dairy, bakehouse, brewhouse, cider mill and smithy.

The importance of Cressing Temple to the Hospitallers in England is indicated by their choice of it as the venue for their annual general chapter in 1381.

It is a widely held view that in the late 14th and 15th centuries many estate owners found it more profitable to lease rather than farm their demesne land because of the difficulty of obtaining labour due to the reduction of the population resulting from the recurring plagues of the 14th century (Dyer 1986, 22; Cantor 1987, 15). During this period there was a trend towards commuting labour services into money rents. In 1414 the Hospitallers were still exacting these services from their manorial tenants at Cressing, but were finding it necessary to lease some of the customary holdings for lack of owners (ERO D/DBw Ql). As the cultivation of their demesne land depended, at least in part, on labour services, it is probable that it was soon after this date that they decided to lease the Cressing Temple demesne. However, no firm evidence to support this has been found prior to the tenancy of John Edmondes in the early 16th century.

The documents connected with the sale of the property by Henry Nevill to Tuke, Winstanley and Sedgewick in 1657, the break-up of the estate, and the acquisition of part of it, including the mansion house, by Sir Thomas Davies provide some information about the organisation of the estate in the 17th century. The demesne land had been divided into a number of holdings which were leased to tenants. The mansion house, stables, coach house, etc, and 30 acres of pasture, were reserved for the owner's use. The largest farm included about 410 acres, the farmhouse and the farm buildings in the vicinity of the mansion house. The other holdings varied from 232 acres to 4½ acres. The larger farms concentrated on arable farming, with only one-third of their acreage given over to pasture and meadow. Their buildings included barns, stables and malthouses. The smaller holdings consisted mainly of pasture and meadowland. All were described as being 'well enclosed with quickset hedges'.

By the mid-19th century the Templars' land was in the hands of seven different landowners, all of whom rented to tenant farmers (ERO D/CT 109, 290, 257 and 405). The largest farm, Cressing Temple Farm, included the site of the ancient manorial complex. Although the greater part of the land was described as arable in the tithe survey of 1842, the information in the farm record books kept by Jeffrey Grimwood's executors indicates that livestock played an important part in the economy of the farm (ERO D/DO B21/7-11). The l9th century Ordnance Survey maps show that the farmyard, like many others in the area, was subdivided into stock yards where cattle were fattened on crops from the fields.

The documentary sources contain no information about the rebuilding of the manor house after it was sacked by the rebels in 1381. It may have been the Hospitallers themselves who rebuilt the house; it may have been one of their tenants. Paul's Hall in Belchamp St Paul was owned by the Dean and Chapter of St Paul's Cathedral, but was considerably extended in the l6th century by Sir John Golding and again by his son Sir Thomas, both of whom held long leases of the property. It is quite possible that Cressing Temple was rebuilt by one of the later 16th century owners. The 'Great House' referred to in the l7th century documents was probably the result of several building phases.

It is still not clear when the chapel and the 'Greate House' were demolished. A chapel was still in existence when John Evelyn visited George Tuke in 1659, and the 'Greate House' was assessed on twenty hearths in 1673. A survey dated by an archivist as c.1675 refers to 'the scite of the Manor house' (ERO D/DU 191/31). Whilst this could be taken as an indication that the mansion had been pulled down, this is not necessarily so, for the wording was a common convention of the period. A mid-l7th century survey of Pauls Hall, a large part of which still survives, also refers to 'the scite of the manor house'. That the mansion was gone by 1758, however, is fairly certain for John Grimwood's lease of Cressing Temple refers to 'All that capital messuage, tenement or farmhouse and farm commonly known as Cressing Temple etc.' (ERO D/DO T390). The actual date and circumstances of its demolition remain a mystery.

APPENDIX 1
A Chronicle of Events Connected with Cressing Temple

1137	Queen Matilda granted the manor of Cressing to the Templars.
1286	Bartholomew de Brianzun held the manor of Kersyng of the Knights of the Temple by service of 5ls 6d per year (Cal Inq Post Mortem Edw 1, II, 378).
1308	The Templars arrested and their lands, including Cressing Temple, taken into the hands of the Crown.
1312	The Order of the Templars suppressed and their lands given to the Hospitallers.
1381	Cressing Temple sacked by the Peasants (*Anonimalle Chronicle*).
1523	John Edmondes assessed for the highest amount to be paid in the Lay Subsidy List for

	the parish of Cressing (ERO T/A 427/1/2).
1532	John Edmondes, gent., left the remainder of his lease of Cressing Temple to his son, John Edmondes, of the Middle Temple (PRO PROB 11/24).
1539	Sir John Smyth leased Cressing Temple (VCH Essex, II, 178).
1540	Hospitallers suppressed and Cressing Temple taken into the hands of the Crown.
1541	Sir William Huse granted Cressing Temple (Morant 1768, II, 113).
1545	Sir John Smyth made his will leaving his lease of Cressing Temple which was to expire twelve years after his death to his son, Thomas (LRO DE 91/53).
1547	Death of Sir John Smyth and will proved (LRO DE 91/53).
1563	Death of Thomas Smyth of Cressing Temple, will proved 1663 (Emmison 1978, 252-3).
1590	Death of Humphrey Blunt, natural half brother of Mary, wife of Francis Harvey, widow of Sir Thomas Smyth and daughter of Sir Thomas Nevill of Holt, Leicestershire (Broughton 1985, 7).
1591	Henry Smyth, eldest surviving son of Thomas Smyth and Mary, took the name of Nevill and succeeded to the Nevill estates in Leicestershire in accordance with the terms of his maternal grandfather's will (Broughton 1985, 7).
1592	Death of Mary, wife of Francis Harvey etc.
1593	Death of Sir Thomas D'Arcy of Tolleshunt D'Arcy. Subsequently Francis Harvey married his widow, Camilla.
1600	Francis Harvey was described as 'of Cressing Temple' in documents concerning a sale of land (LRO DE 91/38).
1604	Will of Francis Harvey of Cressing Temple (Emmison 1978, 210).
1612	Death of Henry Nevill or Smyth.
1612	Thomas Smyth, next surviving son of Thomas Smyth and Mary, succeeded his brother, took the name of Nevill and completed the settlement of Cressing Temple on his brother William for sixty years or until one year after his, William's, death (LRO DE 221/6/2/7).
1626	William Smyth of Cressing Temple given licence to continue services in the chapel by the Bishop of London (GLRO DL/C 342, f20l).
1630	Death of William Smyth.
1633	Death of Dorcas, wife of William Smyth.
1636	Henry Nevill, son of Sir Thomas, assessed in Cressing Ship Money list (ERO T/A 42).
1636	Death of Sir Thomas Nevill.
1644	Henry Nevill taken prisoner by the Parliamentarians (Cal State Papers,

Committee for Composition 1643-46, 863).

1656   Henry Nevill petitions that the decimation may be taken off his estates in Essex so they may be sold in order to pay his debts (Cal of State Papers, Committee for Composition, 1654-59, 3262)

1657   Sale of Cressing Temple by Henry Nevill to Winstanley, Sedgewick and Tuke who were to pay off the mortgages held by Hugh Audley and Lady Judith and Anne Carey, sell the estate and share the profits or losses (LRO DE 91/115; DG5 594).

1659   John Evelyn visited his cousin, George Tuke, at Cressing Temple (Bray 1907, I, 335).

1662-1663   Simon Dixon described as 'of Cressing Temple'. He had acted as agent for Winstanley, Sedgewicke and Tuke in the sale of Cressing manor, etc (LRO DG5 607, 610 and 632).

1662   Death of Hugh Audley. Thomas Davies his nephew was his residuary legatee (PRO PROB 11/309).

1665/6   Death of George Tuke (PRO PROB 11/320).

1659   Marriage of Sir Thomas Davies (Guildhall Library, Noble Coll. L'Anson MS C 78).

1671   Sir Thomas Davies assessed on 20 hearths for Hearth Tax (ERO Q/RTh 5).

1679   Draft agreement for sale of Bulford Mill, part of the Nevills' Cressing estate, by Dame Mary Tuke, widow of Sir Samuel Tuke, the executor and residuary legatee of George Tuke's will, to Sir Thomas Davies, who was one of the executors and residuary legatees of Hugh Audley's will (ERO D/DHf E3).

1680   Death of Sir Thomas Davies.

1703   Thomas, the eldest son of Sir Thomas Davies, was reported to have shot himself at Cressing Temple, and the property sold by his brothers to Herman Olmius (Morant 1768, II, 114).

1718   Death of Herman Olmius, John Olmius inherited (Morant 1768, II, 395).

1731   Death of John Olmius, succeeded by his son John (Morant 1768, II, 395).

1741   Mr Robert Marriage tenant at Cressing Temple (ERO D/P 30/3/6).

1746   Mr Samuel Frost tenant at Cressing Temple (ERO D/P 30/3/6).

1758   Mr John Grimwood tenant at Cressing Temple (ERO D/DO T390).

1762   Death of John Olmius, Baron Waltham, succeeded by his son John Drigue, Lord Waltham (Morant 1768, II, 395).

1830   Mr Jeffrey Grimwood, tenant at Cressing Temple (ERO D/DO T390).

1842   W F H Stuart, great-nephew of Drigue Billiers Olmius, Lord Waltham, owner, Jeffrey Grimwood, occupier (ERO D/CT 109).

1842   Death of Mr Jeffrey Grimwood

1844   Isaac Blythe, tenant at Cressing Temple (ERO A6815).

1852   Mr T. H. Shoobridge, tenant at Cressing Temple (ERO A6815).

1882   Conveyance by S. H. Stuart to Mrs K. M. Ford of his interest in Cressing Temple (ERO A6815).

1905   Mr Officer tenant at Cressing Temple (ERO A6815).

1913   Mr Frank Cullen purchased Cressing Temple from the executors of Mrs Ford (ERO A6815).

1987   Purchase of the medieval farm complex at Cressing Temple by Essex County Council to safeguard this internationally important site.

APPENDIX 2
The Acreage of the Cressing Temple Estate

1309 20th April. Extent of Templar land
(BL Cotton MS. Nero E IV f.303v-4; in Gervers 1982).

Profitable land (terra lucrabili)	1,115 acres
Meadow (in several)	16 acres
Pasture (in several)	52 acres
Woods (in several, of which 10 acres of underwood can be cut and sold each year)	104 acres
	1,287 acres

1313. Inventory of arable land and stock at Cressing Temple
(PRO E 154/1/11)

Wheat	252 acres
Beans	16 acres
Peas	80 acres
Dredge corn	25 acres
Oats	175 acres
Fallow	53 acres
	601 acres

Cattle and sheep		
	13 rams	
25 bullocks	44 sheep	
18 oxen	163 ewes	
9 cows	40 hoggets	
4 heifers	72 [illegible]	
5 calves	240 lambs	
61	572	

[From information contained in Walter of Henley's Husbandry, livestock was pastured on meadows, woodland, fallow and stubble as well as pasture].

1338. Philip de Thame's Report (Larking and Kemble 1857, 168)

Arable	800 acres
Pasture for 32 cattle and 600 sheep	

1656. Particular of Cressing Manor
(ERO D/DAc 96 and 101)

	A	R	P
Arable	618	2	19
Pasture and meadow	513	0	34
Woods	81	2	5
	1,213	1	18

c.1840. **Tithe Awards of Cressing, Rivenhall, White Notley and Witham, land described as Templar land**
Total acreage of Templar land

	A	R	P
Arable	1,111	1	29
Pasture	111	1	29
Woods	57	1	24
Homesteads, etc	30	0	4
	1,310	1	6

Main block of Templar land centred on Cressing Temple

	A	R	P
Arable	666	2	31
Pasture	78	2	8
Woods	37	2	11
Homesteads and occupation roads	14	1	28
	797	0	38

APPENDIX 3
Transcription of Particular of Cressing Temple Manor 1656 (ERO D/DAc 96 and 101)

(ERO D/DAc 96)
Manor of Cressing Temple

A Particular in the County of Essex 2 miles from Witham 8 miles from Maldon 9 miles from Chelmsford 3 miles from Braintree three miles from Coxall all Market Townes & about 34 miles from London well convenienced with food & water with the demeasne wood ffarme ffreehold & copyhold rents ffynes Royalties perquisites & profitts as followeth (vizt)

[In margin] in lease for 12 years newly lett The Temple ffarme with a good dwelling house 2 great barnes & stables Malthouses Cornechambers & all Other conveniences to it in the occupacion of Sam. Ellis gent rent at £300 per annum the particulars as follows.

	A	:R	:P
In primis the north grove past[ure]	03	:2	:00
Church field ar[able]	26	:3	:37

	A	:R	:P
Dovehouse Croft ar	07	:2	:24
Barnefield ar	58	:3	:12
The Higher Bennerley ar	36	:2	:20
Middle Bennerley ar	32	:1	:34
ffurther Bennerley ar	40	:0	:30
Bushey Peightell past	03	:0	:18
The Sheepcottefield ar	24	:0	:18
Upper Moores past	25	:2	:12
The Hither Lower Moores past	09	:3	:16
the furthermost moore past	07	:1	:14
the Hither Meade Meadowe	03	:3	:26
The middle Meade Meadowe	01	:3	:05
The ffurther meade Meadowe	01	:1	:25
Oxshott ar	23	:1	:04
The Impaled ground being past abateing 2a 2r the rest	80	:2	:27
The Ozier ground meadowe	02	:3	:37
Rush meade Meadow the fore Cropp but of 7a & the after Cropp of the wholle	10	:2	:12
Broade Meade the ffore crop of	07	:2	:00
in all	407	:0	:39
	£300	0s	0d

Lands unlett as followeth

[In the margin] *in the owners hands vallued att the rents*

The Further Banley past	20 :1 :39	not valued
the lower Banley	10 :2 :27	20
of Meadowe	10 :0 :00	20
Garland Marsh within 1 mile of Maldon	56 :0 :00	50
		£90

Woods about the house (vizt)
Years growth of underwoods.

		A	:R	:P
10 the 18 acres spring	01	:3	:17
8 oulld Warren spring	02	:1	:02
5 the 18 acre wood	06	:2	:02
4 Churchfield springe	01	:3	:32
3 Oxshot spring	02	:1	:32
3 Barnefield Springe	01	:2	:10
5 further Benley springe	02	:2	:08
6 Sheepcoat field wood & springe	08	:2	:14
8 Banley wood	06	:2	:16
3 Banley Springe	01	:1	:10
3 spring next little Benleys	01	:1	:04
3 spring next the highway	01	:1	:17
12 Brewets Bushes wood	08	:1	:14
7 Brewets Bushes spr	08	:1	:29
6 Crosse spr	02	:3	:18
4 Ashfield spring	01	:0	:25
4 great Ashfield Spring	02	:2	:12
4 long Ashfield spring	01	:2	:18
1 Witstock wood	04	:0	:18
5 Witstock Spring	01	:0	:18
5 Witstock longe Spr	02	:1	:18
	74	:2	:05

in wood 74 acres att xs per acre is £37

The Temple ffarme per annum	£300
The lands in hand per annum	£090
The woods per annum	£037
	£427

[On dorse]
[In a second hand] Cressing Temple 1656
[In a third hand] Mr Nevills particular of Cressing 1656

[ERO D/DAc 101]
[In the same hand as D/DAc 96]
[In the margin] *in lease for 21 yeares about 7 yeares to come* Goodman Saches ffarme with a faire house 3 barnes with stables Maulthouses & other buildings orchards gardens ffishponds & [bac]ksides with 239a of land all well inclosed in parcells with good quicksett hedges
Pasture 38a 1r 14p, Arable 169a 3r 13p, Meadow 25a 0r 10p

Rent £100 0 0

[In margin] *in lease for 21 yeares about 19 yeares to come* Widd Wades ffarme with a faire house Barnes s[tables] Maulthouses & other buildings orchards gardens backsides with 152a 2r 38p land well inclosed with quick sett hedges
Wood 7a, Pasture 42a 3r 35p, Arable 90a 3r 4p, Meadowe 11a 3r 39p

Rent £101 0 0

[In margin] *in lease for 12 yeares some tyme to come* John Bacon for Bulford Mill ffarme a house well built with barnes stables etc with Corne & fhulling Mills orchard & gardens 74a 2r 3p well inclosed with quick sett hedges
Pasture 56a 3r 13p, Arable 8a 2r 9p, Meadowe 6a 3r 32p
Rent £74 6 8

[In margin] *Nott in lease butt to a tenant att will* New ffarme with a new good built house barnes stables & other buildings newe built with 129a 1r besides a ffield called 18 acont 28a 2r 2p all well inclosed
Pasture 36a 0r 0p, Arable 89a 0r 4p, Meadowe 4a 0r 0p
Rent £56 0 0

Goodman Marsh a ffarme house & buildings orchards & gardens with 43a 3r 30p well inclosed
Pasture 41a 3r 10p, Arable 2a 0r 9p

Rent £17 3 4
Raven sen[ior] a ffarme house & buildings orchards & gardens 4a 0r 3p
Arable 4a 2r 9p

Rent £3 10 0
Raven jun[ior] the like buildings with 23a 2r 32p all inclosed
Pasture 20a 0r 5p, Arable 3a 2r 32p

Rent £7 10 0
Widowe Rushe for

Pasture 29a 3r 18p
Rent £8 0 0
[In margin] *in lease for 18 yeares to come*
The greate tythes of Whit Notley in the occupacion of Goodman Wade

Rent for 18 yeares £50 0 0
The quitte rents of this mannor per annum
Rent £25 11 2

The after pasture of Broad Meade conteyning 30 acres lett to Richard Swynburne   Rent £10 0 0

£453 11 0
£427 0 0
£880 11 0

The Copyholds to be valued as appears by the Court Rolles hath beene made of them one yeare with an other for 14 or 15 yeares
All Tymber over & above that [wh]ich must be left for repaires to be pd for likewise the [—]oth of the woods to be valued
Besides all this the Mannor house with gardens & orchards dovehouses & ffishponds & all conveniences belonging to it not mentioned before in the particular
[On dorse in the same hand as the second hand on D/DAc 96] White Notley 1656

NOTE - Whilst these two documents are indexed and catalogued separately they are two sheets of one document and the endorsement White Notley is in part at least incorrect.

APPENDIX 4
Translation of Document No. 3 included in the St. John's Cartulary for Essex transcribed by M. Gervers. (BL Cotton Nero E VI f.289; also in PRO C 66/113 22 Ed I m26)

The King to all whom etc greeting. Although by the record of our beloved and faithful Roger Lestrange and his fellows, our justices lately in eyre for the Pleas of the Forest in the county of Essex it appears that that [wood] of Our beloved in Christ the master and brethren of the Knights Templars in England at Cressynge which is called Stablerswode was newly wasted by the sale which brother Robert Turvill formerly master of the said knights made in the same wood whereby that wood was taken into our hands; and that afterwards it was found by the rolls of Roger de Clifford and his fellows, our justices, later in the court of the Pleas of the Forest in the aforesaid county, that the same wood and similarly the wood of the same master and brothers Kyngeswode were taken into the king's hand for new waste, and were not redeemed within a year and a day of the eyre of Roger de Clyfford and his aforesaid fellows and so it was judged that these woods should remain in our demesne at the second assize of the forest. We, however, wishing to show favour to the aforesaid master and brethren in this matter concede and grant to them from us and our heirs the aforesaid woods: to have and to hold to them and their successors in perpetuity those woods as they were before they were taken into our hand; provided that, nevertheless, those woods which previously were outside the regard of the forest remain within the regard of our aforesaid forest in perpetuity. In these things etc. Witnesses the King at Westminster. By patent of king E[dward] son of king H[enry] in the twenty second year.

Acknowledgements

I am indebted to the staffs of the Public Record Office, the British Library, and the Essex and the Leicestershire Record Offices for their assistance and advice; and to the staff of the Essex Library Service for their diligence in obtaining obscure requests. I would also thank Mrs Janet Gyford for drawing my attention to a number of very useful references.

The Historic Landscape of Cressing Temple and its Environs

by John Hunter

Introduction

The field systems of North and Central Essex

The parish of Cressing lies on the southern limits of the Essex Till, that bouillabaisse of surface geology: chalky clays, gravels and loess, riddled with spring lines and soils which may change their immediate nature and pH in a distance of a few yards. Settlements and their attendant field systems reflect this stew, superficially haphazard and random, and make the landscape analyst long for the seemingly rational landscapes of Midland England, with their nucleated villages, ordered ridge and furrow, and neat overlays of surveyors' roads and hedges.

Yet our Boulder Clay landscapes, despite the depredations following post-war changes in farming practices, have an intrinsic interest precisely because of their apparently haphazard quality, so far little deciphered. In 1974 I posed three landscape types (Hunter *et al.* 1974):-

1) *Direct Enclosure:* irregular ad hoc assart from woodland and waste.
2) *Early Enclosure:* slow enclosure of common fields and commons.
3) *Late Enclosure:* post-1600 field patterns with the straight lines of surveyors' T-squares.

Although an oversimplification these categories remain valid, but their proposition was at a time when the archaeologists had yet to show the extent of prehistoric and Roman clearance, the concomitant level of population and organisation of land holdings, and the residue apparent in later landscapes. Forest clearance then still appeared a post-Roman achievement. Eighteen years is a long time in landscape studies, and I would now include woodland and waste in *Early Enclosure*, and stress the medieval reclearance of lands previously farmed and then abandoned.

Perhaps much land lies in this category - a Dark Age spread of woodland following a considerable decline in population. But if so, woodlands preserve former earthworks, and ditches remain evident under woodland cover however silted. With reclearance the farmer might find it easier to dig out leaf mould than stiff clays, particularly if a part of a rational system of drainage. Continuity as a factor then must be taken into account, either directly in areas where tillage never ceased, or as a rediscovery of former features, particularly major boundaries, as populations recovered, markets for crops expanded and the wooded area shrank.

So far there is little to guide the student of historic field patterns on the Essex Boulder Clays. There are Ken Newton's incomparable studies of Thaxted and Writtle (Newton 1960 and 1970), the latter relevant to Cressing in its demonstration of a huge demesne of open, but not common, fields. Writtle was royal, Cressing the property of a powerful and dynamic international order who could afford the best professional and technical advice. To Newton's studies one must add R. H. Britnell's *Agriculture in a Region of Ancient Enclosure, 1185-1500*, particularly useful as he deals with an area roughly within a five mile radius of Witham where 'in comparison with the detailed information available concerning operations in open field of the Midland type, the enclosed system of Essex is under-recorded'. Two terms were used to describe compact areas of arable land - field and croft. A croft was a small area of up to about twelve acres, while a field might approach 200 acres in size. In practice there was overlap as some land described as 'field' was very small. Britnell considered that 'probably both field and crofts were normally surrounded by hedges'. Smallholders normally divided their land into three or more parts and operated quite small parcels of arable as cropping units; land described might be so subdivided. Large areas of common grazing lay to the south-east of the London to Colchester road on less fertile soils, particularly in the area around Tiptree, whereas in Cressing common grazing was limited to small greens in the northern half of the parish.

Area of Study

The area considered is the parish of Cressing with such parts of Rivenhall to the east where the parish division is irregular and Templar land overlapped. It also includes parts of Witham, Faulkbourne, and White Notley where Templar land also crossed the parish boundaries.

Analysis

The parish boundary (Fig. 5)

The parish of Cressing is a long tract of land bounded to the west by the river Brain. To the north it appears to have been a wooded area and follows the boundary of the Hundred of Witham. Field systems north of the boundary relate to the Roman road of Stane Street (the modern A120), and appear long cleared and farmed, except for a wooded relic called Templeborder Wood. To the south, it will be argued that the boundary is tailored to a pre-existing field pattern in the parishes of Witham and Rivenhall. Except for a strange western incursion of White Notley parish into the Templars' Bannerly Field, it is logical. On the east, however, the border is seemingly chaotic with overlaps and detachments which appear a compromise reached at some early date

Tithe-exempt land (Fig. 6)

The Cressing and Rivenhall surveys for tithe (ERO D/CT 109 and ERO D/CT 405) refer to lands exempted as formerly the property of the Knights Templar. Their exemption lay with the land and not the ownership and was forfeited if the land was leased, but regained if the land came back in hand. Clearly in the 1830s it was more profitable to let the land than avoid the tithes. Morant refers to King Stephen's gift of five hides in Witham and Cressing to the Templars, part in demesne, the other let to divers tenants. I

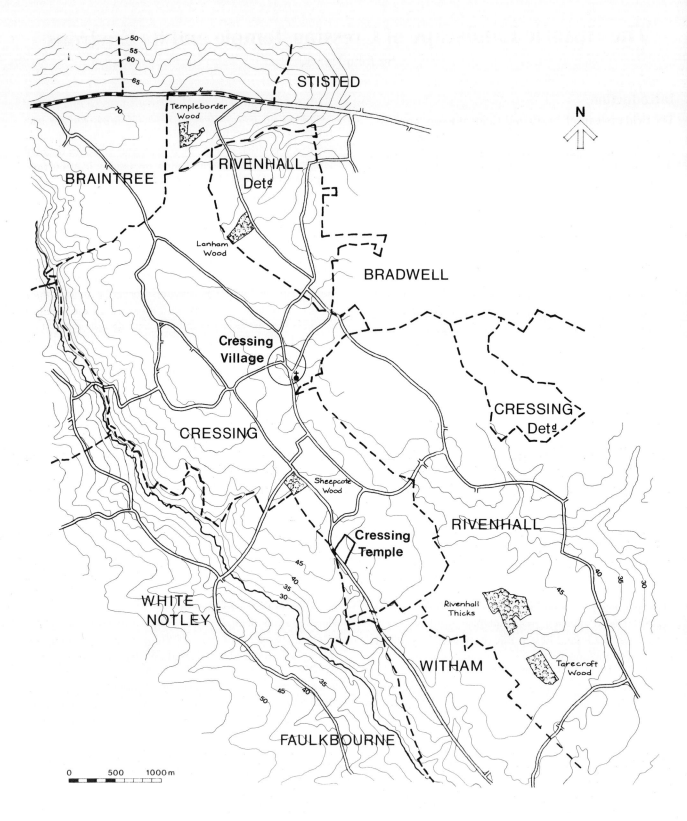

Fig. 5 Cressing parish showing modern roads and natural features (parish boundaries shown with dashed lines)

suggest that the tithe-free land refers to the former and that this is the only reasonable interpretation of the land shown on the tithe maps. So the question arises as to the date on which this valuable privilege was established. Pope Adrian IV (1154-1159) sought to claw back exemptions to the monastic orders, but refrained from doing so to the military orders, and this would seem a *terminus ante quem* for the land so defined (Ollard and Crosse 1912, 595). One can imagine the legal eagles of the time rushing to establish the exact limits of the papal exemption.

So what does this exemption show? First, a consolidation of arable fields around the preceptory - the demesne

Fig. 6 Map of the tithe exempt lands interpreted as forming the original Templar demesne (parish boundaries shown with dotted lines)

home farm. Secondly, the manorial woods in the north of the parish; thirdly scattered properties which include holdings in existing fields including lands related to a water mill and others through escheatment.

Roman Cressing

Warwick Rodwell (Rodwell and Rodwell 1986, 65-66)

describes the landscape from the Late Iron Age as intensively managed with scattered farmsteads. Dominant features were the two Roman roads, now the A12 and A120, and 'away from the main roads, in the valleys of the rivers and streams, lay the villas'. In Rivenhall lay the palatial villa partly excavated by Rodwell, but as yet no villa has

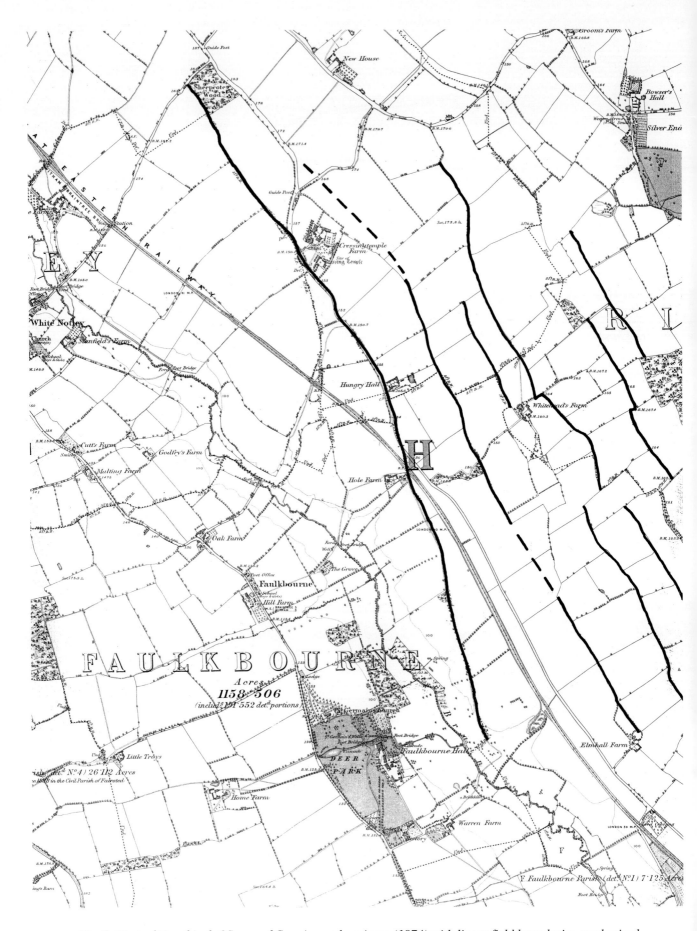

Fig. 7 First edition 6 inch OS map of Cressing and environs (1874) with linear field boundaries emphasised

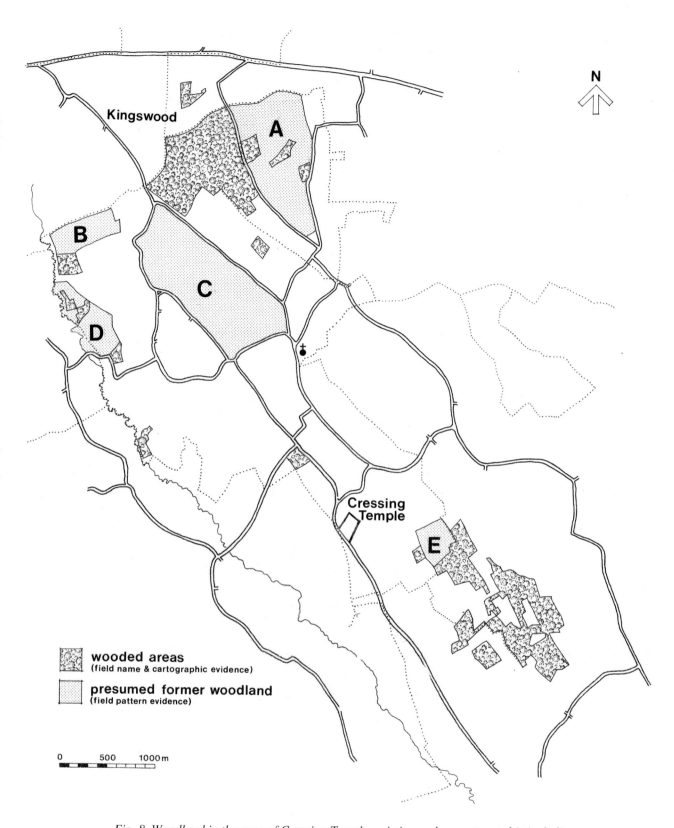

Fig. 8 Woodland in the area of Cressing Temple, existing and reconstructed (stippled)

been located in Cressing parish.

The County Council's Sites and Monuments Record lists pottery and urns along the Brain Valley and a possible Roman bridge at White Notley, but the main known foci are around Cressing church and Cressing Temple. At Cressing Temple, archaeological evidence begins with

Bronze Age ditches and continues with extensive evidence of occupation in the Roman period. Then there is a blank until the establishment of the preceptory. At Cressing village, which is situated on a watercourse (Fig. 5), there is the possibility of continuity beside the church from the Iron Age to the Middle Ages. The adjacent field contains Iron

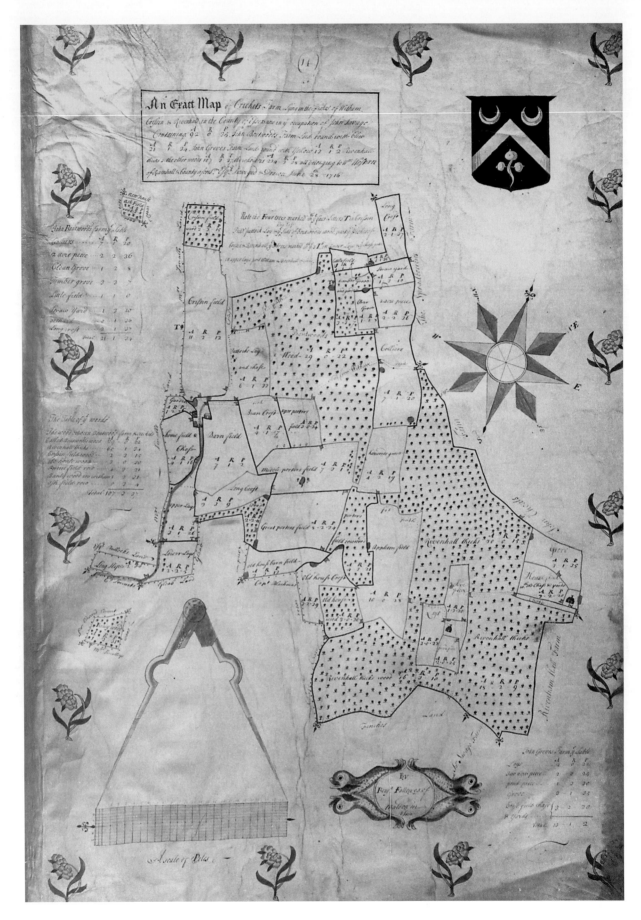

Plate 9 Map of Crickets Farm made by Benjamin Fallowes of Maldon in 1716 for William Western (ERO D/DFg P1-26)

Age and Romano-British features, including a ditch system of a 'planned' nature. Postholes found inside the church may be evidence of a Saxo-Norman building on the same site (Hope 1976, 1978, 1984a, 1984b).

Of a different interest are the parallel field boundaries south of the Temple stretching into the parishes of Witham and Rivenhall. The parish boundaries respect these fields which suggest an early origin. The boundaries shown on Fig. 7 are those recorded on the first edition six inch OS map (1874), and although there are clearly gaps and removal, they retain a resemblance to many early field systems in archaeological surveys. They indeed resemble the Ceide Fields of North Mayo (Caulfield 1978) interpreted as family farms with boundaries well over a kilometre in length and subdivided within for control of pasture and tillage. There are other examples in Britain on Dartmoor and elsewhere. The Cressing/Rivenhall field boundaries follow a ridge which parallels the Brain Valley on a north-west/south-east axis, and merge into the land and field system to the north of Cressing Temple. The wavy nature of these boundaries would have been unsatisfactory to a Roman surveyor and they have the character of planned but unskilled clearance. This perhaps takes them back into a time well before the Empire. Overlain by later woodland expansion, these boundaries re-emerge in still later farming landscapes and a few still survive.

The Extent of Woodland (Fig. 8)

The evidence we have suggests a landscape cleared and farmed in the imperial centuries and indeed earlier, possibly much earlier. The villa economy, however, required a woodland resource (Rackham 1976, 51-52) similar to that of the later manor. Moreover the flora of the surviving southern woodlands, Rivenhall Thicks and Tarecroft, indicates links with primary cover: the small-leaved lime *Tilia cordata* or pry occurs in Tarecroft and also in Lanham Wood, Rivenhall. Dr Rackham comments that pry 'was one of the commonest trees of the prehistoric forest; it is nowadays rather rare on a national scale (Rivenhall is at its southern British limit) and is strongly associated with ancient woodland. Here it occurs, significantly in or very close to those part of the woods which on wood bank evidence are the original woodland. Several stools are over 15ft across and must be several centuries old' (Rackham 1993).

Whatever the reduction in the wooded area in the Roman centuries, the collapse of the Empire saw a dramatic increase. This may be partially reconstructed from the Rivenhall estate maps, field name evidence and the nature of field patterns as recorded on the first edition six inch OS map. Fig. 8 depicts areas where:

1. woodland can be shown to have existed (areas A and E).
2. where it may reasonably be presumed (areas B and D).

Area A. Kingswood, the demesne woodlands of the manor which were the subject of a dispute in 1293. The justices in Eyre for Forest pleas alleged 'waste', to which the Master responded that the woods lay outside the regard

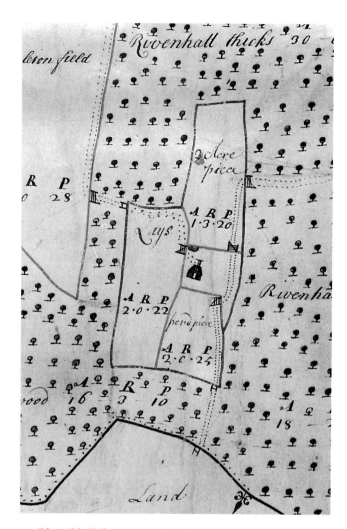

Plate 10 Enlargement from the 1716 map of Crickets Farm showing a croft of medieval origin within Rivenhall Thicks

of the Forest (see Ryan, Appendix 4, in this volume). A substantial remaining area is indicated by Chapman and André on their map of 1777. A further area is suggested eastward to the lane running northwards from Cressing village to Withies Farm. The Rivenhall Tithe Map shows two relic woods and the field patterns suggest phased early enclosure. One of these, Lanham Wood, still survives and is mainly hornbeam coppice with some standard oak.

Area B. Probably reclaimed from woodland, again by phased early enclosure. It lies against the parish boundary and an adjacent demesne field is called Lower Thrift.

Area C. Land with the field pattern character of direct enclosure from woodland, distinctly haphazard and irregular

Area D. An irregular 'nibbled' area of woodland is shown on the Tithe Map (ERO D/CT 109) and the character of the field pattern suggests phased early enclosure.

Area E (Plate 9). A patchwork of woods mostly in the parish of Rivenhall. Tarecroft and Rivenhall Thicks, which survive, have been referred to above, but the complex depicted is that shown on the fine Rivenhall Estate Maps of 1716 (ERO D/DFg 13 and 14) and the Witham Tithe Map (ERO D/CT 405) which depict the woods interspersed with

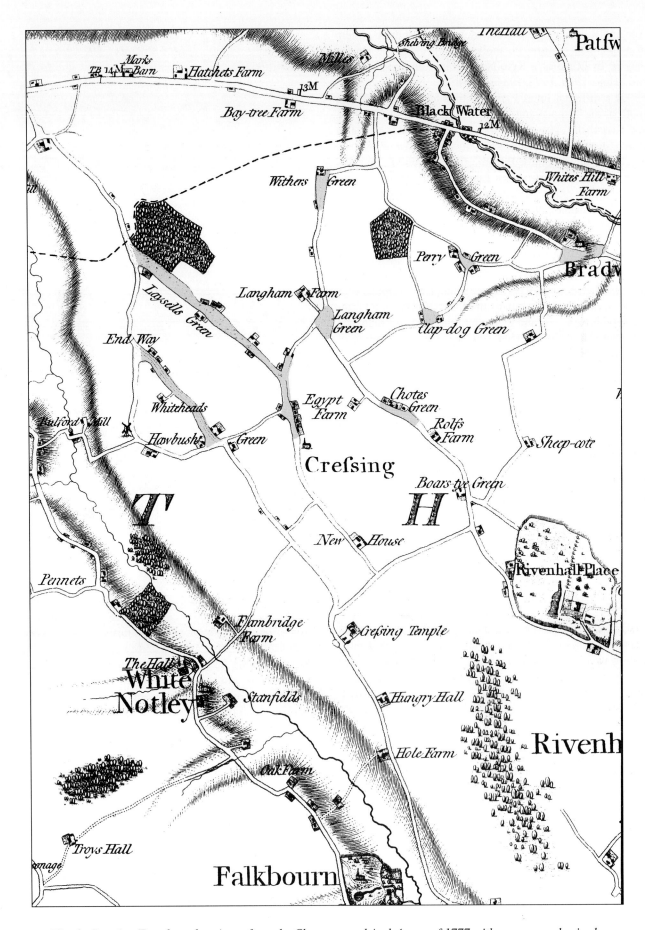

Fig. 9 Cressing Temple and environs from the Chapman and André map of 1777 with greens emphasised.

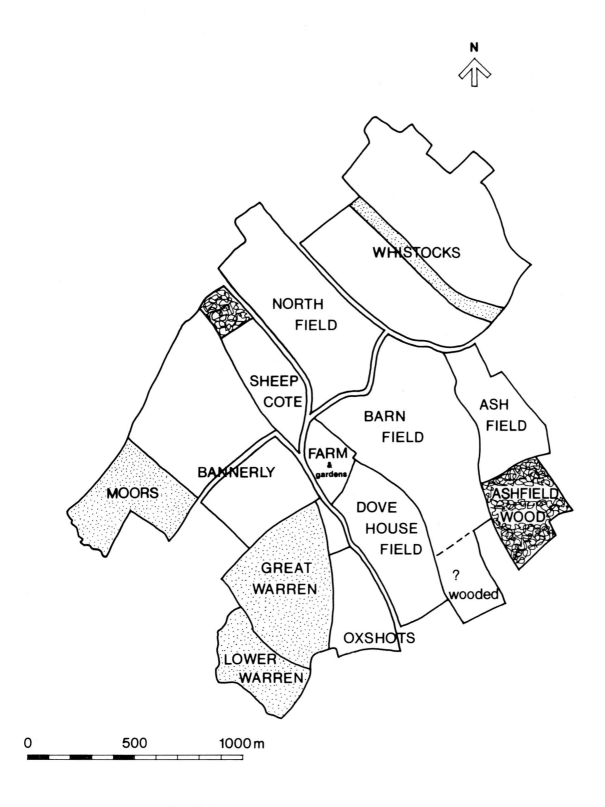

N

Fig. 10 Reconstructed map of the medieval home farm c.1300

small farms and crofts. One croft (Plate 10), formerly surrounded by Rivenhall Thicks, had three small fields, a cottage and a garden, totalling 6 acres. As a holding it had vanished by the time of the tithe map but survives as one field today - its perimeter that of the croft.

Medieval Cressing

The lineaments of medieval Cressing are depicted on Chapman and André's Map of 1777 (Fig. 9), less the extensive woodlands in the north of the parish then in the process of phased clearance. There are two main landscape types divided by a line that may be drawn just to the south of Cressing village and Hawbush Green, then due west to the river Brain. To the north it is an irregular patchwork landscape of farms and crofts in which lie all the surviving

33

listed buildings of pre-1600 date other than those at the Temple. There are two moated sites and one possibly moated, and five greens. Ashes Road and Long Green were a wide linear green known as Laysells Green. Braintree Road through Tye Green was also a linear green. Fields, as described by Britnell, occurred but were small. It was a dense, complex and well settled landscape.

To the south, the landscape appears empty of dwellings except for the Temple; the farms shown by Chapman and André are post-1500 on building evidence. Well over half of this land lay in the Temple demesne.

Further south, and concentrated mostly over the parish boundary, lay the very different wooded landscape described in Area E.

The medieval home farm

Figure 10 is a reconstruction of the medieval home farm derived by working back from the Tithe Maps of Cressing, White Notley and Rivenhall, the estate map of 1794, and the written survey of 1656 (see Ryan, Appendix 3, in this volume). Divisions within fields have been removed as being planted at a later date for more finely tuned rotations; but the boundaries would have been hedged for cattle enclosure after cropping or on the fallow (Britnell 1983, 40 and 54), and may have formed linear belts in some cases. The fields were large even by modern standards, Bannerly some 45 ha (110 acres) and North Field 31 ha (76 acres). The largest appears a common field in both Cressing and Rivenhall approaching 121 ha (300 acres) in size in which Whistocks represents a compact Temple holding. Permanent pasture lay in the Moors beside the River Brain and in meads following a watercourse through Whistocks.

Templars were forbidden to hunt, except apparently for lions (Upton Ward 1992, 33), so there is no deer park, but a considerable warren existed, divided into Great and Lower. This would seem to be the impaled ground described in the 1656 survey when rabbits were still a valuable resource and warrens were still enclosed. It lies on the sandy river terrace above the Brain, land attractive to rabbits for easy burrowing. Rabbits (known as coneys until the 19th century) were natives of Britain in post-glacial times but became extinct. Re-introduction by the Normans followed first on islands and then the mainland, in warrens and 'coney-garths'. 'There was a rapid spread of rabbits across the English mainland in the period 1230-1250; by the early 1300s rabbits were numerous, warrens were valuable and there was an export trade in skins' (Tittensor and Tittensor 1986). The establishment of the Cressing warren in the 13th century seems likely, but there is no corroborative evidence, and although estate warrens remained valuable until the late 18th century, it had been replaced by cropping by the time of the map of 1794.

A feature of the 1656 survey is the number of small woods and springs, 21 in total, and all in active coppice rotation. Mostly they are very small, less than one hectare, and named from adjoining fields. It would seem that these were the narrow belts between enclosures that one frequently finds on the older Essex estate maps and were turned over to arable or pasture when underwood lost its local and commercial value. These belts are described as springs rather than woods and resemble the Wealden shaws and the patterns one sees from the air around Gatwick Airport. They may represent strips of woodland deliberately retained when the land was reclaimed or alternatively, hedgerows were allowed to colonize outwards to a defined limit. They had gone by the time the surveyors prepared the map of 1794 (Plate 8).

It remains to consider the capacity of the barns to contain the estate crops and here I have turned to the valuable and unique research by John Weller (Weller 1986). The arable of the home farm was 666 acres (Ryan in this volume), from which 80a may be deducted for the Warren. The overall tithe-free arable was 1,111a from which deductions must be made for areas of former woodland: King's Wood 190 acres and with Lower Thrift, say, a total of 250a. This gives the following:

Home farm arable:	
586 acres, less ⅓ fallow,	net: 391 acres
Other demesne arable:	
195 acres, less ⅓ fallow,	net: 130 acres
	TOTAL 521 acres

If the warren had not then been created and the land remained arable, the total would be 574 acres. Variables must remain the extent of clearance in the north of the parish in the 13th century and the assumption of ⅓ left fallow.

Weller reckons in an average year there would be 80 sheaves per acre carted to the barns; at 2 cu ft per sheaf this required 160 cu ft per acre. The total requirement for the Temple demesne, then, was 83,360 cu ft. The sheaves would be stacked between the main posts to the height of the tiebeam, leaving the aisles free for ventilation and other storage, and the midstrey also free for threshing. The storage capacity of the Barley Barn (with its present measurements) is 46,560 cu ft (1,319 cu m), and with the Wheat Barn, of similar capacity, we have a total of 93,120 cu ft (2,638 cu m). This would store the sheaves gathered from 582 acres. If, however, the full storage capacity of the barns was required and the aisles brought into use the capacity could be increased by almost a half bringing the total area served to around 863 acres. This would easily accommodate, if necessary, a bumper year without resort to ricks.

My figures of a maximum of 574 acres arable disagree with the 1313 inventory (Ryan in this volume) which gives 601 acres, and also with Britnell's figure for 1310 of 710 acres under crop (Britnell 1983, 50). Nevertheless the fit is close and the two barns could cope with whatever harvest the estate might produce. This lays to rest the possibility of a third barn, analogous to the planning of the preceptory at South Witham in Lincolnshire (Current Archaeology). An earlier barn, however, replaced and perhaps moved, is another matter.

Discussion

A cleared and populated Roman landscape appears to have given way to one largely wooded. The speed of woodland spread on abandoned land is swift given good soils and local seed sources; 40 years may suffice as shown on south Essex plotlands. Tracts of wooded land in Ireland appear long established features of the landscape but are the result of the Famine and emigration. A degree of continuity between the Roman and medieval landscape is generally accepted and the former concept of energetic forest clearance by the Anglo-Saxon newcomers for their advanced ploughs and farming systems well laid to rest. But a population level in 1066, perhaps only half that of the Roman province, must assume a corresponding rise in woodland or wood-pasture. With subsequent reclamation, the infrastructure of former lanes and field drainage systems would be useful for an agriculture not very different in its technology from that which went before.

Granted their new manor, it would seem that the Templars avoided the existing settled area focussed on the church in the north of the manor, although they retained Kingswood for their demesne woodland and land associated with the mill (Bulford). For their demesne farm they chose a site with good surface water drainage, and laid out their field system with regard to existing trackways and former boundaries. Whether this was 'empty' land or eviction was required is a question only archaeology may one day resolve.

One would expect the best advice on efficient estate management available at the time and the plan reconstructed in Fig. 10 would represent a well organised and productive demesne on Boulder Clay land in the 13th century. The building dates of the barns should reflect the phasing of land brought into cultivation and requiring crop storage; if the land was already clear the barns would be of similar date. The boundary ditches were later enlarged to form moats or fishponds for which the natural slope was an inconvenience. New manors of a later date would seek a level site where a wide, impressive and continuous rectangle of water could be created, for example, Rookwood Hall, Abbess Roding.

The preceptory must have been a very pleasant place with its great barns, dovecots, gardens and orchards, fishponds and parading peacocks. Scattered woods and hedged fields, perhaps with the linear springs recorded in 1656, would have provided a verdant tree-covered ambience very different to today's scene of land scorched by the Agriculture Acts and elm disease. Here a retired Templar could reflect in peace on his memories of the heat, dust and dangers of Outremar and prepare his soul, hopefully, for the life hereafter.

Lines of further enquiry must lie with the archaeologists, particularly the relation of existing features with the adjacent landscape and former settlement on the site. Detailed replotting of air photographs at an appropriate scale should enable particular cropmark features to be related to the relict boundaries depicted on Fig 7. It should be possible to arrange trial trenching of such features which might provide dating evidence. Fieldwalking would be invaluable in providing an overview of the date and extent of settlement within the area of relict boundaries. Further cartographic study of the northern part of the parish to establish the extent of small fields would be of interest and a possible subject to contribute at a future conference. Then there is the matter of where the people lived who worked this large farm; if customary tenants, no doubt they were situated in the north of the parish, but if lay brothers or labourers were required in addition, their housing might be expected in or near the centre.

Acknowledgements
I am much indebted to Pat Ryan for her patient analysis of the cartographical and archival evidence on which this paper is largely based. The staff of the Essex Records Office have, as always, been most helpful, and I would also thank Catherine Greetham Cooke for her draughting of the maps.

The Archaeology of Cressing Temple

by Tim Robey

Introduction

Since the acquisition of Cressing Temple by Essex County Council in 1987, the Council's Archaeology Section has maintained an almost continuous presence at the site. Because of the importance of its buildings and long history of occupation, the area of Cressing Temple containing the moats and major buildings, but excluding Dovehouse Field, is now a scheduled ancient monument protected under the Ancient Monuments Act. This reflects the importance placed on the conservation and recording of the archaeology, especially whilst restoration and improvements are under way. The site has, however, a much longer history of archaeological investigation and there are records or finds from excavations as far back as 1934. This paper is a preliminary assessment of the results of archaeological excavations at Cressing Temple over this period, although with an emphasis on the work of the last five years.

The earliest record of an excavation at Cressing Temple comes from The Times for November 1934 (ERO D/DU 1491/1). Work on a pond (presumably that south of the road) revealed 'huge timbers and brick foundations' and refers in passing to '...[brick] remains of a subterranean kitchen... near to the site of the chapel'. A group of photographs associated with the text (ERO D/DU 1491/5) clearly shows that this is the post-medieval cellar re-excavated first by Roy Martin and later by John Hope (see below).

During the 1940s the then farm manager, Mr Bayliss, dug a trench near the western edge of Dovehouse Field from which he recovered a large quantity of Romano-British pottery. No records survive of this excavation, which apparently followed the line of a ditch from which the finds came. He also collected a quantity of medieval and later ceramics from various groundworks, all of which must be regarded as unstratified finds.

In about 1968 Roy Martin, now the site warden, carried out further excavations on Dovehouse Field. These revealed a second ditch, also filled with material containing Romano-British pottery, running almost due south from the northern edge of the field. Another trench exposed a cobbled surface associated with Roman period finds. Martin also excavated a post-medieval brick drain running northeast across the area east of the walled garden, as well as the cellar mentioned above.

The first major excavations at Cressing Temple were carried out between 1978 and 1980 by the Brain Valley Archaeology Society (BVAS) under the direction of John Hope. The interim results of these excavations have been published (Hope 1986, 1987) although the dating of certain features has subsequently been revised (Hope in prep.). The excavations were divided into four areas as follows: Area I, about 100m east of the Granary and immediately south of the modern farm building; Area II, about 20m west of the Granary; Area III, a narrow trench immediately north of the

horse shelter; and Area IV, between the Granary and the walled garden. These sub-divisions are used to locate individual features referred to below. The BVAS excavations located the medieval chapel and associated structures and features, recorded the cellar, and identified the first prehistoric features to be discovered on the site.

Excavations by the County Council Archaeology Section have to a large extent been limited to rescue work in advance of necessary improvement schemes. Thus of the twenty-five separate fieldwork projects undertaken since 1987 (Fig. 11), only six have not been subject to imposed limitations in depth or size, and two of these were only preliminary trial trenches. Although such restrictions tend to limit the dating and interpretative potential of these projects, they have nevertheless generated a considerable body of data that can be used in more general interpretations of the site. Each of the ECC projects is designated by an alpha-numeric code comprising the initials 'CT' and a number, and is referred to thus in the text. Where appropriate, the relevant sub-division of the project is indicated by a trench number.

In order to bring together the results of these excavations into a phased history of the whole site, there follows a summary of the data by period, after which the evidence and its significance is discussed.

Prehistory

Most of the prehistoric finds and features on the site date to either the Bronze or Iron Ages, although there are a few isolated flints which might be earlier. There are several linear features (Fig. 12, P1-4) sectioned in various service trenches which are undated but probably fit into one of these two later periods. In all probability the Bronze Age material dates to the later part of the period (c.1200-c.700 BC) while the Iron Age features are spread through the entire era (c.700BC-AD43).

Bronze Age

Isolated Bronze Age flakes and flint tools have been found in contexts dating to almost all periods across the site, although they appear to be slightly more common in Tudor or earlier deposits. As many contexts contain quantities of imported soil they need not reflect a major Bronze Age presence on the site itself. Below the floor of the chapel in Hope's Area IV was a small circular pit containing crazed flints and Late Bronze Age pottery and interpreted by Hope as a seething pit. Two linear features, probably field boundaries, have been assigned to this period, but both are at present problematic.

The first of these was a shallow ditch with stakeholes in its base (Fig. 12, P5), excavated in Hope's Area IV. It runs from the southern tip of the walled garden south-east across the chapel and reappears to the south of the cellar complex. The northern part of the ditch contained five sherds of

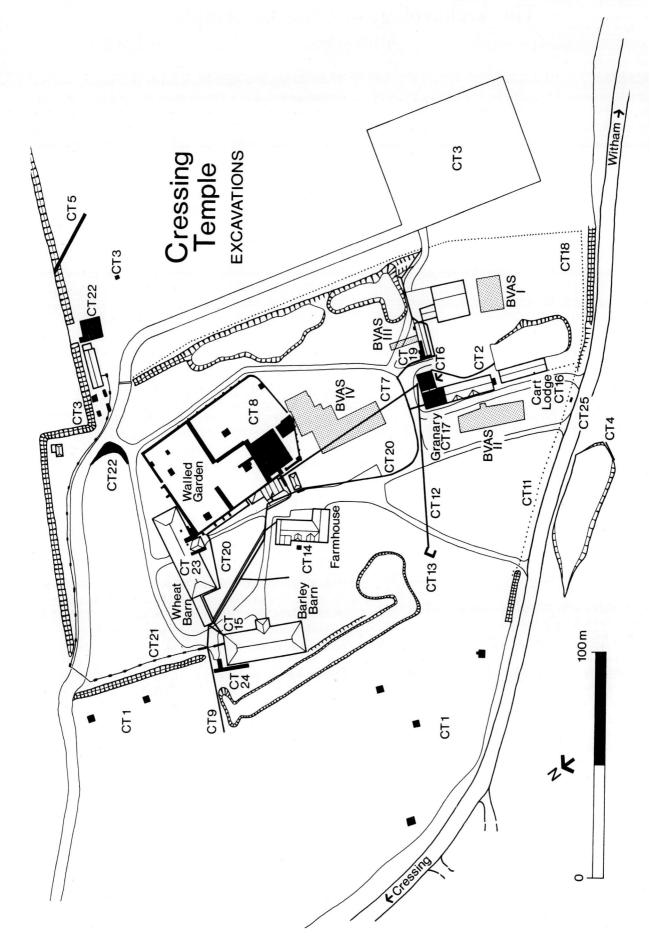

Cressing Temple
EXCAVATIONS

CT 5

CT 22

CT 3

•CT3

CT 3

CT3

CT 22

BVAS I

BVAS III

CT 19

CT6

CT2

CT18

CT 7

BVAS IV

Cart Lodge

CT 8

CT16

Granary CT17

Walled Garden

CT20

CT 25

BVAS II

CT4

CT 22

CT20

CT 12

CT11

Wheat Barn CT 23

CT 15

Barley Barn CT 14

Farmhouse

CT 13

CT21

CT 24

CT9

CT 1

CT 1

CT 1

Cressing

Witham →

N

0   100m

Fig. 11 Plan of Cressing Temple showing excavations by Essex County Council Archaeology Section and the Brain Valley Archaeology Society

Bronze Age pottery and two medieval sherds, but the southern section contained twenty medieval potsherds and only a single Bronze Age flint arrowhead. It seems certain that both sections originally formed a single ditch and it is probable that the excavators missed an intrusive medieval feature. With no way at present to check this, all that can be said with certainty about the ditch and the two postholes is that they are older than the 12th century chapel.

The other feature was located in what is now the walled garden (CT8 Trenches 2, 11, & 12). This was also a shallow ditch (Fig. 3.2, P6), roughly parallel to the other, but containing no sign of stakeholes. One end of the ditch lay against the southern edge of Trench 2, where it was badly damaged by an animal burrow in antiquity. The other (north-eastern) end was cut by a slightly larger Iron Age ditch running in the same direction.

The Iron Age
Several features from this period are known from Cressing Temple and there was residual Iron Age pottery throughout the later deposits.

In Hope's Area III a section of an east-west trench 0.75m deep was located (Fig. 12, P7), with postholes in its base and traces of a bank or collapsed rampart to the north. Area IV contained a single pit with an assemblage of Middle Iron Age pottery in the fill. Within the garden (CT8 Trench 12), a shallow ditch (Fig. 12, P8), aligned with the Bronze Age ditch mentioned above, contained an assemblage of Iron Age pottery. These features were not necessarily contemporary with one another and only indicate an Iron Age presence in the locality. To the east, in Dovehouse Field, a substantial ditch 1.4m deep by 3m wide (Fig. 12, P9) was in use at the end of the Iron Age and filled in the 1st century AD. This ditch ran north for some distance before turning west and was associated with a line of postholes along its western edge. Of more or less the same date was a second pit found by Hope in the area of the chapel, which contained local pottery of the invasion period (Hope 1987).

Plate. 11 Decapitated burial found in the walled garden (CT8), cut by 15th century feature
(photo: E.C.C. Archaeology Section)

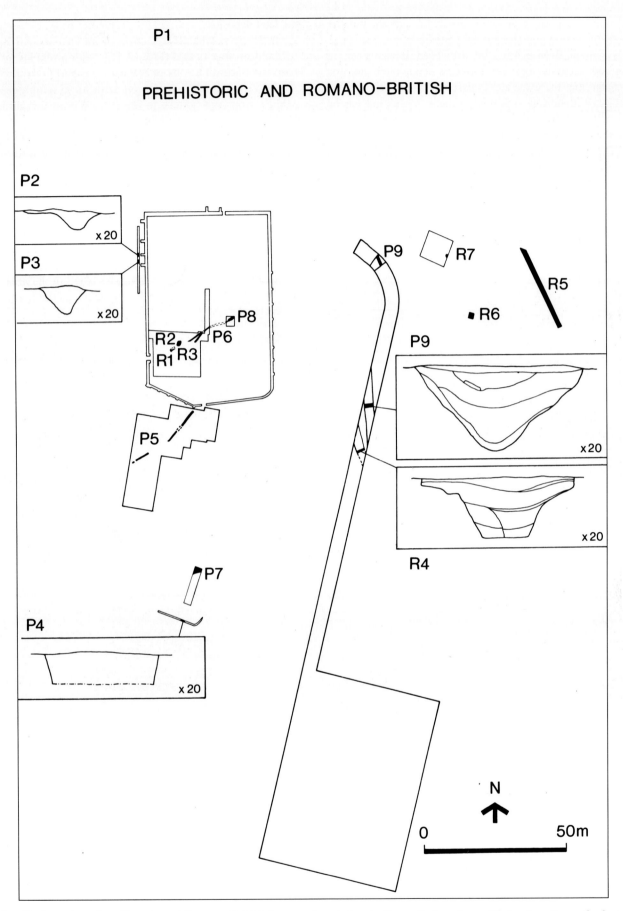

Fig. 12 Location of prehistoric and Romano-British features in relation to the walled garden, with inset sections of selected ditches

Plate 12 View looking up the shaft of the Templar well showing its excellent ashlar masonry (photo: P. Rogers)

Romano-British Settlement

There are no features in the area of the scheduled monument that can be securely dated to the period of the Roman occupation although, as before, occasional Romano-British potsherds have been recovered from later contexts. The pit containing invasion period pottery may of course belong in this period rather than in the Iron Age. A pre-15th century decapitated burial recently unearthed in the garden (CT8 Trench 8) may also be of Romano- British date (Fig. 12, R1; Plate 11), although it contained no datable finds. The attribution of this feature to the Roman period relies largely on typological parallels with dated burials from sites such as Chignall Roman Villa (Clarke forthcoming), although the recognition of two further Romano-British features nearby does strengthen the argument. These are a shallow ditch and a sub-rectangular pit (Fig. 12, R2 & R3), also in the garden (CT8 Trench 2 & Trench 8), which were cut by the same medieval feature as the burial and contained only Roman and prehistoric pottery, although in small quantities.

It is from the excavations on Dovehouse Field (CT3, CT5, & CT22 Trench 6) that definitive evidence of Romano-British settlement has come. During the excavation of the track to the new car park (CT3), the Iron Age ditch already described was found to have been filled in and then replaced by a second, almost parallel, ditch (Fig. 12, R4; Brown & Flook 1990). This in turn was soon filled in and cobbled over, perhaps in the late 2nd or early 3rd century, although this date must only be regarded as an approximation. This new surface suggests a westward expansion or change in focus of the settlement area (Flook, archive report), an idea supported by the later ceramics from Bayliss's trench to the west of the ditches.

To the south there was less evidence of expansion and Romano- British features were limited to 'field ditches and scattered postholes' (Flook, archive report). East of the boundary ditches excavation has been limited, but Martin found another ditch (Fig. 12, R5) and a cobbled surface overlain with Romano-British pottery (Fig. 12, R6). This latter feature was again located during recent excavations

MEDIAEVAL

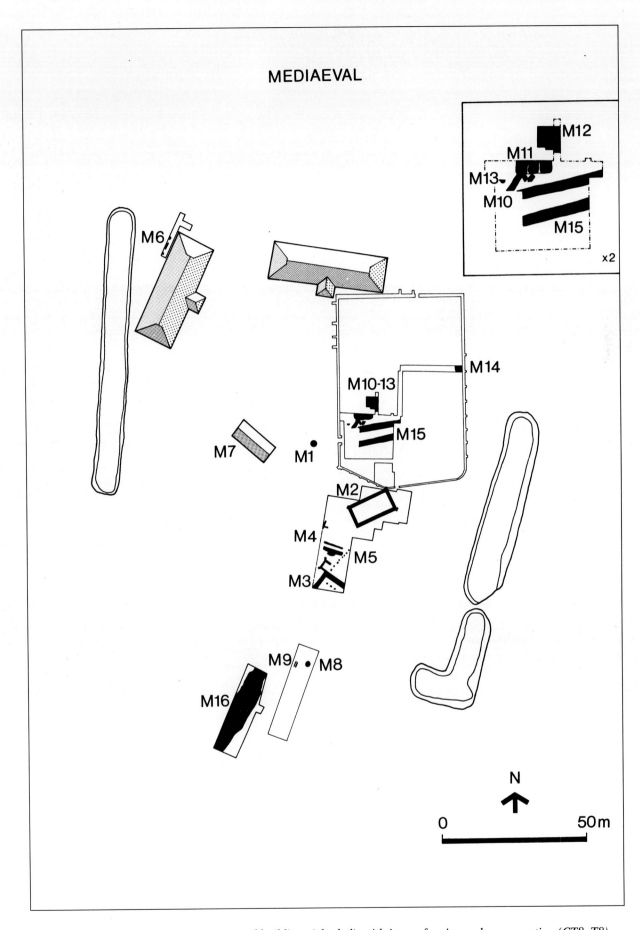

Fig. 13 Location of medieval features and buildings (shaded), with inset of main garden excavation (CT8, T8).

(CT3 Test Pit 5). A shallow trench just west of the milking shed (CT22 Trench 6) exposed some intact Roman soil horizons and a few shallow pits, one of which contained a quantity of burnt daub (Fig. 12, R7).

The Early Middle Ages
This period covers roughly the time from the end of the Roman occupation to the Norman conquest (c.400-1066). Despite the presence of a few Late Saxon potsherds in Hope's Area IV, no firm evidence of Saxon occupation has so far been found at Cressing Temple and it is increasingly likely that this represents a real hiatus at the site, rather than a sampling problem.

The Templars and Hospitallers
The first documentary references to the site relate to the medieval Templar establishment and it is from this period that the earliest known structures date. As with earlier periods, isolated medieval finds occur throughout the site, and a few small features excavated in Dovehouse Field may date to the medieval period (11th - 15th centuries). It is, however, in the area around the existing farm buildings that most medieval activity was centred. This section describes the traces of the medieval buildings and the features associated with them, and other features revealed in the garden and elsewhere on the scheduled monument. The burials associated with the chapel are described here and dealt with more extensively in the final Discussion section of the paper.

The Buildings
The two great barns and the well (Fig. 13, M1; Plate 12), a stone-lined structure 1.7m in diameter and about 15m deep, still survive from the Templar period. In his Area IV excavations, Hope identified the rammed gravel foundations of the chapel (Fig. 13, M2) and a corner of another building (Fig. 13, M3), both of which would have been built of stone. It now seems likely that the stone buildings were preceded by earlier building phases in the same area.

One of these comprised a set of beam slots (Fig. 13, M4) which outlined a rectangular structure on a slightly different alignment to either of the stone buildings. Associated with the beam slots was a group of features thought to be the remains of an oven. This contained a large quantity of 11th or 12th century pottery, which could of course pre-date the Norman conquest but seems more likely to belong to the early part of the Templar occupation. A timber structure almost 11m long was defined by a set of eight to ten postholes forming two rows at right angles (Fig. 13, M5). These were originally thought to belong to a Late Saxon building (Hope 1987) but since most of them contained pottery (recently analysed by S. Tyler) that is more probably post-conquest in date, it is likely that they form part of an early Norman structure instead. Its perfect alignment with the stone building links it with the plan of the later preceptory buildings and indicates another early Templar phase of construction.

The stone building itself, which Hope surmised might be the Templar's hall or guest-house, occupied the southern end of his Area IV excavation. The extent of this structure has now been revealed by both resistivity survey and by parch-marks visible in the dry summer of 1990, although there is some disagreement in the resulting dimensions (16 x 8m from parch-marks and about 21 x 10m from resistivity). In either case it is a substantial structure and must have been one of the main buildings of the preceptory. The open-sided structure added to the north-west corner of the stone building in the 14th century (Hope 1987) must have been an outshot structure, though its purpose is unknown.

The single-cell chapel (15.2 x 7.1m) stood to the north of the other excavated buildings and was identified by the associated burials and its rammed gravel foundations, typical of 12th century churches in Essex. The north-east corner of the chapel was butted by the southernmost tip of the garden wall, and the corner of the foundations has recently been located in the garden excavations, along with part of a nearby grave (CT8 Trench 1). At least 38 inhumations were associated with the chapel, although some of them were post-medieval burials. Three postholes cut by the 12th century chapel foundations are undated. Whilst they and certain of the burials may suggest the presence of an earlier chapel, the evidence is inconclusive (see Discussion, below).

Preliminary excavations in the Wheat Barn (CT23) and outside the northern corner of the Barley Barn (CT24) revealed extensive modern disturbance, and the few possible medieval features found are difficult to interpret with certainty. In the Wheat Barn, three postholes were partly visible beneath the brick plinth of the south wall. These are undated and could relate to repair work, the original construction, or even to an earlier structure. It is suggested elsewhere (Stenning, in this volume) that the Barley Barn has been reduced in size and the excavations there were undertaken in order to define the original outline of the building. Two short beam slots (Fig. 13, M6; see also Fig. 23) cut into the natural clay were discovered lying parallel to and 1.4m west of the Barley Barn. Two postholes, 1.4m deep and 0.8m across containing late medieval tile fragments, were found roughly aligned with the slots and opposite the cross-frames of the barn. These features look as if they marked the original position of the west wall of the barn. However, no similar traces were found on the north side of the building, and it is possible that the beam slots and postholes are traces of repair work and not part of the original construction.

Recent investigations by the County Council Historic Buildings Section in the farmhouse have shown that at least part of the south wing is medieval in date and may once have formed the cross wing of an early 14th century building (Fig. 13, M7). Whether the structure is still in its original position is not yet known.

No other medieval building outlines have been excavated, although the discovery of a circular tiled hearth, 1.65m across (Fig. 13, M8; Plate 13), in the Granary (CT17) indicates the presence of an earlier building there. The hearth cut a shallow feature which contained 13th century ceram-

Plate 13 Excavations inside the Granary (CT17), showing the medieval hearth and the post-medieval steeping pit in the background (photo: D. Bartram)

ics and clearly pre-dates the construction of the Granary probably in the 17th century. The shallow feature in turn cut two parallel linear features, a shallow groove and a round-bottomed trench containing two sherds of Early Medieval Ware (Fig. 13, M9). Other features in this excavation included two pits containing three medieval potsherds between them and a single posthole without finds. All these features cut a soil horizon containing two sherds of medieval pottery but none give any clues as to the nature or purpose of the building which must once have stood there.

The Walled Garden Area

The walled garden itself is a post-medieval construction, but during excavations within it (CT8) several medieval features have come to light, nearly all of them in the south-western corner (Trenches 1, 2, 8, 13, 14, & 15) nearest the buildings described above. Among the earliest of these was a ditch, with a V-shaped profile (Fig. 13, M10), running diagonally across the north-western corner of Trench 8 and containing medieval pottery. This was cut by a group of three intercutting pits (Fig. 13, M11) at the western end of

Trench 2. The easternmost one was roughly circular, but the others continued beyond the limits of the excavation and their shape was unclear, although they were probably similar in outline to the first pit. They were left open for some time and had begun to silt up before all three were filled in in a single operation. The fills contained a large quantity of iron slag and other smithing waste, some bone, and several 13th century potsherds.

Trench 13 proved to be within the fill of a single large feature (Fig. 13, M12). Two small offsets were dug to link the trench with the main excavation and to locate the north and south edges of the feature. These excavations defined the feature as a very large pit, 1.7m deep, 4.2m across, and an estimated 7-10m long. It had nearly vertical and roughly parallel sides, with a flattish but uneven base. The pit was unlined and showed no signs of lengthy exposure before filling commenced with a thick dump of silt and clay dredged from a pond or moat. Settlement of the fill and slumping of the sides at this point indicates a break of several months before filling continued with more pond cleanings and some soil containing, like the pits described

44

above, smithing waste and 13th century pottery. The function of the pit is uncertain.

Several other features of probable medieval date have been excavated in the southern half of the garden. These include three shallow pits (Fig. 13, M13) and at least eleven postholes, not all contemporaneous, in Trench 8, and a pit (Fig. 13, M14) lying beneath the east wall of the garden in Trench 3. It should be noted here that there is residual Romano-British pottery in most of the medieval features and that the pit, ditch and burial described above as possibly of Roman date might as easily be medieval.

What has been interpreted as the remains of a bordered path runs roughly east-west across Trench 8 (Fig. 13, M15). All that remained of the path was a layer of very ashy clay but the borders were clearly defined by a pair of shallow (0.2-0.3m deep), flat-bottomed features filled with a dark clay loam. They showed no signs of silting and have been interpreted as planting trenches. Both had evidently been recut at some point, doubling their width to about 1.5m. The borders have been dated to the 15th century, although they may have survived into the early 16th century. The path appears to be heading towards the well but at least one of the borders ends directly beneath the west wall of the garden (CT 8, Trench 15). Neither the path nor the borders were revealed in a service trench (CT7) dug between the garden wall and the well-house.

Sealing the medieval contexts, and below the early garden deposits, was a gravel surface 50-100mm deep. This layer, covering the northern half of Trench 8, was well preserved in the west but became progressively thinner and more patchy to the east, where it was badly dissected by garden features. The gravel must have been preceded by a phase of levelling, which removed the surface of the path and most of the medieval soils in this part of the trench. Evidence of this levelling may also have been found at the southern tip of the garden, where there was a very shallow grave and the chapel foundations stood proud of the surviving medieval soil. Here, however, there was no gravel surface to separate this levelling episode from any levelling done during the creation of the garden.

The Pond
The BVAS excavation west of the Granary (Hope's Area II) centred on a large oval pond of medieval date (Fig. 13, M16). It cut features containing 12th to 13th century pottery, and the lowest fills incorporated material from the 15th century and earlier. It appeared to have been filled in the 16th or 17th century.

The Post-medieval Great House and Farm
The vast majority of the material excavated at Cressing Temple relates to the post-medieval and modern periods. To list all the drains, ditches, pits and postholes found would be of little value at this stage and I propose to limit discussion here to those finds which relate to the moats, to the dating and function of certain buildings, and to the development of the walled garden.

The Moats
The BVAS excavations on the north side of the horse shelter (Hope's Area III) revealed the existence of a southern arm of the moat system, running from the south-eastern corner of the existing moat towards the north end of the Granary. The trench cut a section across the moat to a maximum depth of about 2m below the present surface level. Hope noted that the upper fills were modern and that only the lowest fill dated to the 17th century. The south side of the moat was cut by the footings for the 19th century horse shelter, whilst the north bank was capped with a brick revetment. This wall, only four courses deep at this point and apparently set on top of the bank, must have been a parapet rather than a moat lining.

Recent excavations in and around the horse shelter (CT19) confirmed most of these findings and showed that since the BVAS dig up to 1m of soil has been dumped into the hollow above the moat fill. In the new excavations the western end of the moat (Fig. 14, F1) was located , with a brick lining extending at least 1m down the side, directly beneath and supporting the west wall of the horse shelter. A machine trench dug along this wall about 15 years ago exposed a 10m length of walling, which then turned back along the north side of the moat towards the section of wall found in Hope's Area III, and into which was set the entrance to a brick culvert (Martin pers. comm.). Inside the horse shelter a partially collapsed brick revetment, at least 4m long and supported by a square buttress, formed the south side of the moat. A second brick culvert provided an overflow to the south about 1.1m below present surface level. These walls completely contain the end of the moat in a manner very similar to the surviving revetment around the north end of the pond behind the cart lodge, except that it appears that the revetment continued as an ornamental parapet along at least the northern side of the moat. The brickwork of the revetment has been dated to the early 17th century and may be an alteration made to the moat system when the Granary was erected.

The L-shaped south-eastern corner of the moat is not shown on the 1794 estate map, but appears on both the 1842 tithe map and the 1875 Ordnance Survey map. It has clearly been shortened since then, and the alignment changed to avoid the horse shelter. The circular pond at the south end of the west moat dates to between 1794 and 1842, whilst the widening of the east moat can be dated from the maps to the third quarter of the 19th century.

The pond on the south side of the main Braintree to Witham road may have been associated with the old moat system. A brick revetment (Fig. 14, F2) which runs along the south-east side is linked with submerged timbers and a brick pillar dredged from the pond. These are believed to be the remains of a bridge or mill, and some early bricks which were removed during cleaning operations seemed to suggest a 16th or 17th century date for the structure. Subsequent investigation has shown that these bricks come from an unmortared structure buttressing the main revetment, which is a 19th century construction.

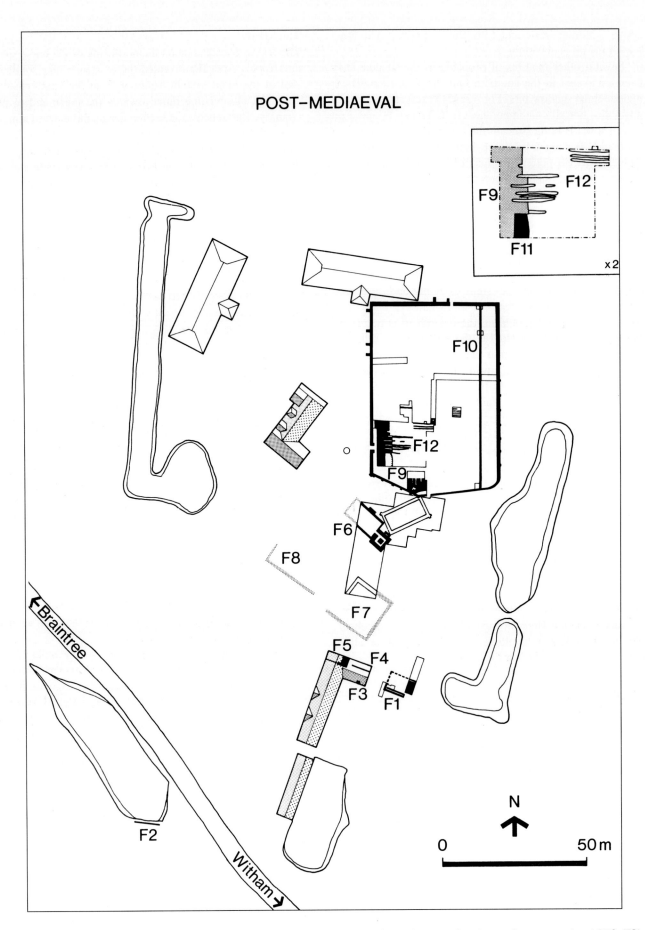

POST-MEDIAEVAL

F9   F12

F11

x2

F10

F12

F9

F6

F8

F7

F5

F4

F3   F1

Braintree

F2

Witham →

N

0   50 m

Fig. 14 Location of selected post-medieval features and buildings (shaded), with inset of main garden excavation (CT8, T8).

*Plate 14 The Tudor brick pavement found in the walled garden (CT8), cut by 18th century planting trenches
(photo: E.C.C. Archaeology Section)*

The Granary and Workshop

CT6 comprised a set of trenches dug by contractors in the old workshop adjacent to the Granary when it was converted for use as public toilets. These were recorded afterwards in section and plan. Apart from one or two possible medieval layers in the northern half of the building and a single feature cut into them, all contexts were clearly post-medieval. The original brick structure dates to the late 17th or 18th centuries, with a floor level some 0.4m lower than the present one. A buttress in the south (farmyard) wall suggests that there may once have been a door at that point. The original north wall (Fig. 14, F3), which aligned with the remains of a wall (Fig. 14, F4) found in a trench just outside the building (CT2), was 1.6m south of the present one. The existing wall was built in the 19th century flush with the north side of the Granary. Most of the excavated contexts relate to the later (19th century) phase.

The excavations in the room at the north end of the Granary, (CT17 Trenches 1, 2 & 4) revealed the medieval hearth described above and included the sunken feature traditionally identified as a steeping pit. This rubble-built, tile-floored pit (Fig. 14, F5) was located in the north-eastern corner of the room and was associated with a brick sluice and drain floored with reused medieval Coggeshall-type

bricks. These features are probably late 17th or 18th century in date, although they appear to have continued in use into the 19th century.

What appeared to be a foundation trench for the west wall of the Granary contained 19th century glass and pottery and is probably only a repair trench. At the south end of the building (where the fire escape now stands), Trench 3 was dug through a thick gravel track over a spread of 19th century rubble including a quantity of broken marble slabs. Below this, at the bottom of the trench, was an eroded clay surface of uncertain date. No foundation trench for the Granary was seen. The brickwork of the plinth-wall was painted with pitch to within two courses of its base and had clearly been exposed to this level.

The Great House

The location of the 16th century manor house on the site remains one of the unsolved mysteries of Cressing Temple. In the BVAS Area IV Hope exposed a Tudor cellar (Fig. 14, F6), the same one partly excavated in 1934, which is thought to be a part of the Great House. Adjacent to the medieval stone building at the southern end of Hope's Area IV further parch marks revealed the existence of a continuation of the structure to the south (Fig. 14, F7). This was aligned with further marks to the west (Fig. 14, F8)

47

between the two driveways. Observations from two service trenches (CT7 & CT20 Trench 1) have shown that the walls which created these marks are brick-built, dating probably to the 16th or 17th centuries. Like the cellar, this structure is a candidate for the missing house or a part of it.

The Walled Garden

Extensive archaeological work in the walled garden (CT8) has enabled the reconstruction in some detail of its development over the last four and a half centuries. Finds from the earliest garden-related deposits gave only an approximate date in the 16th or early 17th centuries for the establishment of the garden. As could be expected in a garden, the quantity of datable artefacts recovered throughout all but the 19th century layers was small and the degree of mixing due to root, worm, and rodent activity correspondingly high. It should be noted that no garden features earlier than the late 18th century have been found north of the (modern) central lawn; all references to early features relate to the southern half of the garden.

The earliest part of the garden sequence consisted of a thick deposit of clay capped by a gravel spread, both laid down as bedding for a wide brick pavement along the western and south-eastern sides of the garden (Fig. 14, F9). Between the pavement and the walls was a 0.6m wide gap interpreted as a flower bed. Beyond the pavement the ground was built up first with a thin spread of rubble, mostly very fragmented brick, tile, and mortar, and then with a thick layer of soil, only thin patches of which have survived, to raise it to the level of the pavement. Later tilling has erased any recognisable traces of early beds, which may in any event have been largely raised above the level of the paths. It has not therefore been possible to decipher any pattern to the early garden layout. Running the full length of the garden, parallel to and 6m from the east wall, are the remains of a retaining wall, 0.5m wide, which must once have supported a broad terrace (Fig. 14, F10). This perhaps carried another section of brick pavement, bordered with flower beds, along the eastern side of the garden but all evidence for the terrace surface has been eradicated by later landscaping.

Judging by the worn state of the brickwork and the extensive repairs to it, the pavement continued in use for many years before finally being covered with gravel in the late 17th century. There was little other evidence of late 17th or early 18th century activity apart from a few irregular planting holes south of the western doorway and a single rectangular cut (Fig. 14, F11) in Trench 2 which may belong in this period. There was, however, a relatively undisturbed soil horizon across most of Trench 8 and it may be that this area was under lawn at this time.

In the mid- to late 18th century the northern half of the garden was dug over, in most places right down to the Boulder Clay subsoil, destroying all traces of earlier features. To the south the damage was less severe as some soil was imported or redistributed to level up this part of the garden. The southern end was then given over to some form of kitchen gardening and the area was dissected by rows of parallel planting trenches (Fig. 14, F12). A few

postholes associated with the trenches might indicate that some were for climbing plants, but this is far from certain. No similar features were found in the northern half of the garden; indeed there is little evidence of any features at all, and it is likely that this area contained a few very large beds or was perhaps cleared for an orchard.

At some time around 1800 the garden was once more redesigned. It is probable that at this time the terrace was levelled and the oblique wall across the south-west corner of the garden was built, although both of these events could be somewhat earlier. Certainly a thick layer of topsoil was put down and the surface sloped up to cover the remains of the terrace. Initially the area covered by Trench 8 was laid out with a number of small beds, both circular and rectangular. This was soon overprinted with a more formal layout, marked by a new series of brick drains and by the first gravel paths. A small brick-lined pond and a shallow bonfire pit date to this phase of development. This pattern seems to have been made increasingly more regular, with the paths defining a pattern of rectangular beds which was the basis for the modern layout. The 1875 map shows this pattern and documents the establishment of an orchard along the eastern side of the garden. The central and south-western lawns were laid at this time, although both have undergone subsequent alteration.

It was only in this century that the garden took on its present form. The orchard was reduced, the lawns expanded, the main paths paved or grassed over and a new brick terrace built along the east wall.

Other Features

Various excavations and watching briefs have shown that, as in the garden, the modern topography of the site is the result of gradual evolution, punctuated by a series of major landscaping episodes over the last 350 or so years. Hope (1987) notes that the area south of the walled garden was landscaped in the late 17th century. The hollow between the two barns has been enlarged and greatly accentuated through late 18th and 19th century activity, while the farmyard east of the Granary and the lawn west of the farmhouse (the 'rose garden') were created by 20th century levelling. All the gravel tracks and driveways investigated so far date to the 19th or early 20th centuries. The 1875 Ordnance Survey map also shows two animal sheds and a lean-to projecting from the barns which were demolished earlier this century.

Discussion

The story of human activity at Cressing Temple spans some 3000 years. Archaeological excavations here have revealed traces of Bronze Age fields, probably fairly minor subdivisions of a larger field system. On the basis of the few finds recovered, it seems likely that this system dates to the Late Bronze Age, and may have continued in use into the early part of the Iron Age. Although the seething pit south of the garden does suggest the presence of at least a temporary camp it is insufficient evidence on which to postulate more permanent settlement in the Bronze Age. Traces of a palisade or bank and ditch just north of the horse shelter are thought to date from the Middle Iron Age. Since no further signs of it have been found in more recent excavations to the west, this was probably a small feature, such as a stock pen, rather than a full settlement enclosure. As with the earlier seething pit, such a feature might have been situated out in the fields and need not indicate habitation close by.

The first sure signs of settlement on the site are the pre-Roman ditch and postholes in the Dovehouse Field. This part of the site remained the focus of settlement throughout the period of Roman occupation. The continuation of settlement and the scarcity among the finds recovered of both Roman building materials and fine ceramics suggests a native agricultural settlement rather than a villa or military site. Better definition of the status of the settlement must await further excavation.

In the period between the end of the Roman occupation and the Norman conquest there is no evidence of settlement or agricultural activity at Cressing Temple in all the areas sampled to date. Whilst some information may have been lost as a result of later levelling, the total absence of features that can reliably be dated to the Saxon period seems to indicate that a hiatus in occupation occurred during that time.

The siting of a major Templar preceptory on the site was clearly the high point in the history of Cressing Temple. Comparison with other excavated Templar establishments such as South Witham in Lincolnshire (Current Archaeology 1968) suggests that there should have been an extensive range of buildings at Cressing Temple, a conclusion supported by the documentary evidence. Yet so far only six broadly contemporaneous structures, including the barns, have been found. The main buildings were preceded by at least two building phases, the earliest phase including the structure outlined by beamslots and containing the 'oven'. This was followed by other timber structures, represented by the postholes beneath the chapel and the other stone building found in the BVAS excavations. As the Templars became more affluent and influential, these buildings were replaced by more prestigious stone structures and the great barns. The south wing of the present farmhouse and perhaps the building over the tiled hearth were added during the Hospitallers' ownership of the manor. The focus of occupation was in the area south of the walled garden, extending across in front of the modern farmhouse.

There is general consensus on the identification of the chapel but the associated burials contain little by way of pottery or other datable materials and pose a considerable problem in phasing. Most are contained within the chapel walls, but a few are outside and it is likely that there was a small churchyard around the building, the northern boundary of which may have coincided with the late medieval bordered path in CT8. Several were cut by the east wall of the chapel, which, however, was rebuilt in the Tudor period and 'almost completely obliterated ... the original gravel footings' (Hope in prep). It is tempting to suggest that the medieval chapel may once have been longer, in which case all these graves would have been within the structure. No

definite evidence of such an extension has been recognised either in CT8, where other features have removed any trace of a foundation trench, or in the BVAS excavations, which however did not penetrate to the natural in this area. If the extension existed, then most of the evidence for an earlier chapel on the site would disappear, leaving only three postholes and about thirty unarticulated fragments of human bone in two features supposedly cut by the north wall of the chapel.

Between the chapel yard, the well, and the barns there is little evidence for medieval activity, and it seems plausible that most of this too was open yard. The group of 13th century pits and the large feature in CT8 Trench 13 lie on the southern edge of this area and the presence in their fills of large quantities of slag may indicate that the blacksmith's workshop stood somewhere nearby. The pond excavated to the west of the Granary is clearly medieval, but the dating and original plan of the moat system is still obscure.

The 16th and early 17th centuries were a time of substantial change at Cressing Temple. The Great House was built and the walled garden established, requiring the redefinition of various internal boundaries across the site and probably the demolition of several medieval buildings. At the same time new buildings sprang up to replace the old, the Granary and the first phases of the farmhouse being among them. Tudor brickwork in the garage walls indicates another, as yet undefined, building there. A network of covered brick drains was put in around the buildings and the moat system was altered and improved. Numerous pieces of fine imported glassware and some good quality ceramics of this period from the BVAS excavations add to the general impression of prosperity.

Hope (1987) initially suggested that the Tudor period cellar in Area IV was once connected to the present farmhouse to form the main wing of the Great House. He has subsequently revised this opinion, since the two are out of alignment, and it is now clear that the farmhouse is a combination of two separate buildings which were joined in the 17th century. The Area IV cellar could, however, still be part of the Great House in view of its position adjoining the chapel, which Evelyn's diary mentions as 'in the house'.

It is also likely that the Tudor walls connected with the medieval stone house formed part of a large building which thus incorporated the earlier structure. It is probable that this building was linked by a long wing with the cellar to form the Great House. Whilst this is still largely supposition, such a grand house would not be out of keeping with the scale of building works and landscaping on the site as a whole.

At the end of the 17th century, the site appears to have gone into a period of decline, and through most of the following century the evidence indicates a far less grand approach to works on the site. Documentary evidence suggests that the Great House was demolished early in this period, and was superseded as a residence by the present farmhouse. The brick path in the garden was covered with gravel and by the mid-18th century the garden had been turned into a utilitarian kitchen garden. Alterations were made to the Granary and a new brick building (the workshop/toilet block) was added to the north-east corner of it.

The traditional identification of the rectangular structure in the Granary as a steeping pit, used for soaking barley when making malt, and the contemporary construction of the adjacent brick building, have led to the suggestion that the two together were used as a maltings. This is an attractive interpretation, although the only other evidence in its support remains a documentary reference to the existence of a maltings beneath a granary. There was no trace of a kiln or baked floor in the workshop and no grain recorded in either CT6 or CT17. Perhaps the remains of the kiln may yet be found beneath the floor of one of the modern stables at the south end of the building.

Towards the end of the 18th and through the early 19th century, the appearance of the farm began once more to change. The cartlodge was built, new gravel tracks were laid, the walled garden was laid out again, and a lean-to bakehouse was added to the rear of the farmhouse. Throughout the 19th century and into the present one this process has slowly continued with further landscaping, the digging of new ponds, and the construction of better tracks and new outbuildings.

Acknowledgements

As a synthesis of research done at Cressing Temple over a great many years, this paper clearly owes a great deal to the work of a number of individuals. Although the final interpretations and any errors herein are those of the author, the contributions of both data and ideas by previous excavators are gratefully acknowledged. In particular, thanks are due to Roy Martin and John Hope for their co-operation and assistance. Likewise I wish to acknowledge the work and assistance of my predecessors in the County Council Archaeology Section: Roland Flook, Deborah Priddy, Steve Godbold, and Nigel Brown. Thanks are due also to the many members of the excavation team, especially those whose association with the site has been long or significant: Jason Walker, Alec Wade, Katherine White, Andy Letch, and Barry Crouch. The contributions made by many other members of the County Council Archaeology Section, particularly the finds staff, should be noted here, and I would like to extend special thanks to Pat Ryan for her work on both the historic records and on the excavated brick and tile remains. Finally, I wish to thank all those who have read and commented on various drafts of this paper for their suggestions and guidance. The figures that accompany this paper are the work of Barry Crouch.

The Cressing Barns and the Early Development of Barns in South-east England

by Dave Stenning

Introduction

The two great 13th century barns constitute the most obvious and significant standing structures at Cressing Temple. The purchase of the site by Essex County Council facilitated a detailed and on-going process of investigation and recording, which is providing a greater understanding of their particular characteristics.

Whilst each barn can, and should be, enjoyed as a self-sufficient, majestic structure, interpretation requires a wider view. It seems reasonable to suppose that the barns were not totally unique creations, but were two particular manifestations of a gradually evolving building type.

With this in view, it is clearly necessary to identify and compare other related structures and to try to piece together this development process. Logic, together with experience, suggests that this process is unlikely to have been entirely straightforward and that a number of strands may have existed in parallel.

Remnants of some extremely early buildings certainly survive, but the evidence is, at the present time, sketchy in the extreme and greater understanding will need to await further discoveries. It has to be admitted that even for the 13th century, the picture is far from clear, with most surviving examples being mere incoherent fragments. As will be seen, the hazy picture that can be discerned is substantially reliant on the utilitarian conservation of earlier generations. Thus most early work survives as reused components in later barns and it is usually difficult to untangle the various constituent structures.

It is obviously tempting to widen the field of investigation to include the contemporary aisled houses, which fortunately survive in somewhat greater numbers. Whilst such an exercise has some value, caution should be exercised as the functional differences may ultimately distort the argument. Similarly, the late 13th century and early 14th century great stone barns of the Midlands and the West (e.g. Great Coxwell, Oxfordshire; Bredon, Worcestershire) are suggestive of later development, but their rubble walled aisles required different structural and assembly systems. Their relative remoteness, from East Anglia and from each other, suggests the possibility of a wider pattern of influence and this perhaps can be discerned from their particular attributes. Nevertheless they do provide useful evidence as to the longevity of the notched-lap joint and of other archaic features, and of the gradual introduction of more diverse regional styles. It is sad to note that the body of evidence continues to shrink. The barn at Abbess Warley Hall (see below) has vanished, apparently without trace, and reused 13th century fragments at Hatfield Heath were destroyed in a recent fire. This clearly underlines the need for protection and this can best be assisted by a thorough understanding of our building heritage.

Structural evidence for early barns elsewhere

Barn at Paul's Hall, Belchamp St. Paul, Essex [1]

The manor at Belchamp St. Paul was granted to the Dean and Chapter of St. Paul's, London by king Athelstan (925-940), and was held by them until modern times (Morant 1768, II, 328). A lease (Hale 1858, 138) drawn up in the time of Hugh de Marini, who was Dean of St Paul's about 1160-81 (Morant 1768, I, 406), contains a dimensioned description of two substantial barns. That described as the 'Oat Barn' most nearly fits the components that survive reused in a late medieval barn on the site, and forms the basis for the reconstruction drawing (Fig. 15) of a typical truss. The other, named as the 'Wheat Barn', was of wider span and had aisles of unequal size.

Once later joints are eliminated from the reused timbers, a structure can be identified that is fundamentally similar to our Cressing barns. It will be noticed that all the timbers are straight rather than curved and this is a distinguishing feature of all our early timber structures. Open notched-lap joints, another diagnostic early feature, are used in a number of locations, and are of the earlier form with simple triangular notches (Fig. 16). Such lap joints have the advantage that the timber on which they are worked can be placed in position after the principal member has been fixed in place. It seems reasonable to suppose that these surviving components are of a building of pre-1181, and thus the earliest barn that will be considered in this article.

The arcade-braces and braces to the tiebeam are set at an angle of 45 degrees, slightly shallower than in the Cressing barns. The aisle framing is of the reversed assembly type with the arcade plate superimposed on the aisle-tie, and this seems the prevalent arrangement in early barns. The aisles were infilled with heavy, butt-jointed planks which fitted into a groove in the underside of the wall plate. One such elm board survives reused in the barn and is 0.5m in width and of a substantial thickness. The remnants suggest that small studs were placed about one metre apart, there being two boards between each stud. The one unique feature of this otherwise straightforward structure are the large raking struts that once supported the posts. Mr C. A. Hewett has suggested that these were originally earth-fast and acted as permanent shores during the process of erection (Hewett 1980, 23-4, 32-34). Although no physical evidence survives, it is clear from the written description that the barn terminated in simple aisles of similar dimensions to the surviving side aisles.

Unfortunately, the one surviving section of top plate is without a contemporary scarf joint and all the surviving scarf joints date from a later rebuilding, probably in the early 14th century.

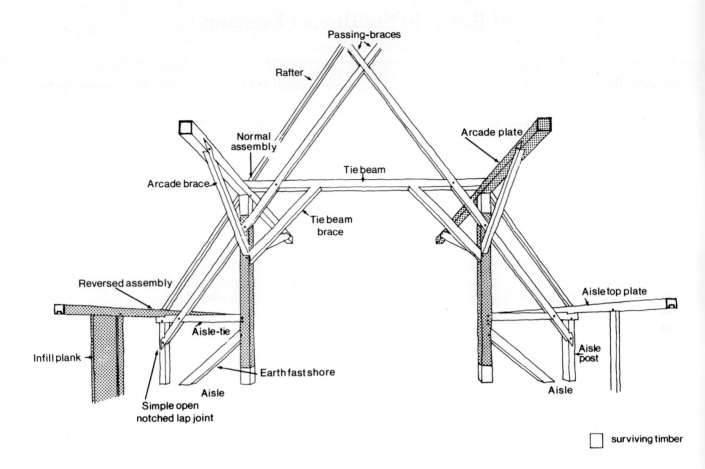

Fig. 15 The 'Oat Barn', Belchamp St. Paul

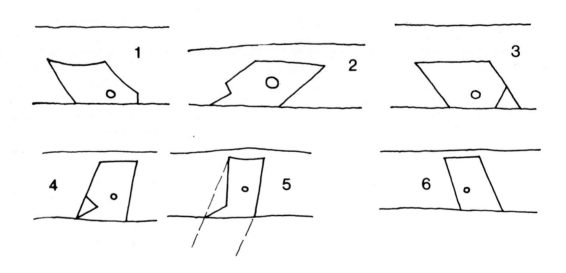

Fig. 16 Notched-lap joints: 1) basic (barn at Brices, Birds Green, Clavering); 2) with refined entry (Copton Manor barn, Sheldwich, Kent); 3) secret notched-lap (Cressing Wheat Barn); 4) and 5) secret notched-laps with refined entry (large barn at Sandonbury, Herts.); 6) notchless lap joint, small barn at Sandonbury, Herts.)

Barn at Stantons Hall, Black Notley, Essex

Stantons is generally identified with one of the Domesday manors in the Notleys, though by Morant's time it was a farm belonging to Black Notley Hall (Morant 1768, II, 124). The quality of construction of Stantons Hall (RCHM 1921, 19), a remarkably complete aisled house of the early 14th century, implies that it was originally of manorial status.

The nearby barn contains components that are similar in concept to the previous example (Fig. 17). Again, the notched-lap joints are of the early form (Fig. 16) with markedly curved profiles to their terminal edges. However, in place of the raking shores, there were little notched-lap angle-braces, rising up between post and aisle-tie. One aisle-tie shows evidence for a wattle and daub infilling, and in this assembly the angle-brace is omitted.

It would appear that the aisle walls also had wattle and daub infilling between widely spaced studs and thus some form of ground-cill must have been employed. If my interpretation is correct, the barn had simple terminal aisles and a section of top plate from these aisles has survived, reused. This has normal assembly and evidence for an external angle-brace rising up from the corner post. Such angle braces will be encountered again, and were normally located on those major structural posts that lacked any other form of angled bracing. The other aisle-posts were restrained by the long passing-braces.

A noticeable feature of this barn is that the tenons, where aisle-tie meets arcade-post, are off-set to one side. This feature, which will be noted again, seems to be the result of the 'side lap' mentality. Where arcade-braces have upper notched-laps, it is perfectly sensible to provide off-set tenons at the base where they enter the posts. There is no real practical reason for applying this to the aisle-tie situation, but an established working habit is seen to have its effect.

Long Barn, Whiston Hall, Rotherham, South Yorkshire

This was a manorial barn which may have been erected by the Furnival family (Jones 1980). Tree-ring dating by Jennifer Hillam of Sheffield University gave dates in the range 1146-1204, with a felling date after 1214. The height to the underside of the tie beams is 4.9m.

Whiston Barn originally consisted of five equal bays, later extended at one end. The arcade-posts mostly survive in their original positions and stand on low, stepped, stone stylobates. Each post is noticeably tapered, the timber utilised in its 'natural' position, with the root bole to the base. The general structural assembly is similar to Stantons barn but with a few significant differences. Open notched-lap joints are of the early unrefined profile, with noticeable curving of sides. Each post has, on its inward facing flank, a small blocked mortice, a short distance up from the base. These 'lifting holes' are here assumed to be associated with the stone stylobates and a so far undiscovered assembly procedure. Each post also has a large square unpegged hole, right through the post, and these have also been interpreted as serving a similar function. However, some of these holes penetrate from front to back and one, at least,

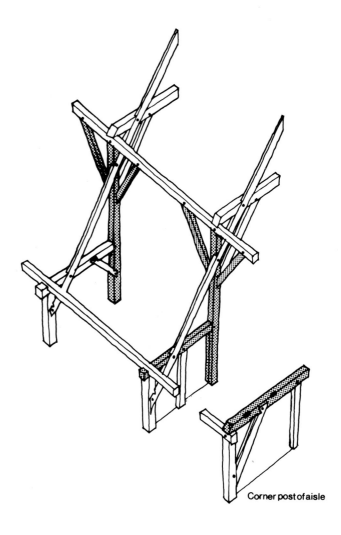

Corner post of aisle

Fig. 17 Barn at Stantons, Black Notley. Reconstruction of part of the east side

passes through the flanks, so a later rebuilding seems a more probable explanation. Surprisingly, in view of the antiquity of the barn, one arcade-plate survives for almost its complete length. This is seen to be made up of three timbers of almost equal lengths with two relatively perfect splayed scarf joints. From this it can be deduced that assembly began with pairs of central posts, with the outer pairs of posts added later. The scarf joints are relatively unsophisticated, being splayed and pegged with a vertical table in the centre (Fig. 20).

The surviving remains suggest that the aisle walls were originally timber-framed, in that a geometry similar to our other examples seems probable. The later (?16th century) extensions were certainly timber-framed and one wall post survives, half buried in the later red sandstone walls which now enclose the total building. The original configuration of the ends remains in doubt as the surviving terminal posts show no evidence for cantilevered ends or for longitudinal aisle ties. Several reused rafters carry collar halvings and one has a second collar mortice, suggestive of an original gablet.

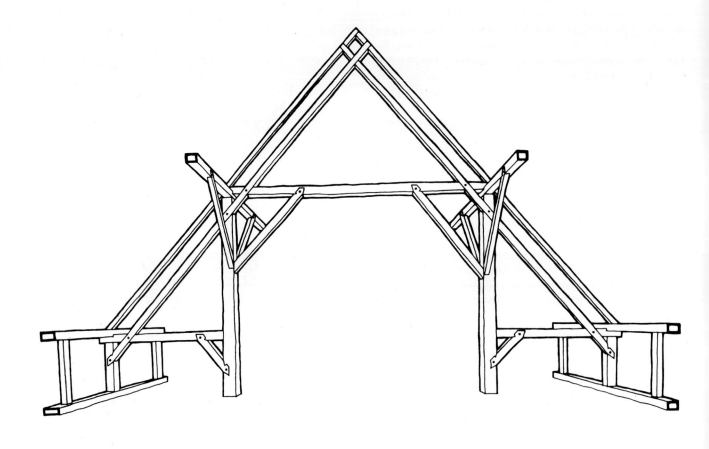

Fig. 18 Grange Barn, Little Coggeshall. Reconstruction of truss

The existence of a second set of lifting holes at the base of the posts suggests that the barn has been erected twice, and that this second operation involved a slightly different technique. It seems also worth noting that, in its present state, the ground slopes sharply beyond the western aisle wall, leaving insufficient room for the supposed original width aisle. The total lack of original lateral tie members must also be borne in mind. It seems therefore distinctly probable that the barn has been reused from another site. As indicated above, the barn forms part of the manorial complex of the Furnival family who may have been the original builders. However, a mere six miles away lay the Cistercian Abbey of Roche, which was destroyed and plundered immediately after it was dissolved. As an Elizabethan commentator stated: 'it seemeth that every person bent himself to filch and spoil what he could' (Butler and Given-Wilson 1979). The possibility that the barn was brought here from a grange belonging to Roche is reinforced by the similarity between it and the Grange Barn at Coggeshall (see below) which was undoubtedly a Cistercian building. Seen together these barns could be regarded as circumstantial evidence for the existence of a Cistercian school of carpentry.

Grange Farm Barn, Little Coggeshall, Essex

This barn belonged to Little Coggeshall Abbey, originally a Savignac house founded *c.*1140 but Cistercian from 1148 subsequent to the disbandment of the Savignac order (Gardner 1955). The barn has been published by Hewett (1980, 47-9). Limited recording was carried out at the time of the major restoration carried out in 1983-84 (Andrews and Boutwood 1983-84).

The original dimensions of the barn are uncertain. It was of at least seven bays. Today it measures 45ft 6in (13.5m) internally in overall width. The tiebeam span is 26ft (7.8m), the bay width 18ft (5.3m), and the height of the arcade posts is 16ft 8in (4.8m).

The Grange Barn shows evidence for numerous rebuildings and repairs, unsurprising in view of its great age. Although considerably larger, the main posts of the Grange Barn are strikingly similar in appearance to those of Whiston Barn, Rotherham. In its present recently renovated state, it represents an accurate rebuilding of the barn as it was prior to its almost total collapse in the late 1970s.

The ancient structure that survives consists of twelve standing posts, one aisle tiebeam, numerous arcade and tiebeam braces, two aisle-posts and a length of passing-brace. Various other timbers survive not *in situ*, including an original corner post and parts of an arcade-plate with simple splayed and pegged scarf joints. From the surviving material it is possible to produce a reconstruction drawing (Fig. 18) showing the general configuration of the structure.

Inspection suggests that the posts are almost certainly not in their original position (all but two of the posts have their passing-braces away from the centre rather than towards the centre as at the other barns examined), and the total lack of contemporary tiebeams and top-plates means that the original bay dimensions must remain in doubt. The arcade-posts have, as at Whiston, a slight but noticeable taper from base to top, and it seems probable that they may have suffered some shaving off of material at top or bottom. Considerable use is made of open notched-lap jointing, all with refined entry, and some with a slight curving of the profile (Fig. 16). It will be noted that the arcade and tie-beam braces strike up at an angle of about 45 degrees and this, together with the relatively broad, low central span, produces a comfortably relaxed proportion. The reversed assembly configuration of the aisle-plate (as reconstructed in 1984 at the north-east corner), is unquestionably correct, but the lack of convincing wall-studs or aisle-plates prevents any accurate reconstruction of the original side walling. However, the two aisle-posts each have a small unpegged and round-ended mortice in one face and notches for wattle and daub, but these, of course,

could be secondary.

Lying on the floor of the barn is one very weathered and eroded former corner post from the original build. Inspection reveals that as originally constructed, the barn had a return aisle at the ends, with a passing-brace, at right angles, stopping at this post. It would appear that reversed assembly at the aisle eaves was general throughout the barn, including the return aisle at the ends. The present day south-east post is another former corner post, though now rotated through 90 degrees. This post is quite unlike all the others in being relatively slim and having its aisle-tie mortices at a slightly higher level (Fig. 19). It is suggested that this post, in other respects similar to the other corner post, represents a slightly later extension, or rebuilding, incorporating normal assembly at the aisle-plate level.

From the foregoing, it is concluded that, as first constructed, the barn had relatively simple hipped ends, without the cantilevered arcade-plates that were formerly present at both the Cressing barns.

An earlier investigation, prior to the second reconstruction of the barn, provided somewhat controversial information. Some of the arcade-posts were discovered to be standing on blocks or pads; some of a hard, mortar-like material and others of a brownish, shelly, crystalline stone (Hewett 1980). These stylobates were about an inch larger

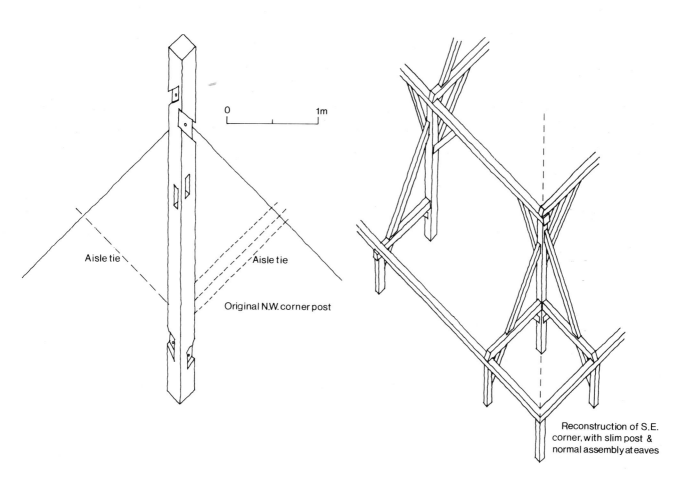

Fig. 19 Grange Barn, Little Coggeshall. Reconstruction of south-east corner

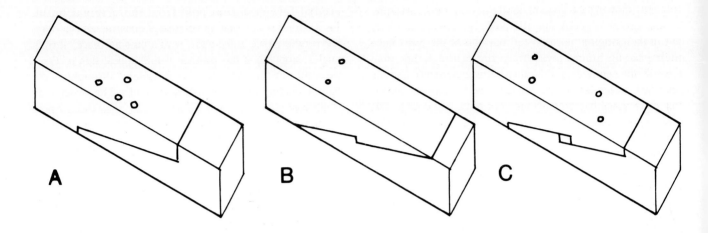

Fig. 20 Scarf joints: A) Grange Barn, Coggeshall; B) Whiston arcade-plate, and Cressing Wheat Barn purlins; C) Cressing Wheat Barn aisle- and arcade-plates

than the base of their posts and the latter were seen to be planed smooth without any indication of additional fixings. During the restoration work, the County Archaeologist sought traces of such stylobates, but found nothing to confirm the earlier discovery. One post was seen to be tenoned to a short timber which projected towards the centre of the barn in a somewhat surprising manner. The complete absence of lifting holes may be relevant to this issue, if only we could ascertain their precise original function. As has been previously mentioned, two pieces of old top-plate survive now in storage on the site. One appears to represent a simple pegged scarf, and the other is splayed and pegged with substantial vertical abutments (Fig. 20).

The present author believes that the existing aisle-tie sole-plates are all later additions, and that an original constructional method involving some form of pad, perhaps of limited height, at the foot of the arcade-posts is most likely.

Wanborough Barn, Surrey

This barn is thought to have belonged to a grange of the nearby Cistercian abbey at Waverley. The mid- to late 14th century building contains three reused posts, a tiebeam and remnants of aisle-ties of a 13th century structure. The early barn represented by these fragments was clearly a larger building, comparable in size to the Cressing Barley Barn, and the posts and tiebeam have been truncated to fit into the more normal-sized existing building.

The surviving posts are all similar and suggest an arrangement as reconstructed in Fig. 21, with a passing brace stopping at the post and a short angle-brace above. No mortices for aisle-ties are visible and this suggests that the posts, which have been reduced in girth, have also been cut off at the base. The notched-lap joints are all of the refined profile type and a mid-13th century date is suggested.

A roof of this size, without passing-braces, is difficult to envisage and unfortunately the present roof seems to provide no clues. One aisle-tie fragment (A), probably from

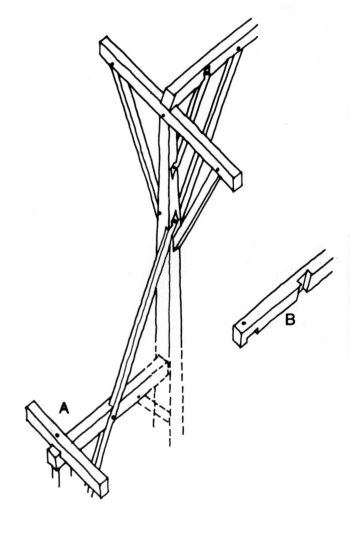

Fig. 21 Wanborough barn, Surrey, reconstruction of framing represented by reused timbers (not to scale)

this structure, involved reversed assembly at the eaves. An otherwise similar example (B), however, is of normal assembly type suggesting that the barn was terminated by simple return-aisles.

This barn would seem to represent a logical development from the Grange Barn, Coggeshall, but compared to the Cressing barns seems relatively conservative. More detailed inspection of the reused parts could throw more light on the earliest phase, which was probably more complex than the story presented here suggests. Also reused in the barn are two octagonal posts, presumably 13th century arcade-posts, and the probable remains of a domestic aisled hall.

The 14th century rebuilding of the barn could also have been Cistercian work. It involved passing braces of the Netteswellbury type (Plate 16) between the tiebeams and aisle-posts. All the bracing is curved, the arcade-posts are without jowls, and the roof has crown-posts with substantial braces. The exterior walls, judging by the surviving north aisle, had grooves for vertical boarding, but markedly inset from the face of the wall. The central bay seems to have been the contemporary entrance with doors beneath the aisle-plate and a pair of massive door posts abutting the adjoining aisle-posts.

Copton Manor Barn, Sheldwich, Kent

This barn originally belonged to Christ Church Priory, Canterbury. Intriguing and ambiguous timbers survive, incorporated to form one end of a small well-built 14th century barn. Three unjowled main posts exist, of typical 13th century form, as well as two lengths of aisle top-plate, grooved on the underside to receive thick external boarding. Three main aisle-posts perform more or less their original purpose and have narrow vertical slots in each flank. The presence of a similar slot on an original, but truncated, aisle corner post suggests that the boarding was rebated with the narrow rebated edge fitting into the vertical grooves (Fig. 22).

A short length of probable tiebeam now serves duty as an aisle-tie, and has the usual passing-brace slot, a refined notched-lap joint for a tiebeam brace, and a mortice for an angle-tie. However, this presents a difficulty in that the timber in question seems ludicrously undersized for this important purpose but nevertheless, it is difficult to suggest a convincing alternative role. One of the three main posts at point 'B' on Fig. 22 has a notched-lap joint in place of a passing-brace slot. It is suggested that this post originally supported the cantilevered end tiebeam as shown in Fig. 22. Such central end posts are a common feature of early Kentish barns, and post 'C' has this function in the existing rebuilt barn. This notched-lap post, surprisingly, carries three original brace mortices and so must have carried a short interconnecting tiebeam. If this hypothesis is correct,

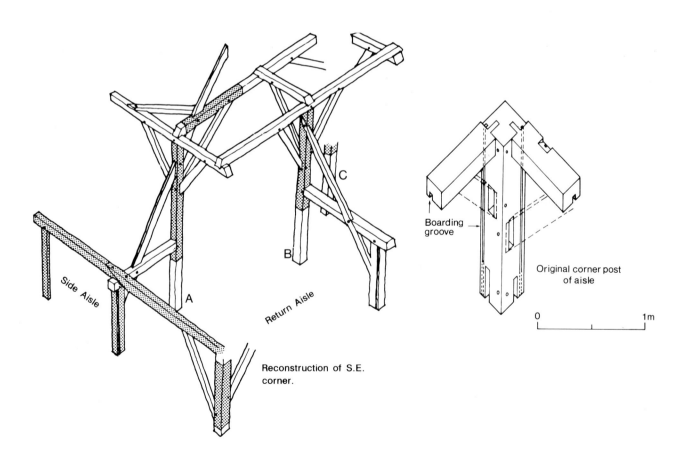

Fig. 22 Reconstruction of barn at Copton Manor, Sheldwich, Kent

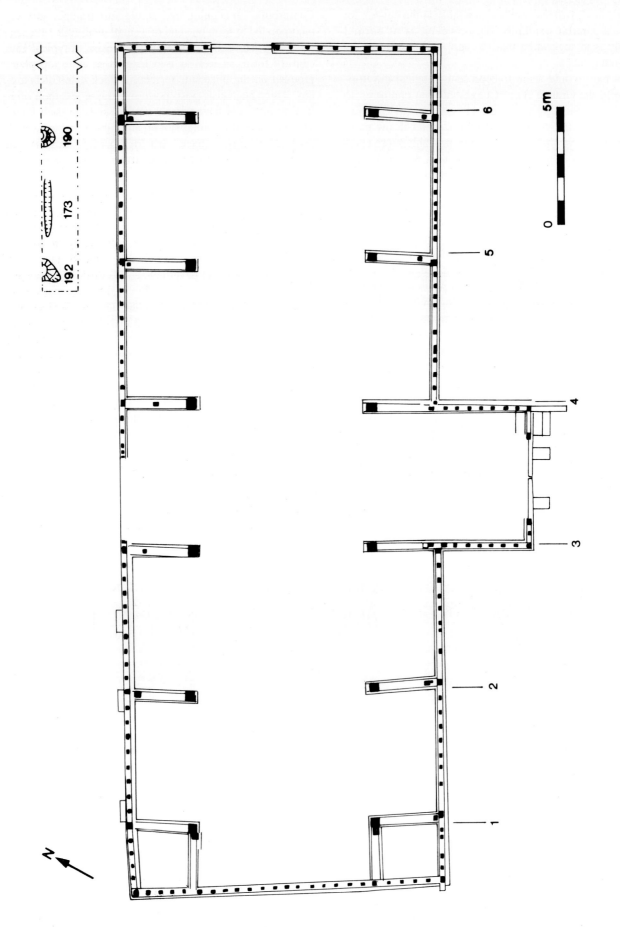

Fig. 23 Cressing Barley Barn, plan

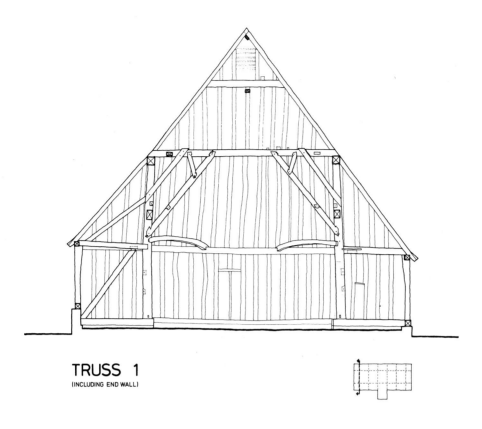

TRUSS 1
(INCLUDING END WALL)

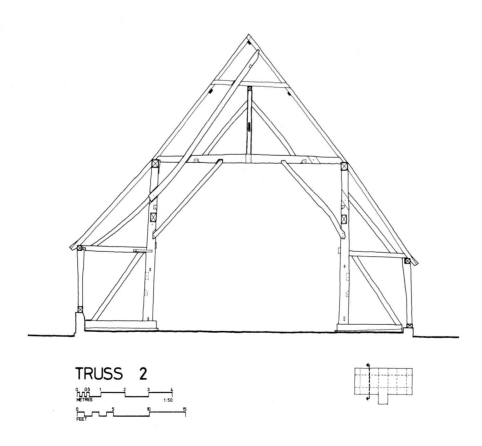

TRUSS 2

0 05 1 2 3 4
METRES 1:50

0 5 10 15
FEET

Fig. 24 Cressing Barley Barn, trusses 1 and 2

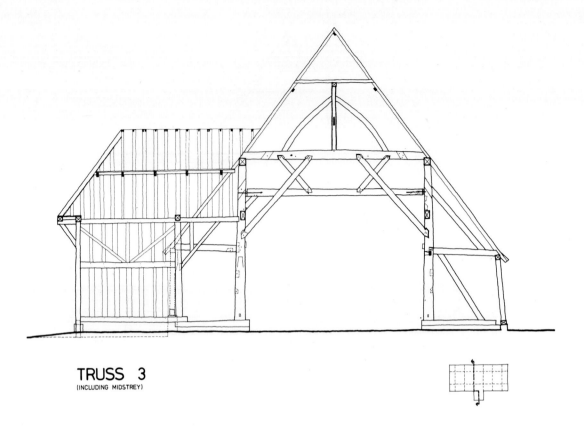

TRUSS 3
(INCLUDING MIDSTREY)

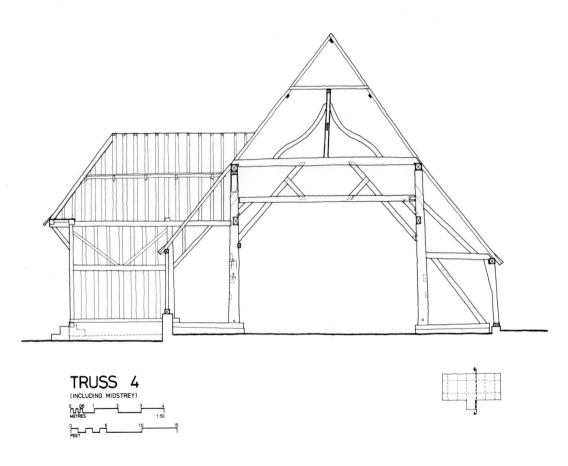

TRUSS 4
(INCLUDING MIDSTREY)

Fig. 25 Cressing barley barn, trusses 3 and 4

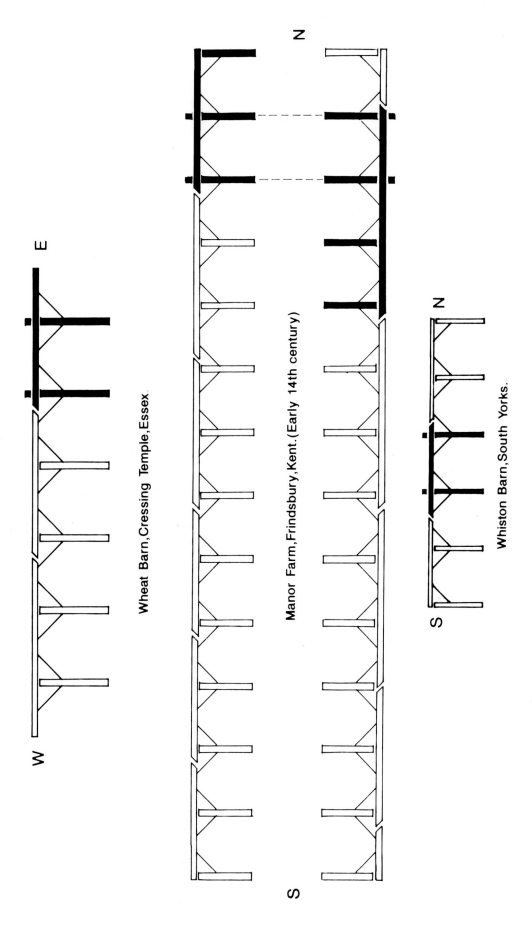

W

E

Wheat Barn, Cressing Temple, Essex.

N

S

Manor Farm, Frindsbury, Kent. (Early 14th century)

N

S

Whiston Barn, South Yorks.

Fig. 26 Suggested erection sequences for the Cressing Barley Barn, the Whiston barn, and the Frindsbury barn. Black indicates the first units to be erected

then we can interpret the structure as an experimental form, with this central axial post helping to support a daring new cantilevered end.

It could be said that the short passing-brace, stopping at the post-head, is the structural equivalent of the short aisle passing-braces in the Grange Barn, Coggeshall, but separated out to support the new cantilevered ends. Nevertheless, it has to be admitted that this particular post with its peculiar truncated passing-brace may have served some other purpose. The aisle top-plate has a simple splayed scarf joint and there appears to have been a single wall-stud at the centre of each bay. It is suggested that Copton Manor Barn is possibly older than the Cressing Barley Barn, and a plausible prototype for cantilevered end aisles.

The Barley Barn, Cressing Temple

Having placed the foregoing buildings in developmental sequence (possibly also a chronological sequence) we now arrive at the Cressing Barley Barn. We should already know something of what to expect if the previous sequence is substantially correct.

This is a manorial barn originally built by the Knights Templars. Tree-ring analysis by Ian Tyers gives a felling date of 1205-35 (Tyers 1992a; and see Tyers in this volume). It is of five equal bays, with the aisles returned at the ends. Internally it measures 36.3m by 13.6m. The average bay width is 5.76m, and the average nave clear span 7.73m. The height to the underside of the tiebeams is c.7m. The barn is considerably larger than all the previous examples, saving the Grange Barn, Coggeshall, which has a similar cross-section. Close examination shows that it has been reduced in width and also at both ends, and that the roof structure has been substantially rebuilt. Figures 23-25 are taken from a recent measured survey and show typical cross sections and a ground plan of the barn as it is today.

Whilst the general concept of the structure follows the well established lines, the trusses can be seen to be of two distinct types. It is here suggested that the building team, responsible for this barn, were perhaps being faced with a problem outside their previous experience. They clearly felt it was necessary to differentiate their trusses and add additional strengthening members to cope with a building of this size. The two central trusses were given an additional lower tiebeam and cruciform bracing between this and the tiebeam proper. Whilst all of the arcade-plates have been replaced, it seems probable that a system akin to Whiston Barn may be postulated, with the two rigid central trusses being the first to be erected, providing a solid central starting point. The other four trusses are more commonplace, but have additional short struts to triangulate the spandrels. In passing, it seems worth suggesting that such spandrel bracing may well be the origins of the similar short spandrel struts in buildings of the 14th century.

As has been already suggested, the arcade-plates of the Barley Barn appear to have been replaced. With the loss of this evidence, the erection sequence is put in doubt, but fortunately in other cases some of the evidence is intact. It is usually assumed that the *lower* half of a splayed scarf joint is the first to be raised into position. Figure 26 demon-

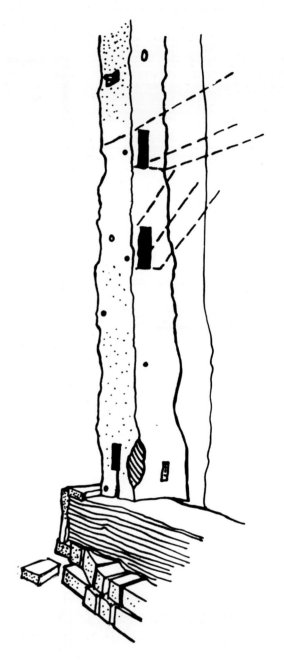

Fig. 27 Cressing Barley Barn, the existing south-west corner post showing mortices

strates likely erection sequences for the Wheat Barn, the Whiston Long Barn, and the early 14th century Frindsbury Barn in Kent (Rigold 1966, 10-11). In the Whiston case, the central pair of posts were the first to be erected, whereas Frindsbury and the Wheat Barn involve erection from one end. As will be seen, the scarf joint is usually located between the top of an arcade-post and an arcade-brace, and other examples only reinforce this observation.

In the Barley Barn, open notched-lap joints of refined profile are abundantly used, but a brand new form of joint makes its first appearance. The tops of the arcade-braces where they meet with the arcade-plate have a form of mortice and tenon with a V-shaped profile. Similar V-shaped mortices can be found elsewhere in the structure and the advantage they offered can readily be determined. Such a joint acted as a lap joint substitute and like a lap joint allowed the particular member to be placed in position following the erection of the principal timbers. Presumably certain disadvantages of the lap joint had been detected, such as its proneness to sheer at the point of contact. V-shaped mortices avoided this problem but could be said to rely unduly on the strength of the fixing peg. It should be noted that all but two of the arcade-braces have a peg hole in their soffit and this may have provided a locating point when they were manoeuvred into position.

As has been previously noted at Stantons Barn, the conventional mortice and tenon joints have offset tenons. In the Barley Barn this phenomenon is particularly marked and there seems to be an attempt to locate the aisle-tie-tenon in a direct vertical alignment, over the strut mortice below (Fig. 27).

Examination of the ends of the barn show that the original construction involved cantilevered top-plates as we have seen before in the barn at Sheldwich. Again, as at Sheldwich, the penultimate tiebeam carried angled corner-ties, but in this particular case on both faces of the tiebeam. I think we can assume that this is again an early use of the cantilevered principle which had the effect of increasing the volume of the return aisles in a way that was economic in timber.

At first sight, the use of notched-lap joints at the lower end of the very long tiebeam braces seems anachronistic, but this is probably one of many indicators that the carpenter was anxious to reduce the primary structure to the minimum. By this process, the tiebeam braces became secondary members, fitted after the principal frame was in place.

In the past, surprise has been expressed that the posts at each end carry no longitudinal aisle-ties (unlike the Wheat Barn). Moreover the lack of such aisle-ties has led to the suggestion that the barn must surely have had a further pair of posts at each end. However, examination of the surviving carpenters' marks tends to undermine this theory (see Fig. 28). These come in two forms, a circle or a half circle, which seem to differentiate each side of the barn. It will be noted that these are only provided on the two central trusses and those at the present-day ends. There would not seem to be any real reason for so marking penultimate posts, if the building has really been shortened. It will also be noted that the carpenters' marks on post 'X' do not follow the general pattern, which would seem to suggest that this is not in its intended position. The somewhat surprising fact that it cannot, in reality, be swapped for any of the posts, suggests that this fault in the marking was an error by the original carpenter.

Returning to the question of the cantilevered ends, the apparent lack of any original aisle components was for a long time a major obstacle to reconstructing how they were built. Fortunately, part of an original aisle top-plate has now been identified, reused as a longitudinal aisle-tie from the present-day north-east post. The soffit of this timber shows a mortice for an aisle post, a pair of V-shaped mortices for straight arch braces, and an upegged stud mortice.

Unfortunately there is no evidence for any form of cladding. Of even greater interest is the top face of this plate for, along with the expected rafter notches, there is an interesting angled dovetail. The lack of longitudinal aisle-ties is thus almost certainly to be explained by a reliance on short corner angle-ties to stabilise the structure.

A feature of great interest in this barn is the presence of lifting holes in both flanks of each post (cf. Whiston). All but two of these are rectangular in shape and still retain in situ slightly tapered wooden blocks. The other two posts have on their innermost faces circular holes which must have served the same function. Hewett (1969, 31-32) suggested that the lifting holes were provided to anchor the post feet during the process of erection. The presence at Whiston of a lifting hole on only one face of the post somewhat complicates the matter. It is here suggested that such lifting holes were intended to receive the ends of short levers, to allow the posts to be finally manoeuvred into their intended positions.

It is also suggested that the Barley Barn, together with all of the examples previously cited, was originally erected without structural aisle sole-plates connecting the post bases to the aisle walls. Where no lifting holes are present, the posts would originally have stood on thickish pads of damp-proof material, such as those discovered at Coggeshall barn. On the other hand, where lifting holes are present, the posts would have stood on substantial stone stylobates and the lifting holes would have allowed them to be raised into position. It should be noted that in areas of England where stone was readily available, arcade-posts generally stand on stone stylobates and lifting holes are invariably provided.

The Barley Barn contains a number of other still unexplained features that need to be considered. Each arcade-post carries a large peg hole, in each flank, immediately below the arcade-brace mortices. Such peg holes serve no obvious purpose, but they appear to be original and so it is probable that they had some role in the assembly process. Perhaps they were a form of datum line to check the geometry or hitching positions for the fixing of halyards. Similarly most of the posts have a small shallow mortice in one face which may possibly have been used to fix a positioning template.

One more important structural feature should now be considered. The lower tiebeams that span between the two central pairs of arcade-posts have one intriguing detail. Whilst at one end they have a one-sided mortice and tenon, the other end has a free tenon. Clearly these beams were not provided to link opposed posts at the primary erection stage, but were added at a secondary stage to stiffen the assembly. The total lack of original arcade-plates makes for difficulties in assessing the likely assembly procedure. It does seem possible that this could have involved single-post erection (as opposed to the system proposed by Hewett 1969, fig. 6), and the pair of lifting holes might strengthen this theory. If this were the case, then the strainer beams could have stabilised the pairs of posts whilst the first section of arcade-plate was lowered into position. The

Carpenters Marks

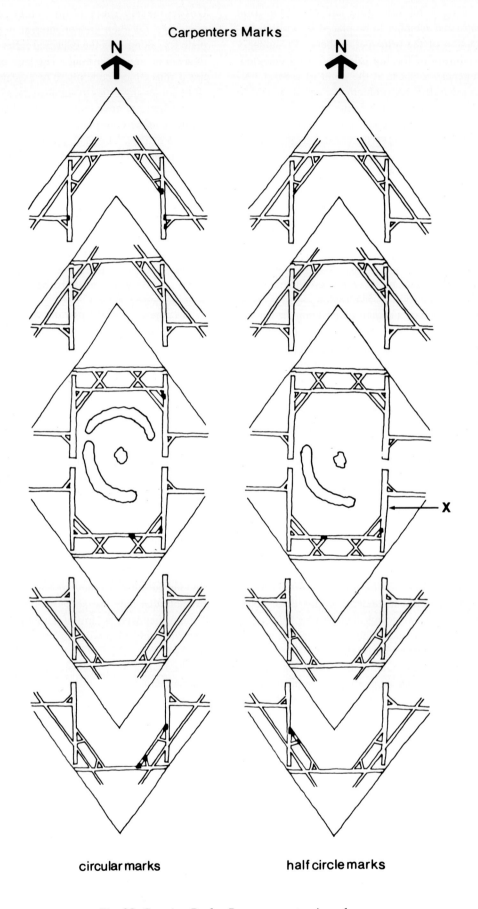

circular marks   half circle marks

Fig. 28 Cressing Barley Barn, carpenters' marks

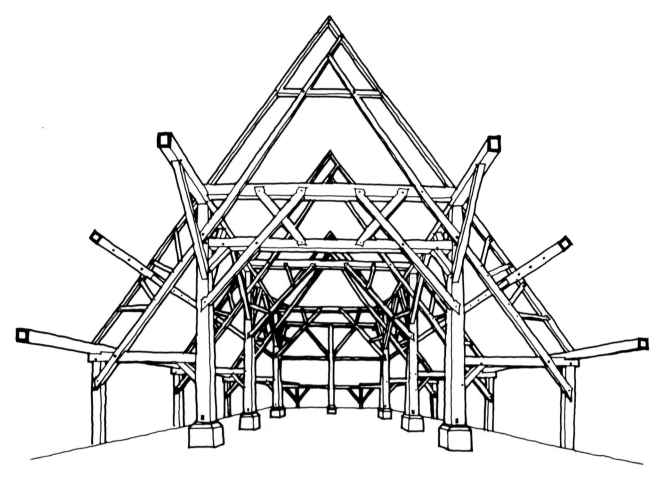

Fig. 29 Reconstructed perspective view looking down the interior of the Cressing Barley Barn.

substantial aisled barn that formerly stood at Parkbury Farm, Hertfordshire, certainly represented single-post construction. This seven-bayed barn was ascribed by Gibson (1974-76) to the late 14th century, but a mid-14th century date might seem equally plausible. The aisle-plates and arcade-plates had in each bay a simple splayed and tabled scarf joint, requiring each post to be erected separately. Gibson argued a possible connection with the cruck framing tradition, and certainly cruck frames exist not far away from this Hertfordshire barn.

Such a system clearly depends on the carpenter erecting an extreme minimum of structure at each stage in the process. The long passing-braces, of which a pair were provided for every truss, survive only as four small fragments. Whilst such passing-braces normally cross above the collar level to fasten to a rafter, that is not the case in the one determinable example. Here, one passing-brace passes the collar and terminates in a notched-lap against the flank of its pair. Whether all couples were of this asymmetrical form or whether this was one exception cannot, unfortunately, now be determined.

As a result of the numerous repairs and rebuildings that have affected the Barley Barn during its long life, there are now a number of reused timbers scattered throughout the structure. New information obtained since the conference at which this paper was given has enabled at least some of these to be explained. An archaeological excavation outside the western flank of the barn revealed a slot and two postholes which seemed to represent the line of the footings of a much wider original aisle than had previously been thought (Fig. 23). This prompted an assessment of the reused timbers, and the geometry of the sides of the barn began to fall into place.

One previously unexplained timber, currently reused as a rafter, has been interpreted as a principal aisle rafter, and another, reused as an aisle-tie strut, as part of a passing-brace. Careful measuring and reassembly of these features on paper produced Fig. 29 which is a perspective depiction of one half of the barn, and also made it clear that the slot found by excavation was unrelated to the original construction of the barn. Instead, the aisle walls seem to have lain just outside their present position, standing just 300mm or 1ft wider than the present aisles. As reconstructed, the aisles required triangulated strutting, echoing the tiebeam brace strutting already noted. A peg hole, centrally placed on the soffit of the reused rafter, suggests an in-plane roof purlin, necessary to support the very long rafters. The use of in-plane roof purlins, or purlins of any form, at such an early date, had been previously unsuspected. Clearly it was also necessary to support the underside of such a purlin, and short timber struts, as at the 14th century barn at Widdington in Essex, were the probable solution.

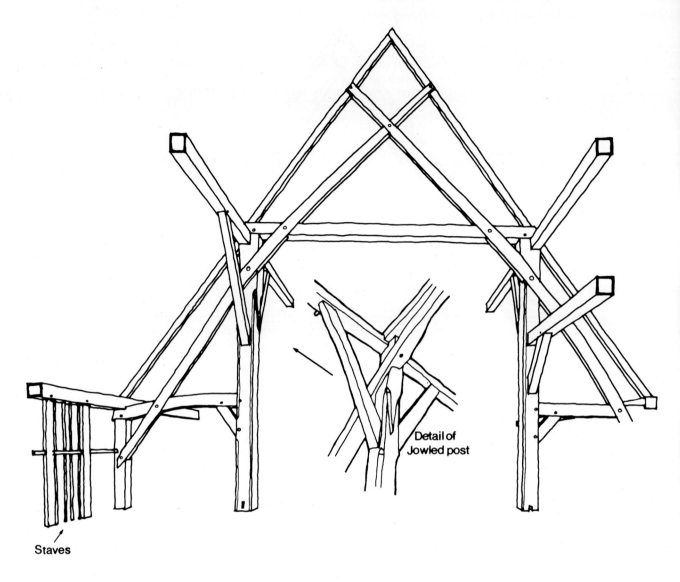

Staves

Fig. 30 Colesden Grange Barn, Bedfordshire, reconstruction

Detail of
Jowled post

As can be seen in the surviving fragments, the passing-braces projected well proud of the timbers they intersected (Fig. 29). This was surely also the case at the end joint on the aisle-posts, where a conventional notched-lap would have looked extremely awkward. Logic again suggests that some form of concealed notched-lap, within the depth of the timber, was probably utilised, perhaps a prototype of the later secret form (see discussion of the Wheat Barn below).

Such an interpretation of the side aisles obviously suggests that the end aisles were of similar design. Logically, they would also require a purlin, which in turn would require support. The means of achieving this are severely limited. The most likely solution is one analogous to Sheldwich in Kent, with central posts in the end aisles, here supplied with side-aisle-like trussed rafters.

This new understanding of the complete structural system enables the Barley Barn to be seen in a new light. Whilst it bore a degree of resemblance to our other early barns, the differences are more striking than the similarities. The later alterations to the Barley Barn are a complex

story in themselves and will be treated later in this paper.

Barns illustrating structural developments between the Cressing Barley and Wheat Barns

Having described the Barley Barn from the point of view of its original construction, our task is now to consider the continuing evolution of this building type. The Cressing Wheat Barn is altogether more sophisticated and a notable advance. Fortunately there are other structures that help signal the changes that occurred between the erection of these two barns.

Colesden Grange Barn, Bedfordshire
The original proprietor of this barn is unknown, but it may well have been monastic. The span between the tiebeams is 5.5m, the total internal width being approximately 10.5m. The height to the underside of tiebeams is *c*.5.4 metres.

Colesden Grange Barn today is, at first sight, a late medieval aisled barn structure with a 20th century roof. However, incorporated in this are five early posts, two contemporary tiebeams and various other remnants. One truss survives substantially *in situ* (see Fig. 30), suggesting by its completeness that it may be in its original location. Although much smaller, there are striking similarities with the Barley Barn and a number of intriguing differences. The aisle-tie bracing pattern is virtually identical and raising holes appear in the base of each post. The short brace between arcade-post and aisle-tie has a post mortice of the V-shaped type which is clearly visible in one of the independent posts. The most important difference is that the posts have jowls and those on the west side are of an unusual decorative form (see insert, Fig. 30). The arcade-posts are also very well finished with stopped chamfers between significant features. The lack of braces between arcade-posts and tiebeam may be a response to the small size but may also be part of a general trend.

Two of the arcade posts are now linked by a low bay width tiebeam, supported on short raking braces. One end of this tiebeam appears to have been refixed, throwing doubt on its value as a bay size determinant. It is suggested that this tiebeam represents part of a midstrey framing and that the two decorative jowls would have been seen through the open doors. The notched-lap joint on the one surviving aisle-post is almost certainly of the secret type but is now seriously decayed. The much renewed arcade-plate has one splayed scarf joint with sallied and under-squinted abutments. Two lengths of what appears to be aisle top-plate survive, reused in other locations. These have widely spaced stud mortices and a series of circular mortices, pre-

sumably for circular staves for some form of wattle and daub walling.

Colesden Grange Barn seems therefore to post-date the Barley Barn but by an uncertain period of time. Such features as the reversed aisle assembly, the V-shaped mortices and the raising holes suggest a relatively small time gap, but the fully developed jowls suggest a different story. A scarf joint with undersquinting of its abutments makes its first appearance in our sequence, but the sallied butts seem a later development of the splayed scarf concept, indicating a late 13th century date.

Barn at Greys Hall, Rectory Road, Sible Hedingham, Essex

Greys Hall was a sub-manor of Sible Hedingham which was held of the De Veres by the Grey family in the 13th and 14th centuries. It was sold by the De Veres in 1586 to a local yeoman (Morant 1768, II, 285).

The barn is a five bay, unaisled, structure of the late 16th century, recently converted into a dwelling. There is much reused timber including a former arcade-post of relevant type, now inserted in a side wall. This post has mortices for an aisle-tie, braces to tiebeam and arcade-plate, and a passing-brace slot. During the conversion, part of the base (formerly the top) of the post was removed when plate level was raised. The apparently unjowled post seems to have formed part of a small aisled barn of Barley Barn type but of unknown date. The post also has a V-shaped mortice for a short raking brace to support the aisle-tie in an

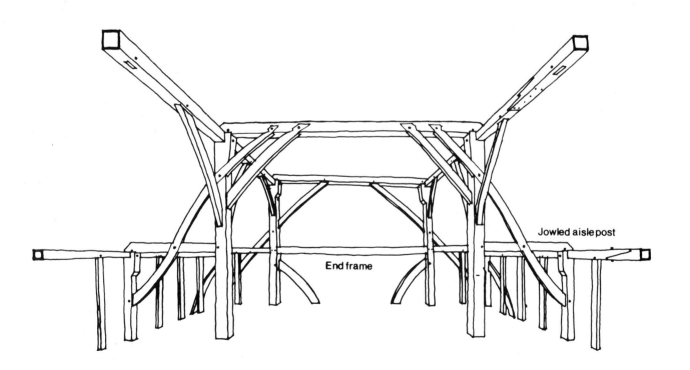

Fig. 31 Church Hall Farm barn, Kelvedon, reconstruction

arrangement similar to the Barley Barn. It is interesting to note that the V-shaped mortice here, as at Colesden Grange Barn, is in the vertical post rather than in horizontal soffits as at Cressing. Another reused timber, now a top-plate, has remains of what is probably a notched-lap joint. It is interesting to discover that V-shaped mortices are now being identified in contemporary non-barn carpentry, such as the wing of an aisled hall in Ware (Herts.)

Barn at Church Hall Farm, Kelvedon, Essex

This manor originally belonged to Westminster Abbey (Morant 1768, II, 150). The barn is a late medieval or immediately post-medieval aisled building, incorporating much reused material. Part of the structure clearly represents an early barn, with passing-braces, but as usual, the individual elements have been reassembled. This early barn had fully developed jowled arcade- and aisle-posts and normal assembly at the eaves. The passing-braces had conventional mortice and tenon joints at aisle-post ends, and this and the other features suggest a post-1300 date. However, a former tiebeam, now used as a wall-post, displays pairs of open notched-lap joints with refined profile. Whilst this may have belonged to our barn, it could also have belonged to some other structure. In Fig. 31 it is assumed to be authentic, and can certainly be made to fit our present reconstruction.

Two posts survive with slots for passing-braces low on their flanks, and these are obviously end-posts. This arrangement suggests a gable or hip above tiebeam termination and an economical and effective way of bracing the structure. The Monks' Barn at Netteswellbury, Harlow, which was built in the 15th century by Waltham Abbey, utilises this form of passing-brace for all its trusses (Plate 16). The existing aisle-posts have notches for wattle and daub walling as has been noticed elsewhere.

Church Hall Barn is another example of offset aisle-tie tenons, and therefore is thus related to the earlier Barley Barn. One arcade-plate scarf joint survives reused, and is an undersquinted *trait de Jupiter* with the usual table wedge. One aisle-plate scarf also survives. It is splayed with undersquinted abutments, and is a simpler joint for a less demanding location.

The Barn, Abbess Warley Hall, Great Warley, Essex

This manor took its name from the abbess of Barking, who held it from before the Norman Conquest until the Dissolution (Morant 1768, I, 111). The barn, which was fortunately described and illustrated by Hewett (1969, 51-52) has long since been demolished. It appears to have been similar to Church Hall Farm, Kelvedon, with long curving passing-braces terminating at each tiebeam with secret notched-lap joints. The base of each passing-brace had chase tenons, but the aisle eaves were made with reversed assembly, with side-facing jowled aisle-posts. The arcade-posts were also jowled, and the wall framing included curved tension bracing.

Barn at Layer Marney Towers, Essex

This manor was held by the Marney family from the 12th to the 16th century. A prominent member of the family in the 12th century was Hugh de Marini, Dean of St Paul's at the time of the lease which describes the barn at Belchamp St Paul which has been examined above. There is a 16th century reference to the manor being held of the bishop of London (Morant 1768, I, 406).

A number of now isolated timbers survive, of probable late 13th century date, reused in a relatively modern barn. The remnants suggest a barn of the Church Hall Farm, Kelvedon type, with low mounted passing-braces in its original ends. A scarf joint of the wedged *trait-de-Jupiter* type performs its original function, and the posts appear to have been unjowled. Two former arcade-posts, now serving as tiebeams, suggest that the structure was of comparable size to the Cressing Barley Barn.

The Wheat Barn, Cressing Temple

This was a manorial barn built by the Knights Templars. Tree-ring analysis of some of its original timbers has given a felling date of 1257-1290 (Tyers 1992b; and see Tyers in this volume). The barn measures 39.75m by 12.2m internally. The clear span of the nave is 6.6m, and the average bay width is 5.6m. The height to the tiebeams is 6.4m.

The Cressing Wheat Barn is probably, in chronological terms, older than the four preceding examples, but is in most technological aspects something of an advance (Fig. 32). The others all retain some conservative features akin to the Barley Barn, and are possibly more vernacular in character. Of five bays plus cantilevered ends, this barn has survived remarkably complete, leaving less room for speculative rumination. The principal technological advance concerns the design of the aisles which, from the first, utilised lateral sole-plates. In this respect, the Wheat Barn is the first truly framed building amongst those considered here, with the arcade-post structure firmly linked to the peripheral walls. Short raking struts link sole-plate with aisle-ties, and their gently curved profile forms a stylistic innovation.

The upper roof slope utilises side-purlins and, until the rethinking of the framing of the Barley Barn described above, these were thought to be the earliest used in a barn. Unlike the Barley Barn, the purlins lie parallel with the ground plane. They are clamped in an ingenious manner between collar, rafter and strut, and clearly resisted any tendency to rack. Given the considerable width of the bays, additional central support was required and a sub-truss, with collar and soulace piece, was the effective solution (it is revealing that these are the only collars in the roof). Such sub-trusses, a sensible precaution with side-purlins, saw further development in the Midlands and West, but were without obvious successors in the immediate locality. The side-purlin concept was also slow to take hold in Essex and the South-East, where the crown-post roof, with its one central purlin, was long the preferred option as a solution to racking.

The design of the cantilevered ends is both a simplification and an improvement over that found in the Barley Barn, and logical evolution can be seen. The end arcade-posts carry longitudinal aisle ties, as at Coggeshall Grange Barn, but the cantilevered technique required them to be

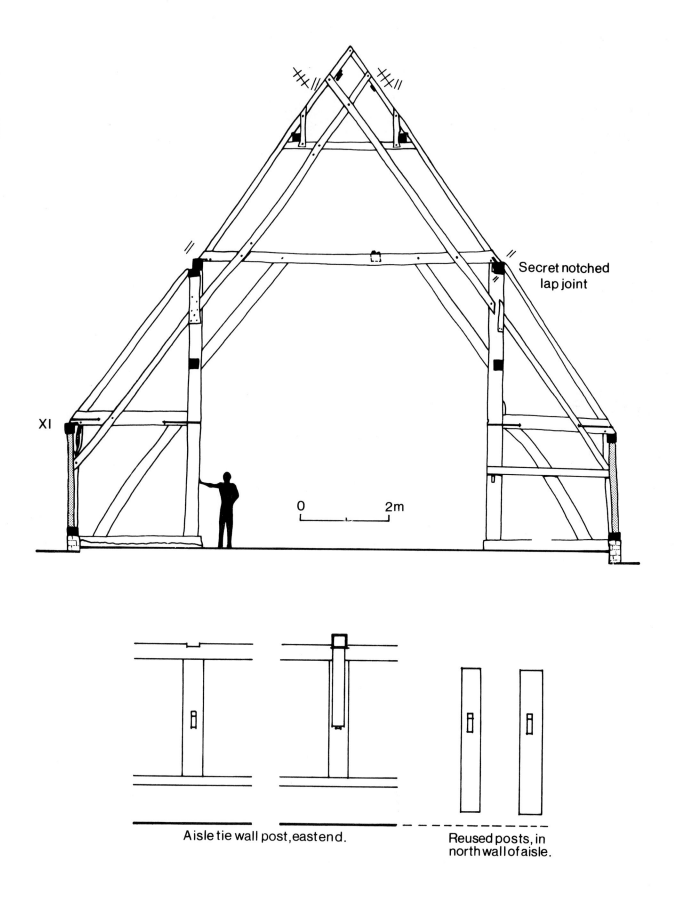

Secret notched
lap joint

XI

0   2m

Fig. 32 Cressing Wheat Barn, truss with detail (not to scale) of aisle posts, existing and apparently reused

Aisle tie wall post, east end.

Reused posts, in
north wall of aisle.

Plate 15. Detail of boarded wall at Manor Farm, Frindsbury, Kent. Note the outer aisle post for the attachment of the boarding, the reversed assembly at the eaves, and the Kentish style raking shore brace (photo: D. Andrews)

exceedingly long. The relatively narrow width of the aisles, together with, no doubt, greater confidence on the part of the carpenters, resulted in the omission of central end-posts.[2] Curiously, many centuries later, central-end posts were introduced into this barn as part of a general process of strengthening it. It will be noticed also that the angle-ties between arcade-plate and tiebeam have been moved out to the ends, thus stabilising the extremities of the frame.

The majority of the notched-lap joints are now of the secret form, but surprisingly some still retain the open version of this joint. It is possible that this represents the idiosyncrasies of a particular carpenter who had little faith in the recently invented variant.

It will be seen that the passing-braces trusses are each of two lengths of timber skilfully aligned so as to appear as one. This is probably a device to avoid the need for overlong scantlings, and may be seen as foreshadowing the end of the passing-brace system.

All the original post-heads, whether to the arcade or to the aisles, have a form of upstand jowl. Such jowled posts generally represent upturned trees with their jowls shaped from the root bole of the tree. Very effective in achieving a 'three-way joint' the more developed jowls, such as at Colesden Grange and Kelvedon, were the logical and eventual outcome.

Carpenters' marks of the familiar Roman numeral kind can be seen in abundance throughout the barn. The arcade-posts and immediate attached timbers were so marked, in a clockwise direction, starting from the south-easternmost post. The five main posts in the eastern aisle wall are numbered consecutively from north to south I-V, and the south wall studs, excluding the main aisle-posts, are numbered from the east. Curiously three apparently original aisle-ties, all in the western half of the barn, are without such Roman numerals and an explanation is difficult to find.

Unlike the majority of our previous examples, normal eaves assembly is generally employed. The original aisle walling method can, fortunately, still be deduced by examining the less altered eastern half. Wall-studs are relatively widely spaced and the spaces in between were originally infilled with vertical planks. Although no planks survive, the top-plates retain the necessary groove and these are possibly detectable in the flanks of the studs. Clearly such a form of construction suffers a fundamental defect in that a decayed board is virtually impossible to replace. The barn at Manor Farm, Frindsbury, Kent, is of the early 14th century and fortunately retains some original vertical boards in its aisle walls (Plate 15). Here the structural system is somewhat different in that the boarding is fixed to a separate aisle-post theoretically detachable from the main structural members. Whilst such a system may well have been designed to assist the erection process, repairs would also have been somewhat easier. It is interesting to note that, whilst most of the plank boards are clearly replacements, the part where old boards survive at the south-west corner lacks this 'double post' detail.

Similar scarf joints are employed in the arcade and aisle plates and are true *trait-de-Jupiters*, splayed with wedged tables and undersquinted abutments (Fig. 20). The side-purlin scarf joints, relatively unstressed in their particular locations, have straightforward splays and a central table. This, of course, is the form of scarf used in the Whiston arcade-plates and thus in a more structurally critical location. The process is surely illustrated whereby a new improved joint relegates the old, easier to make, version to a less important location. The Frindsbury barn, already mentioned, has splayed scarf joints with sallied and undersquinted abutments, each having a prominent vertical key. This seems to be a slightly more advanced variant of the joint noted in Bedfordshire and a developmental process can be perceived.

Later alterations to the Cressing Barley Barn
The Barley Barn has suffered numerous alterations which, together with the casual loss of individual members, makes for difficulties in imagining its original appearance.

It seems possible that at some stage in its life, the barn was approaching dereliction and perhaps had partially collapsed, necessitating a major programme of repair. However, the southern half of the structure is marginally more complete and possibly survived this phase without such drastic disturbance of timbers.

The tree-ring evidence suggests that this major restructuring took place some time in the 15th or 16th century (Tyers 1992a), but the sequence of changes is far from clear. One fundamental alteration involved the shortening of the building, by removing the cantilevered ends of the arcade top plates.

Probably this was seen as an expedient rationalisation of the structure involving only a minor loss of usable floor-space. Possibly, at the same time, the roof was rebuilt incorporating crown-posts and collar-purlin of late medieval type (Fig. 24, 25). Two tiebeams were also replaced and one of these was provided with new, curved, arch braces. One crown-post has now been tentatively dated by dendrochronology to *c.*1510, a date that is convincing on stylistic grounds.

At some time, the side aisles were also narrowed, a process that was echoed in numerous, domestic, aisled halls. The original aisle-ties were removed and new, normal assembly equivalents were provided at a markedly higher level. Somewhat surprisingly, in view of the usual tendency to reuse substantial timbers, with the exception of a single fragment, none of these old ties seem to survive.

The existing jowled aisle posts provided a dendrochronological felling date range of 1410-1445 which is nearly a century earlier than the crown post, and suggests that the aisles were renewed prior to the rebuilding of the roof. This, in itself, seems surprising as rebuilding of the aisles would have necessitated the removal of the passing-

braces and the existing aisle-posts show this to be the case. The loss of these passing-braces would have endangered the stability of the roof unless some other form of structure had taken their place. In the circumstances, it seems unlikely that a temporary expedient was adopted, later to be replaced by the existing crown posts. Perhaps, however unlikely it may seem, the present jowled aisle posts were reused from another building, something which would explain why they are earlier than the crown-post roof.

The aisle walls, in the present form, show numerous renewals, but the various phases are difficult to disentangle. The east wall, itself of two such phases, probably represents the most recent work and incorporates stud-interrupting tension braces of late 17th century character.

The large midstrey centred on the east wall is clearly an addition and is an excellent example of carpentry in its own right. Stylistic grounds again suggest late 17th or 18th century work and dendrochronological analysis might again prove useful. Such sampling was successfully undertaken in respect of the two terminal splint posts which reinforce the arcade-posts at the southern end of the barn. These, together with an inserted part of the eastern aisle top-plate, gave a date range of 1737-1775.

Later alterations to the Cressing Wheat Barn
The one major alteration to the Wheat Barn involved the complete rebuilding of the three aisle walls west of the barn's central bay. Why this work took place is now difficult to ascertain, but it may have been because of instability resulting from this end of the barn being constructed on what seems to be a partly artificial platform. Recent dendrochronological analysis has indicated a felling date between 1420-50 for these works (Tyers 1992b; and see Tyers in this volume), which is somewhat earlier than was previously thought.

In this rebuilding, the main structure survived relatively undisturbed and all but one of the lateral aisle ties were carefully re-employed. In its general appearance, the new work resembles the old aisle walling, to the extent that a conscious imitation seems to have been intended. As first constructed, the new stud walling was infilled with wattle and daub and the fixings for this can be detected. Presumably, by this stage, all the old plank walling of the 13th century work had succumbed to decay and has also been replaced with similar wattle and daub. The new aisle-posts differ in that they employ fully developed emphatic jowls, and the aisle-tie ends were modified to fit this new requirement. Each bay of new aisle framing had regularly spaced substantial studs, the centre one of each bay slightly larger than its fellows. The two aisle corner posts are 'L' shaped on plan, and are jowled in two directions to carry the two-level aisle-plates.

The straight compression bracing of the west end wall is, at first sight, a direct reflection of the earlier work. However, these braces have mortice and tenon joints at both ends and are extremely thick with double halvings at each stud, each stud halving being matched by a similar halving in the brace itself. Such a technique is occasionally seen in early 14th century Essex buildings, but is more

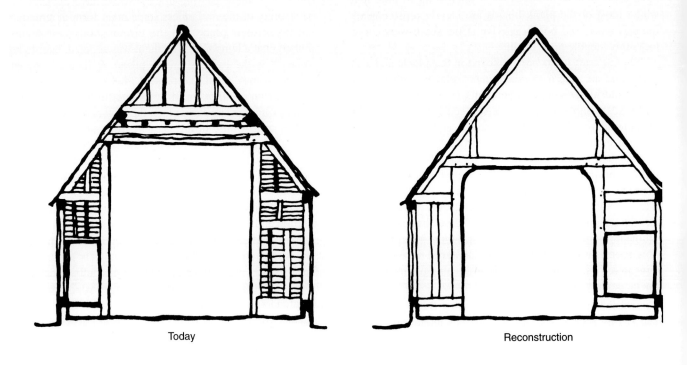

| Today | Reconstruction |

Fig. 33 Cressing Wheat Barn, the porch as existing and reconstructed

commonly encountered in other areas of England. Exceptionally, a mid-16th century barn, north of Maldon in Essex, makes use of this device, and it may represent a previously unnoticed vernacular feature. Compression bracing is, in itself, unusual in mid-Essex in this period. Whilst such bracing was general in the 13th century, tension bracing soon took its place (see Kelvedon Church Hall barn). The question remains, is this work a conscious example of historical revivalism, or is it the work of an outside carpenter, from an area where compression bracing was still in vogue?

Close examination reveals that a number of the studs of the rebuilt aisle are reused from the original work. Two, in particular, in the north wall, bear compression brace mortices and appear to be the principal aisle-tie posts from the old west wall. Comparison of these with the existing east wall-posts shows that they are slightly longer (see Fig. 32). It is possible that the east wall posts were originally as long and were shortened as a result of earlier decay. However, it remains a possibility that the sole-plates were originally at a lower level at this western end, responding to the natural drop in ground level from east to west along the length of the barn, something which suggests its west end stands on an artificial terrace or platform. The outline of small brick piers can be traced in the brickwork of the plinth at the west end of the barn, perhaps representing temporary supports placed in position before the sole-plates were raised.

The existing midstrey, centred on the southern wall, has now been subject to dendrochronological dating and gave a

felling date between 1410-50 (Tyers 1992b). A reasonable correlation between this and the western aisles suggests that this was part of the same building campaign. Its east wall has been rebuilt, but the original stud spacing matched that of the original east end. Grooves for boarded infill are noticeably absent, and instead wattle and daub was clearly intended. The western wall closely follows the stud spacing of the western aisles and was also wattle and daub infilled. Perhaps we have another example of 'keeping in keeping', a surprising phenomenon for the 15th century.

The timbers forming the southern entrance elevation of the midstrey have clearly been re-arranged and supplemented during its long history (Fig. 33). Close examination allows for a plausible reconstruction of its original 15th century design. This appears to have consisted of an asymmetrical arrangement of waggon entrance and pedestrian door, the pintles of the latter surviving *in situ*. The upper part appears to have been gabled, rather than fly-hipped as it is at present. The alterations, which may have been of more than one phase, achieved a wider and taller waggon entrance, no doubt reflecting the increasing size of waggons.

The character of the south-eastern corner post of the midstrey, and the dendrochronological date obtained for it, combine to indicate that it was reused from the original barn. This serves to underline the probability that the porch was erected contemporaneously with the rebuilding of the western aisles.

All the external walls now have brick nogging which

Fig. 34 Comparative chart showing the carpentry features of the barns discussed in the text

Barns in text order →	Open notched laps	Open notched laps refined entry	Secret notched laps	Raising holes	Aisle eaves reversed assembly	Aisle eaves normal assembly	Vertical plank walling	Wattle and daub walling	Unjowled posts	Jowled posts	Simple return aisles	Cantilevered arcade plates	Aisle-less ends	Scarfs with under-squinted abutments	Trait de Jupiter scarf joints
Paul's Hall, Belchamp St. Paul, Essex	■				■		■		■		■				
Stantons Farm, Black Notley, Essex	■				■			■	■		■				
Manor Barn, Whiston, South Yorkshire	■			■					■		■				
Grange Barn, Lt. Coggeshall, Essex		■			■			■	■		■				
Copton Manor, Sheldwich, Kent		■			■		■		■			■			
Barley Barn, Cressing Temple, Essex		■		■					■			■			
Colesden Grange, Bedfordshire			■		■			■		■					
Greys Hall, Sible Hedingham, Essex									■						
Church Hall, Kelvedon, Essex		■			■	■		■	■				■	■	
Abbess Warley Hall, Essex			■		■			■		■					
Layer Marney Towers, Essex									■				■	■	■
Wheat Barn, Cressing Temple, Essex		■	■			■	■			■		■		■	■

73

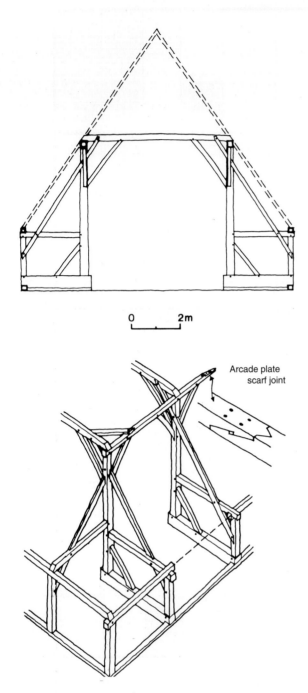

Fig. 35 The large barn at Sandonbury, Hertfordshire

seems to date from the 16th century (see Ryan and Andrews in this volume).

Conclusions

We have examined a sequence of aisled barns that represent almost a century of development. Throughout this period, there is a marked similarity of approach with the barns differing more in size, than in detail, but with Cressing Wheat Barn showing the most notable innovations (Fig. 34). The majority of the buildings had an ecclesiastical or monastic origin and are clearly representative of high status work. If a Cistercian connection has been correctly identified at Whiston, then we are possibly witnessing standard, workshop, lay-brother practice and the similarities

with Coggeshall and Wanborough are to be expected. There are a number of points in the Rule of the Templars (Upton Ward 1991) where craftsmen brothers are mentioned, and in two instances the term mason is specifically utilised. Whether such specialists belonging to the Order would have erected the Cressing barns remains an interesting question.

Roche Abbey itself, which may have been responsible for the construction of Whiston Barn, has the strong north-eastern French Cistercian connections (Fergusson 1974) of the period and the carpentry may also be related. The jowled post-head may in itself be a French concept, but was relatively little used as a result of the French predilection for reversed assembly of the main arcade. It seems unlikely that any of the barns considered actually pioneered any of the technological advances they show, and features such as the secret notched-lap joint and the jowled post were certainly used earlier than our sequence would suggest.

The use of raking struts seems to be common to the three St. Paul's barns, and may again denote specific workshop practice. The somewhat similar raking struts, but between sole-plate and aisle tie, displayed in the Cressing Wheat Barn may demonstrate how influences travelled from one workshop to another. The distinctive multiple triangulation of the Cressing Barley Barn may be particularly significant, and may possibly relate to a North European tradition. However, it seems probable that the carpentry technique, which has so much to do with assembly method, is all related to a common North European methodology. This would itself develop specific characteristics, either locally based or within the works of individual religious orders, which would help to explain the differences observed and discussed in this paper.

Certain other large monastic barns of our period, such as the stone walled Great Coxwell Barn (Oxfordshire), show a marked contrast in appearance and seem much more closely related to a mainstream French carpentry style, involving reversed assembly and true principal rafters. The Wheat Barn, thus, may be a hybrid, combining north European tradition with a subtle overlay of more advanced French influence. The examples show an intriguing mixture of walling methods with plank infilling being a high specification solution, probably with very ancient origins. The later examples, whilst still high status in origin, probably represent a more vernacular approach that leads on to greater diversity in the following century. This diversity can be detected in buildings of all types and seems to represent differing levels of progress in different parts of the realm and continues to become more evident as time goes by.

POSTSCRIPT. Sandonbury Barns, Sandon, Hertfordshire; and the date of the barn at Belchamp St. Paul

The barns at Sandonbury were examined subsequent to the preparation of this paper. This led to discoveries that provoked a reappraisal of the Paul's Hall barn at Belchamp St.

74

Paul, which in turn sheds a new light on the argument contained in the first half of this paper.

Sandonbury was a manor belonging to the Dean and Chapter of St. Paul's. Of the two surviving barns, it is the larger that is of most interest to us. It is of five aisled bays, with a span of *c*.19 ft (5.6m). The face orientation of the passing-braces in particular suggests that there were two entrances and that it probably functioned as a dual unit. The ends had simple return aisles with passing braces, akin to those of the Coggeshall Grange Barn, but with normal assembly of the return aisle-plates (Fig. 35).

The roof, now replaced, was probably of basic collar/rafter type with passing-braces terminating at each tiebeam. The intermediate tiebeams have notched-lap joints, of a somewhat peculiar type, but the terminal tiebeams utilise mortices and tenons. The scarf joints (the arcade-plates survive complete) are splayed, tabled and wedged with vertical sallied abutments. The arrangement suggests that the four central posts were individually erected. The overall character indicates a structure of the second half of the 13th century, in some ways more advanced, and in others more archaic, than the Wheat Barn.

A feature of great interest is that each arcade-post had a raking shore against its back jointed in to the contemporary sole-plates. Such a feature is immediately reminiscent of the Paul's Hall barn (Fig. 15), although at Sandonbury the posts clearly were not earth-fast. Since this shed doubt on the claimed great antiquity of the Paul's Hall barn, a tree-ring date was obtained by Ian Tyers for some of the older timbers in that barn. The two early arcade-posts and fragment of tiebeam produced similar results, with a felling date of *c*.1240. Clearly these fragments do not in fact belong to the Oat Barn described in the late 12th century lease, but are from a building somewhat younger than the Cressing Barley Barn. Obviously, the opening part of this paper has to be reviewed in the light of these results, but most of the other findings remain relevant. However, the raking shores, seen in this perspective, were less likely to have been earth-fast, and aisle-plates, as at Sandonbury, were probably used.

At Sandonbury, there is also a smaller barn built in the 17th century which incorporates some 13th century timbers. The surviving elements suggest a building smaller than but virtually identical to the larger barn, although its exact original dimensions cannot now be ascertained. The only substantial variation lies in the form of the lap joints, which are entirely without notches. Such notch-less lap joints have been noted in various Suffolk barns and generally have been claimed to represent a 14th century development.

Notes

1. The account of this barn has been superseded by research carried out since the conference at which this paper was given. These new results can be found in the Postscript at the end of this article.
2. It appears that central end posts continued to be used in Kent, where they are found in the probably 14th century barns at Lenham and elsewhere which lack cantilevered end

Acknowledgements

This research could not have been carried out without the co-operation of the owners of the various barns discussed here. Their patience and forbearance is acknowledged with great gratitude. I should also like to thank Adrian Gibson for discussing various points, particularly about the Cressing Barley Barn, and for providing information about Hertfordshire barns. The Barley Barn survey drawings are the work of Paul Skeet and Kirsten Kingsley. The Wheat Barn truss was drawn by Barry Crouch. The other drawings have been prepared for publication by Stuart McNeil.

Tree-ring Dating at Cressing and the Essex Curve

by Ian Tyers

Introduction

Twenty years of tree-ring studies in the British Isles has completed a composite chronology that covers the last 7000 years. This, in theory, allows for the accurate dating of suitable samples from oak timbers used in buildings and recovered from archaeological features throughout the British Isles. However, by reviewing the geographic coverage of the chronologies it is apparent that some areas are under-represented.

For these areas it is clear that the samples obtained during the routine analysis of buildings and archaeological features are inadequate for dating and chronology construction purposes. Thus a different strategy must be adopted to obtain suitable material. This paper presents details of the success of one strategy for filling in the sequences from one of the problem areas and perhaps provides a model for dealing with similar situations in other parts of the country.

First it is worth reviewing the areas that are under-represented in the chronologies of the last millenium. Possible reasons why areas are under-represented are then discussed and the case is made for trying to improve the situation.

Local tree-ring chronologies in England covering the period c.AD1000 to the present day are usually derived from three distinct components. Firstly 'modern' chronologies constructed from cores taken from living trees or slices from recently felled trees. These chronologies range from c.100 to c.400 years in length and have been produced from all parts of the country. These provide the anchors for the reference sequences and they have been extended back through time either by samples from archaeological sites or from building timbers. The vast bulk of the archaeological material is derived from waterlogged sites in the main urban areas, since that is where the majority of archaeological work has been undertaken over the past decades; smaller quantities have been produced from many excavations across the country. By contrast standing building timbers are widespread but are more commonly available from non-urban centres.

This extensive sampling has produced poor coverage in a number of geographical areas: Essex/Suffolk/Norfolk, Devon/Cornwall, and Cumbria/Northumbria are the main ones. This suggests that geographical location is in some way related to the problem. It is possible that the deep valleys of the latter two areas, and the extensive rain shadow effects within the first area are important influences. An additional factor which must be borne in mind in the Essex/Suffolk/Norfolk area, and also many other areas around the large medieval towns, are patterns of past woodland exploitation and/or management which has tended to produce structures built with faster grown, younger and less sensitive trees.

Why is it important to completely cover the country in an extensive and well-replicated matrix of tree-ring sequences? The most immediate use is that it would be more likely to be able to date subsequent samples from the same area, thus helping archaeologists and building historians to understand sites and buildings better in those areas. Secondly, it is potentially useful in understanding past woodland economies and changes in tree utilisation pattern through time; e.g. size, species, and age-structure. Thirdly, the availability of widespread local chronologies may highlight material that has been transported within the country; this is of particular relevance to the study of the economy of medieval towns, such as London, and appreciating their effects upon large areas of countryside around them. Lastly climatic reconstructions from variations in tree-ring sequences will need as extensive a set of chronologies as is obtainable. In order to undertake these studies in the future the production of suitable local tree-ring sequences needs to be initiated at this stage.

This paper therefore deals with several aspects of the extensive tree-ring analyses undertaken at Cressing Temple, and their wider applicability. The methodology of tree-ring dating is briefly explained, with particular emphasis laid upon the types of samples required for successful dating and the difficulty of obtaining suitable samples from Essex buildings. The results of the various samples taken from Cressing are explained and the importance of this site for providing the first samples from Essex to be successfully dated is highlighted. Lastly, as a result of the Cressing tree-ring chronologies a number of other buildings have been successfully dated, the results are briefly described, the current extent of tree-ring chronologies from the county covering the last millenium is shown, and the procedure for completing the sequences is discussed.

Tree-ring dating: potential and problems

Tree-ring dating, or dendrochronology, relies upon the observed behaviour of trees in temperate parts of the world to have a growing season and a resting season. Most British hardwood trees drop their leaves during the autumn and wait until the following year before beginning to grow again. Anatomically this shows up within the trunk or branch as a 'tree-ring'.

The pattern of growth on a year to year basis is reflected in the widths of successive rings. For trees growing through comtemporaneous periods this pattern is sufficiently similar to allow the correlations between them to be the basis of an independent and potentially precise dating system.

Chronologies of precisely known date (reference chronologies) are constructed by starting with sequences from modern trees and extended backwards by using increasingly older samples. The ring pattern of samples for which dates are required are measured and this pattern is compared at each point to a wide variety of reference chronologies until a match is found.

There are however several details that need to be clearly understood. For example, not all samples are datable, the most obvious problem being where samples are of a species of wood for which no chronologies are available. In Britain most chronologies are of oak *(Quercus sp.)*. Other species are rarely present in buildings and it is thus more difficult to build long chronologies for them. The next problem is availability of chronologies that are sufficiently local and of contemporary date - it is hopefully obvious that it is not possible to date Roman timbers until Roman chronologies have been constructed. Similarly, for any area of the country it is necessary that several contemporaneous chronologies exist to provide sufficiently reliable cross-matching.

Because sequences of pattern are being matched there are statistical minima to the number of rings that are required; no sample of less than 50 rings is of use when attempting to provide a date, and more than 100 is preferable. In addition it is significantly better to be able to sample many timbers per phase in any structure, attempt to match each sequence together, and then date the resulting composite mean.

Lastly, many apparently suitable samples are found not to date at all. This is presumably because the climate related part of the growth pattern of the sample is too weak to match any dated chronologies. Samples from pollarded trees are an example of a ring pattern dominated by non-climatic factors and such samples are rarely datable.

For all these reasons, in order to date any structure by dendrochronology, it is necessary to be able to take multiple samples from contemporaneous parts of the structure of a single species of timber. For both archaeological features and standing buildings the minimum requirement is 6-8 samples per phase, each with more than 50 rings; the more samples taken and the more rings in them the better the chance of a date. In order to maximise the information derived from the analysis, the importance of the proper recording of the structures cannot be over-emphasised. Only when each dated timber is properly understood within the context of the construction and modification of the structure is the usefulness of the tree-ring analysis fully disclosed.

Finally, although the accuracy of the resulting date is absolute it is not always very precise. Although the dates of chronologies are accurate to the year the precision of any interpretation is reliant upon the type of sample dated and in particular on the presence of the outer sapwood and bark of the timber. The softer and usually crumbly sapwood of many building timbers is often impossible to sample successfully and this results in a less precise date being provided because allowances have to be made for missing sapwood. The full interpretation is reliant upon an understanding of the structure, but problems will result from unrecognised re-use of older timbers, or from the long-term storage of timbers prior to use.

Cressing: the Essex chronology initiated

As outlined in the introduction, suitable samples with enough rings from buildings in Essex have proved difficult to obtain. Many buildings have been studied, mostly by colleagues at the Sheffield University Tree-ring Laboratory, but very few timbers were located with enough

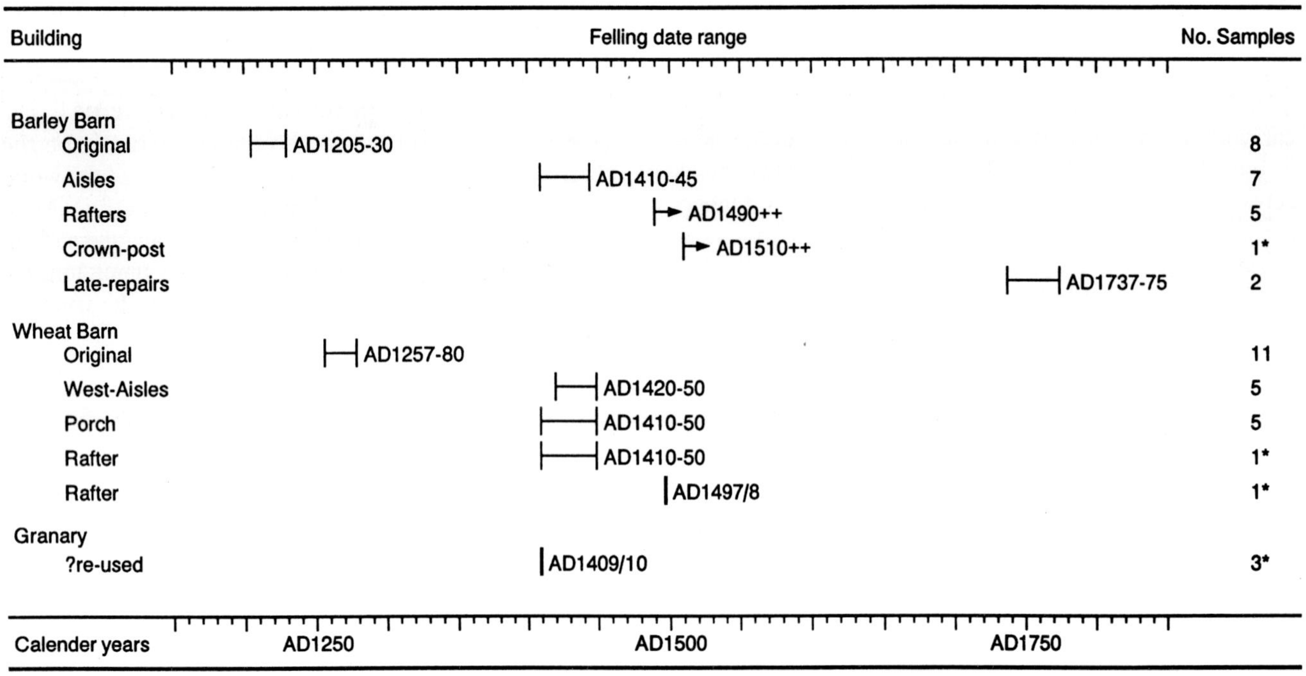

Building	Felling date range	No. Samples
Barley Barn		
Original	AD1205-30	8
Aisles	AD1410-45	7
Rafters	AD1490++	5
Crown-post	AD1510++	1*
Late-repairs	AD1737-75	2
Wheat Barn		
Original	AD1257-80	11
West-Aisles	AD1420-50	5
Porch	AD1410-50	5
Rafter	AD1410-50	1*
Rafter	AD1497/8	1*
Granary		
?re-used	AD1409/10	3*
Calender years	AD1250 AD1500 AD1750	

Fig. 36 Results of the tree-ring analysis of buildings at Cressing Temple

78

rings to be datable, and virtually none had been dated.

The opportunity to analyse timbers from the buildings at Cressing Temple was therefore seized because all the criteria felt necessary to counteract the problems were available there. The favourable circumstances include:-

1. the buildings on the site covered a number of periods, and several have a series of modifications. Thus any chronologies produced were likely to be extensive.

2. the buildings could all be well recorded, and multiple samples were likely to be available, thus providing a good opportunity to replicate the chronologies produced.

3. the buildings contained some large timbers which were likely to contain sufficient rings to be datable.

4. the buildings were in the hands of a sympathetic owner (Essex County Council). It was therefore likely that there would be the opportunity to integrate our work with many other aspects of research on the site and to continue to sample as questions were refined and the understanding of the structures grew.

5. lastly, since the original owners held extensive land in the vicinity there is a high probability that the chronologies produced are very local to the site.

The tree-ring results from the site are summarised in Figure 36. Their significance for the buildings is dealt with by Stenning in this volume. Tree-ring work at Cressing has been undertaken in three phases. The first was involved exclusively with timbers replaced following the gale damage of 1987. The result of this work from a tree-ring viewpoint was the production of the first sequence from Essex to be dated, but from the viewpoint of understanding the buildings the samples analysed were not always well provenanced and were obviously not targeted at all phases of the structure. Hence, in 1991 and 1992 two further analyses were undertaken on the Barley and Wheat Barns respectively (Tyers 1992a and 1992b). These involved close consultation with Dave Stenning and Oliver Rackham and others, and were planned to deal with the main phases of the respective buildings. The interpretations obtained thus far are given in Figure 36, along with the number of samples contributing to each date. This shows that several phases are now very securely dated, but that several are based on only single or poorly located samples (marked with an asterisk). Of these the phase most in need of re-sampling is the Barley Barn's crown-post roof. Several other features within the barns remain undated, including the stylobates in both barns and the Barley Barn porch. In addition, two important timber buildings on the site, the Granary and the farmhouse, await examination.

Many aspects that are of interest have appeared. Clearly the two barns are about 50 years apart in date, and other papers in this volume by Stenning and Rackham detail the technological changes and other differences that are of relevance to this point. In addition, a very major

series of changes occurred to both barns in the early 15th century. At present, the dates of these changes appear to be contemporaneous, but the lack of precision of the dating (through lack of sapwood) may be masking several distinct phases. The aisles of both barns were changed in this period, those at the western end of the Wheat Barn as well as those around all sides of the Barley Barn being rebuilt. The porch of the Wheat Barn is apparently identical in date to all this activity, as are at least some of the rafters in the Wheat Barn. The only dated material from the Granary is also apparently of this period, though this must be assumed to be reused timbers until more complete sampling is undertaken of this building. Aspects of the interpretation of the dates from the buildings are discussed in Stenning in this volume.

Extending the Essex sequences

The overall objective of producing a local Essex tree-ring sequence has been well served by the Cressing material. The site has provided 90 samples thus far (60 cores and 30 slices), although many more timbers have been examined and rejected prior to sampling. 67 samples were considered potentially useful and 49 of these have been dated to produce the information outlined in Figure 36. The combined chronologies from the site cover the periods AD1106-1249, AD1320-1501 and AD1661-1737.

Following the first phase of sampling at Cressing, all previous samples from Essex were re-checked with the new sequences, and the Coggeshall Grange Barn samples (processed many years earlier by Ruth Morgan) were found to link with the early phase chronology from Cressing. Unfortunately, not much is now known about the precise origin of the samples and the interpretation is somewhat unclear. One additional sample (a main post base) from the Coggeshall Grange Barn was fortuitously located and found to date just earlier than the Barley Barn, although the other two dated sequences lie between the Barley and Wheat Barns in date. (The Grange Barn is discussed by Stenning in this volume).

Several other buildings from Essex that had previously been sampled provided sequences that did not date to the new chronologies (Cathy Groves pers. comm.). However, between 1988 and 1992 several more single or double samples from buildings in the county have been taken and three of these are dated. Rivenhall church provides a 13th century sample, Thaxted Guildhall provides some 15th century material, and an excavated post from Coggeshall is 18th century in date. Several other buildings in Essex have been sampled and dated since the start of the Cressing tree-ring work. The barn at Belchamp St. Paul (see Stenning in this volume) was sampled, and although the timbers only produced short sequences, they convincingly cross-match with both the Barley and Wheat Barns at Cressing and the Coggeshall Grange Barn. Thaxted church roof was dated from samples taken during repairs in 1989/90. These provide two sequences, one of which cross-matches with the middle Cressing sequence and extends it to 1526, whilst the other cross-matches with the late Cressing sequence and extends that to 1813. Analysis of Rookwood Hall Barn in Abbess Roding (see Rackham in this volume) has dated that to *c.*1538; it cross-matches with both Thaxted and Cressing and extends the curve to 1537. Queen Elizabeth's Hunting Lodge in Chingford (formerly in Essex, now 200m inside Greater London) has produced a well replicated sequence that matches Cressing, Thaxted and Rookwood, and extends the county sequence to 1542. Lastly, recent archaeological work at Tilbury Fort has produced a well replicated late 17th-early 18th century sequence (Cathy Groves pers. comm.).

Completing the sequence

The current extent of all the building and archaeological tree-ring sequences from Essex, covering the last millenium, is shown in Figure 37. The Cressing 1, 2, and 3 sequences reflect the combined data sets from all stages of analysis at the site as discussed above. It can be seen that several gaps are still present. The sampling of buildings of appropriate dates will be required in order to remove them. The work at Cressing thus far shows that the only sensible strategy in Essex is by the location of buildings containing suitable timber and extensively sampling them, in combination with other structural recording by appropriate specialists.

Reviewing previous work demonstrates that the analysis of small numbers of samples from a large number of buildings has failed to provide material that covers all periods. In addition, the timbers in most Essex buildings are not of sufficient quality to date to reference chronologies outside the immediate area, and are themselves inadequate for use in building local reference chronologies. The Granary and farmhouse at Cressing are perhaps the most accessible material. The timbers in them are probably capable of closing the gap between the Essex 2 and 3 chronologies.

Once the sequence is completed, perhaps many of the buildings that can only provide a few samples will then be found to be datable, although it seems likely that the success rate on such material is always going to be low.

Conclusions

The analysis of extensive tree-ring samples from Cressing Temple has provided dates for the construction phases of the two barns, as well as the dates of a number of the modifications to them. The success of the work is due to a unique combination of circumstances allowing an extensive multi-disciplinary approach to the understanding of the buildings.

In addition, the analyses provided the key elements required for the initiation of a local tree-ring sequence. This has already allowed several other buildings from Essex, where only small numbers of samples could be removed, to be successfully dated. Future work at Cressing and elsewhere in the county should complete the sequence and provide significantly improved dating potential for other local timbers. The work at Cressing provides one model for the production of tree-ring chronologies from areas that are under-represented, or perceived as 'difficult'. The production of a local tree-ring chronology for Essex is also of use for the surrounding areas and will prove valuable for future research objectives.

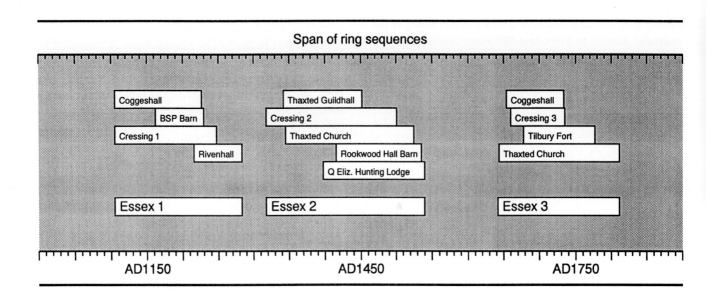

Fig. 37 The Essex tree-ring sequence to date

Appendix. List of tree-ring samples from Essex

In the 1980s, an attempt was made by Essex County Council in collaboration with the Sheffield University Tree Ring Laboratory and the Museum of London Tree Ring Laboratory to analyse timbers from buildings in course of reconstruction and from archaeological deposits. The value of fixed dates for the understanding of timber-framed buildings and of archaeological sequences does not need to be underlined. Many of these analyses were unsuccessful, but some were not, and with the recent progress made on the Essex curve using the material from Cressing, those that initially could not be dated may eventually fall into place. This list brings these analyses, mostly hitherto unpublished, together, and includes all other analyses of Essex material of which we are aware.

	Date	Analyst	Date obtained	Notes
Mersea, piles from causeway	1980	J. Hillam Sheffield	*c.*693	EAH 1982, 14, 80-86.
Foulness ?fishing weir	1981	M. German	*c.*1483-89	EAH 1981, 13, 70. Based on Fletcher's chronologies. Needs re-assessment.
Coggeshall Grange Barn, arcade post	1984	R. Morgan Sheffield	after *c.*1235	EAH 1984-85, 16, 150
Cressing Temple 1) Barley Barn 2) Wheat Barn 3) Granary	1984	J. Fletcher Oxford	after 1220 *c.*1280 after 1575	VA 1985, 16, 41 Provenance of samples in these buildings uncertain
Fyfield Hall 1) Saxo-Norman post 2) brace 3) 2nd phase post	1985	J. Pilcher Belfast	No 1140-85 1390-1425	Wood friable, cores broke Cross-matched to Cressing by I. Tyers
Coggeshall ex-fire station site, Stoneham Street	1986	R. Morgan Sheffield	No	EAH 1987, 18, 94
Rochford Hall 1) window lintel 2) door lintel 3) lintel of inserted door	1987	R. Morgan Sheffield	No No *c.*1582	Probably 1550s Ditto
Rochford, Horners Corner	1987	C. Groves Sheffield	No	Probably late 16th century
Southchurch Hall 1) 1st phase bridge & revetment 2) 2nd phase bridge 3) 3rd phase bridge	1987	R. Morgan Sheffield	No No No	Harwell C14 dates: 1st phase revetment 1265-1355; 2nd phase bridge 1360-1460
Maldon, 160-162 High Street (Wealden houses)	1988	C. Groves Sheffield	No	2 storey posts & a stud. Probably *c.*1400. EAH 1989, 20, 103.
Belchamp St. Paul, Paul's Hall 1) floor joist 2) tiebeam	1988	C. Groves Sheffield	No No	Probably 16th-17th century Ditto
Barking Abbey 1) well	1988	I. Tyers London	after 800	Passmore Edwards Museum excavations

	Date	Analyst	Date obtained	Notes
2) well			*c.*730	
3) rebuild well 2			800-835	
4) timber leet, 3 phases			705; 745; after 768	
Cressing Temple Wheat Barn	1989	I. Tyers London		
1) original build			*c.*1260	Arcade plate and rafters
2) inserted rafter			*c.*1410-50	
Cressing Temple Granary, reused rafter	1989	I. Tyers London	*c.*1410	
Thaxted church	1989	I. Tyers		
1) reused rafters		London	No	?reused from earlier church
2) existing roof			*c.*1530-65	i.e. timber original to roof
3) repair to existing roof			1813	
Harlowbury, excavated watermill	1991	I. Tyers London	No	?16th-17th century
Coggeshall Grange Barn	1991	I. Tyers London	*c.*1180-1225	Arcade post
Rivenhall church	1991	I. Tyers London	after 1295	Chancel wall plate
Cressing Barley Barn	1991-2	I. Tyers		
1) original build		London	*c.*1205-35	
2) rebuild side walls			*c.*1410-45	
3) crown-post roof			?*c.*1510	
4) late repairs			*c.*1735-75	
Coggeshall, pile in West Street	1992	I. Tyers London	after 1734	EAH 1992, 23, 159-61
Thaxted Guildhall	1992	I. Tyers London	*c.*1430-1460	
Rookwood Hall, Abbess Roding. 1) barn	1992	I. Tyers London	1539	
2) 'granary'			No	Carpentry resembles that of barn
Maldon, D'Arcy Tower	1992	I. Tyers London	No	Floor joist. Probably 1530s
Heybridge Hall	1992	I. Tyers		
1) 14th century hall		London	No	
2) 16th century cross-wing			No	
Sible Hedingham church	1992	I. Tyers London	No	Post in vestry. ?post-medieval
Belchamp St. Paul, barn at Paul's Hall, reused timber	1992	I. Tyers London	*c.*1240-75	
Cressing Temple Wheat Barn	1992	I. Tyers London		

	Date	Analyst	Date obtained	Notes
1) original build			*c*.1259-80	
2) rebuild of west end			*c*.1420-50	
3) porch			*c*.1410-50	
Queen Elizabeth's	1993	I. Tyers		
Hunting Lodge, Chingford		London	1543	

Abbreviations: EAH Essex Archaeology and History
VA   Vernacular Architecture

Medieval Timber Economy
as Illustrated by the Cressing Temple Barns
by Oliver Rackham

Introduction

This paper deals almost exclusively with oak. This was the commonest (and also the most expensive) timber in the Middle Ages, and upper class structures like great barns are usually built exclusively of it. The second commonest is elm; the proportion of elm is a good indicator of social status. At Cressing the earliest elm is the braces of the second phase of the late medieval rebuilding of the aisle walls of the Barley Barn. I have sometimes found elm used for exceptionally big timbers, but the elms around Cressing are of one of the 'East Anglian' kinds, and would not have grown bigger than oak. With rare exceptions, the woods of Essex were not oakwoods: only the timber trees were oak, the underwood being a variety of other species.

Woods, wood-pastures, and non-woodland trees are all possible sources for the timbers of the great barns. It is my impression that the greatest number of timber trees was in woodland. In wood-pastures most trees were pollarded, and the timber trees (if any) were allowed to grow longer before felling than in woodland. Both practices were the result of grazing, which made it more difficult to replace the trees if felled. Hedgerow and farmland trees were certainly commonplace in medieval Essex (e.g. in the court rolls of Woodford, the Donylands, and Writtle).

The period between the Cressing Barley and Wheat Barns may have been one of transition. Essex woodland since the mid-13th century has been dominated by coppice-woods intensively managed for underwood, with timber as a by-product. Wood-pastures, though much more extensive than now, have been subordinate. This cannot, however, have gone on for long before 1250, since Domesday Book tells a very different story. Unfortunately, Domesday in Essex hides the information about the extent of woodland under the number of swine it was supposed to fatten, but I have estimated Essex in 1086 was about 20% woodland and wood-pasture. This was rather more than average for England, and twice as much as there was in Suffolk. (This was not, of course, wildwood: as is observed in the paper on the landscape in this volume, much of it would have sprung up during the Anglo-Saxon period on abandoned Roman farmland.)

This would have been too much woodland for all of it to be intensively managed by the population at the time. Although there have been coppice-woods since the Neolithic period, the proportion of them has varied over time. As we learn from what Domesday says about counties such as Lincolnshire, only a proportion - in Essex perhaps 4-5% of the land area - would have been coppice-woods in 1086, and the rest wood-pasture.

Between 1086 and 1250 the increase of population led to some of the woodland being grubbed or grazed away. In Essex this is best documented for the woods on the site of Stansted Airport. At the same time, the management of the remaining woodland and wood-pasture would have been intensified. For any one wood there may have been a transition from a less-intensive to a more-intensive form of management. One way for this to happen would be for a former wood-pasture to become a coppice-wood as, for example, with the encoppicing of the woods in Hatfield Forest.

Another aspect of the transition is illustrated by what happened to the woods of Norwich Cathedral Priory at Hindolveston (Norfolk). In the mid-13th century the 300 acres of woods produced about £4 a year from sales of underwood. In 1272 there was a huge sale of £214 worth of timber at once; the reason was that the Priory had just been sacked by the revolting townspeople, and needed the money. From 1294 onwards we find the woods producing an average of £24 a year from selling underwood. Several things happen at much the same time: the making of a great earthwork round the perimeter of both woods; planting a hedge on it; providing bridges, gates and padlocks at the entrances; and appointing a woodward. Evidently before 1272 the woods had been producing mainly timber and not much underwood. The monks took advantage of the big sale to convert them to producing mainly underwood and less timber. This involved paying attention to boundaries and security, because underwood is more likely than timber to disappear on dark and rainy nights, and the young shoots are liable to be browsed by cattle.

Timber Analysis of the Barley Barn

There is a fundamental difference between medieval and modern carpentry. Today we expect timbers to be shaped more or less like elongated bricks; in the Middle Ages carpenters expected them to be shaped more or less like trees. It is obvious that in the Barley Barn every original timber represents a whole oaktree with four faces *scappled* (trimmed flat) and the corners left rounded or *waney*. Because God did not intend oak trees to grow straight, any bend in the tree is almost bound to cause the waney surface to intrude at some point along the length of the timber.

It is, therefore, comparatively easy to count how many trees, and of what size, went into the Barley Barn. For each timber we need:

1. to verify that it does, indeed, represent a whole log, rather than a half or a quarter.
2. to measure the dimensions.
3. to estimate the degree of wane - the extent by which the diameter of the tree exceeded, or fell short of, the ideal diagonal of the timber.
4. to consider whether the timber represents the whole of the useful length of the tree. Sometimes there

will be a top-length left over which can be used for some other timber. Top-lengths tend to be more crooked than the butt-lengths, and full of knots; they can often be identified, especially in the case of collars. The simplest procedure is to count every butt-length as one tree and not to count the top-lengths as trees. I propose also to treat every timber shorter than, say, 7 ft as being a leftover, not requiring the felling of a tree.

With barns there is the complication of repairs and alterations. Every 80-100 years the tile-battens rot and the roof needs re-tiling; and (as happened with the Wheat and Barley barns in 1988) a few timbers get replaced. Less often but still predictably, there is a long period of neglect with the results that we find in a survey of one of the former Waltham Abbey farmsteads in 1566:

> "Item the greate wheate barne lacketh Twentie foote of Resyn and one pece of Tymber called a sleper, Syx thousand of Tyles. The weste ende of the said barne must of necessitie be taken downe and newe sett up....Item the litle barne wanteth by estymacon Twentie thousande Tyles besydes Sande lathe and nayles ....Item we fynde that the quenes ma[jes]tie ought to repaire the same.... .[1]

Both these fates have befallen the Barley Barn. Repairs call for an unpredictable quantity of timber to be produced in a hurry, and often this is reused timber. This may involve recycling timber from one place to another within the original building. When the Barley Barn was reduced in size, the rafters of the low-roofs could be shortened and reused, but the posts of the original walls would have been too short to use in the new walls. I reckon that although only ten rafters of the original high-roof remain *in situ*, many others have been reused in the present low-roofs and in the ends of the high-roof. Many of the present wall-studs are parts of original rafters. (I cannot explain why so little of the original aisle top-plates should survive). Besides this, there are many rafters whose pattern of joints shows that they must have been reused from some other building roughly contemporary with the Barley Barn.

Although only about 35% of the original components of the Barley Barn survive, it is possible to reconstruct almost the whole of it. The subsequent calculations are based on the information available to me at the time of writing (August 1992). I reconstruct the original structure on the basis that it was half a bay longer at each end, and 3 ft wider at each side than it is now. This takes no account of subsequent excavations, and will doubtless have to be revised further as more information turns up. New discoveries will result in minor amendments to the statistics, but are unlikely to change the conclusions radically.

Sizes and shapes of trees

The Barley Barn is made of great numbers of what we would call smallish oak trees. Every rafter represents an oak tree between 9 and 11 inches in diameter under the bark at the big end. The rafters were originally 21 ft long (high and low roofs alike) and there are often signs that the useful length of the tree was not much longer than this. Many of them taper at the top end (which is an architectural, though not a structural, advantage). They are relatively straight (as oaks go) and therefore were somewhat constrained by other trees growing beside them. The pattern of knots shows that the branches came out mainly at the top, but also often throughout the upper half of the tree and sometimes lower still. They were felled at about 50 years growth - I have counted between 40 and 47 annual rings - before they had reached their full size. In terms of woodland I reckon that these were standard oaks set rather closely among underwood in a coppice-wood. An alternative would be areas of land (arable or heath) abandoned and allowed to turn into woodland, in which oak could well be the commonest tree. However, this is inherently unlikely in the 12th century, a time of great pressure on land. There is a much smaller number of bigger trees. At the other extreme, each of the great posts, 16 inches square, represents an oak some 2 feet in diameter: a rather crooked, branchy tree still only 21 feet in useful length. They are fast-grown, with very wide annual rings; the smaller posts of the Coggeshall Grange Barn were only about 100 years old. My impression is that these came from free-standing, probably hedgerow, trees.

Trees and area of woodland

To relate trees to woodland I devised a system of size-classes (Rackham 1972). A class 1 oak is between $6\frac{1}{2}$ and $8\frac{1}{2}$ inches basal diameter, and I shall suppose that it represents 50 years' occupation of $\frac{1}{100}$ acre of an average coppice-wood, which is one unit of occupancy. A class 2 oak tree is from 9 to $12\frac{1}{2}$ inches basal diameter. The average class 2 oak has twice the cross section area of the average class 1 oak, and represents 2 units of occupancy (e.g. it occupies $\frac{1}{100}$ acre of woodland for 100 years). A class 3 oak has four times the cross section area of a class 1 oak and represents 4 units of occupancy, and so on (Table 1). Any oak of 6 inches diameter or less is class 0, and represents $\frac{1}{2}$ unit of occupancy. Table 2 illustrates this calculation for two kinds of component, and Table 3 summarizes the calculation for the whole barn.

Table 1. Size classes of trees

	Range of diameters of trees, inches	Units of occupancy of woodland
Class 0		$\frac{1}{2}$
Class 1	$6\frac{1}{2}$-$8\frac{1}{2}$	1
Class 2	9-$12\frac{1}{2}$	2
Class 3	13-$17\frac{1}{2}$	4
Class 4	18-$25\frac{1}{2}$	8
Class 5	26-$36\frac{1}{2}$	16
Class 6	37	32

Table 2. Calculation of timber content and sizes of trees for the rafters and principal posts of the Barley Barn

Full length rafters:-

originally = 196 (92 in high-roof, 104 in low-roof)

surviving (*in situ* or reused as rafters; excluding rafters reused as other components) = 51½

original dimensions: high roof = 21½ft x 7½in x 6½in; low roof = 20ft x 7½in x 6½in

average timber content = 7.1 cubic feet per rafter (nominal, ignoring effects of taper and waney corners)

total timber content = 1394 cu ft.

diagonal measurement of timber, ignoring waney corners = 10in

basal diameter of log = 8½ to 11 in

original number of trees = 194 (approximately 25 class 1, 169 class 2)

Principal posts:-

originally = 12, all surviving dimensions = 20ft 10 in x 16in by 16in

timber content = 31.2 cubic feet each (ignoring taper and waney corners)

total timber content = 374 cu ft

diagonal measurement of timber, ignoring waney corners = 22½in

basal diameter of log = 24in

original number of trees = 12 of class 4.

Table 4. Woodland occupancy of the oaks that went into the Barley Barn

	Number of trees	Units of occupancy
Class 1	57½	57½
Class 2	311½	623
Class 3	87	348
Class 4	24	192
TOTAL	480	1220½

As Table 3 shows, the Barley Barn originally contained about 600 timber parts, representing some 480 oak trees. By far the greatest number of these are in class 2, the commonest diameter being 9-10 inches. They add up (Table 4) to rather more than 1100 units of occupancy. This means that a coppice-wood of 110 acres could have produced one Barley Barn every five years for ever.

I emphasise that this is a rough calculation. The number of trees in the structure is reasonably certain; what is uncertain is the number of trees per acre of woodland, which (as we know from documents of a later period) could fluctuate very widely.

Length of timbers

The ordinary timbers are about 21ft, which is a little longer than usual for medieval buildings, but there are a few much longer. In the Barley Barn one of the arcade-plates was probably originally 50ft long. This is difficult to be certain of, because much of the middle has been patched. If true, it would make it one of the longest medieval timbers on record outside cathedrals. All the surviving arcade-plates -

Table 3. Total timber and tree content of the Barley Barn as originally built

	Original number	Number surviving	Total cubic feet	Class 1	Class 2	Class 3	Class 4
Roofs: rafters*	314	130	1849	28	254	-	-
collars	46	5	126	23	23	-	-
Frames: posts	12	12	374	-	-	-	12
tiebeams	6	4	130	-	-	6	-
strainer beams	2	2	31	-	-	2	-
passing-braces	12	½	285	-	-	12	-
aisle tiebeams**	16	0	141	-	-	16	-
sole-plates	12	9	151	-	-	-	12
arcade-plates	6	6 (parts)	206	-	-	6	-
braces	80	39	229	-	-	36	-
Walls: top plates	14	1	175	-	14	-	-
groundsills	14	1	175	-	14	-	-
principal posts***	18	0	70	-	-	9	-
studs**	51	0	89	6½	6½	-	-
TOTAL	603	209½	4031	57½	311½	87	24

*Includes short rafters at ends and corners, some of which do not count as trees

**Numbers and sizes inferred from surviving traces

***Conjectural

the shortest being 33 feet long - show signs of getting the utmost length out of the available trees.

The next longest were the twelve passing-braces, each 40-42ft long. Only a fragment of one can definitely be identified, which shows it to have been an oak tree rather thicker than those forming the rafters. The tiebeams are 26 ft long and even these taper markedly at the little end.

The Wheat Barn

The Wheat Barn is easier to analyse because much more of the present fabric is original. It is, however, rather more difficult to assess its original timber content because the timbers are more accurately square - less waney - and therefore less of the shape of the original tree can be seen. For example, in the Barley Barn, a typical rafter is $6\frac{1}{2}$ x $7\frac{1}{2}$ inches, scappled out of $9\frac{1}{2}$ inch tree, leaving the corners rounded. In the Wheat Barn, it is 5 x $5\frac{3}{4}$ inches, scappled out of an 8 inch tree, leaving perhaps only one corner rounded.

Repeating the calculation, I find that the Wheat Barn has rather fewer components and involves 472 trees, almost exactly the same number (Table 5). As in the Barley Barn, the great majority of the trees were of small diameter. The diameter distributions in the two barns are much the same, except that the whole distribution in the Wheat Barn is shifted towards smaller sizes. In occupancy terms (Table 6), the Wheat Barn made about 20% less demand on woodland than the Barley Barn. In area it was 13% smaller.

The longest timbers in the Wheat Barn appear to be the arcade-plates, one of which is 46 feet long. Perhaps significantly, instead of very long passing-braces, there are two separate braces end to end. The tiebeams are $1\frac{1}{2}$ ft shorter than in the Barley Barn. To put the barns in context, the Barley Barn represents (in terms of occupancy of wood-

land) about four average hall-houses or half a cathedral roof; the Wheat Barn is about three hall-houses or one-third of a cathedral.

The two barns together tell of a distribution of sizes of oaks very different from what we find now. To make a replica today, the difficulty would be in finding, not (as popularly supposed) the big timbers, but the small ones. Very few woods now have hundreds of oaks less than 10 inches thick. This applies to nearly all medieval buildings. As I have remarked elsewhere (e.g. Rackham 1980), medieval woods were similar in composition to coppice-woods now, but different in structure. There was then a rapid turnover of small oaks and no difficulty with replacement. Oak has changed its ecology, and now no longer comes up readily within existing woods, although it still does so in non-woodland sites. I conjecture that the main reason is the introduction of oak mildew from America, but a strong contributory factor is that oak, as a pioneer tree, thrives on felling, and woods are now less often cut down than they were in the Middle Ages (Rackham 1980, chap. 17).

The two barns appear to represent the limits of what can be constructed using ordinary oak trees, rather than exceptional oak trees brought from a distance. A cathedral roof, for example, involved several hundred oaks at least 30 ft long, which were often brought from somewhere like Cumberland or the Forest of Dean. Here, I regard the long timbers as representing the normal limits of variation. Oak being a genetically variable tree, if one cuts down 700 oaks there are likely to be fifteen or so that are twice as long as the average. A possible exception are the great posts. These could well have come from a different source - hedges or a park - from the rest of the timber.

I infer that for each barn the carpenter felled most of the

Table 5. Tree content of Wheat Barn as originally built

	Number of components	Class 1	Number of trees: Class 2	Class 3	Class 4
Roofs: rafters	276	227	33	-	-
collars (2 to a tree)	7	$3\frac{1}{2}$	-	-	-
side-purlins	10	-	10	-	-
purlin-traps	14	-	-	-	-
wind-braces (2 to a tree)	20	10	-	-	-
Frames: posts	12	-	-	-	12
tiebeams	8	-	-	8	-
passing-braces	24	-	24	-	-
aisle tiebeams	12	-	-	12	-
sole-plates	12	-	-	-	12
arcade-plates	6	-	-	6	-
braces	52	-	48	-	-
Walls: top-plates	10	-	10	-	-
groundsills	10	-	10	-	-
principal posts	18	-	9	9	-
studs	28	14	14	-	-
braces	36	-	-	-	-
TOTAL	555	$254\frac{1}{2}$	158	35	24

Table 6. Comparison of the Cressing Barley and Wheat Barns and three other barns

	Barley Barn	Wheat Barn	Netteswellbury	Writtle	Rookwood Hall
External dimensions:					
length (ft)	139	144	87	110	89
width (ft, with aisles but not porches)	51	43	38 ½	32 ⅔	25 ½
area (sq ft)	7100	5216	3350	3600	2500
Length of longest timber (ft)	50 (arcade-plate)	46 (arcade-plate)	*c* 26 (arcade-plate)	39 (crown-purlin)	25 ½ (tie-beam)
Diameter of thickest tree (in)	24 (post)	22 (post)	18 ½ (post)	18 ½ (post)	42 (4 posts)
Number of trees:					
Class 0	-	-	110	136	-
Class 1	57 ½	254 ½	138 ½	138	100
Class 2	311 ½	158	96 ½	102 ½	56
Class 3	87	35	33	70	15 ½
Class 4	24	24	14	14	18
Class 5	-	-	-	-	12
Class 6	-	-	-	-	4 ½
Total number of trees	480	471 ½	392	460 ½	206
Occupancy units:					
Class 0	-	-	55	68	-
Class 1	57 ½	254 ½	138 ½	138	100
Class 2	623	316	193	205	112
Class 3	348	140	132	280	62
Class 4	192	192	112	112	144
Class 5	-	-	-	-	192
Class 6	-	-	-	-	144
Total occupancy	1220 ½	902 ½	630 ½	803	754
Acres of woodland at 50 years' production	12.2	9.0	6.3	8.0	7.5

trees, except perhaps the great posts, from the same source. The biggest trees were set aside for arcade-plates, passing-braces, and tiebeams. To us it seems unnecessary to make the arcade-plates more than one bay long, but perhaps this was done in order to integrate the bays and compensate for the scarcity of horizontal bracing. The maximum size of the barn is set by the length of the worst tree available for tiebeams: for the Barley Barn this would be the 24th longest oak, and for the Wheat Barn (which lacks continuous passing-braces) the 12th longest. One might expect some knot-free oaks to have been set aside to split into laths for tiling and probably for the wall infill, although in practice, as we shall see, both these items could have been bought in.

This analysis has not fulfilled my prediction that the two barns might represent very different kinds of woodland. The Barley Barn, as well as the Wheat Barn, comes from managed woodland. The difference is that every component in the Wheat Barn is a little smaller. It might be claimed that this results from an increasing population managing its woodlands more intensively, making big trees scarcer - leading into the 14th century, when exceptionally big trees appear to have been more difficult to get than ever

before or since. This may be true, but it is not the whole story. In building the Wheat Barn the Knights Templars did use smaller oaks, which would have been less expensive to buy, but not from motives of economy. They did not make the most of each tree. On the contrary, they paid the carpenter to cut away nearly half of each log in reducing it to a square section, instead of one-third as in the Barley Barn.

I see the differences between the two barns as partly a matter of architecture - the difference between the rough, robust Norman and the more elegant, highly finished Early English. The Barley Barn is the Durham Cathedral among barns, the Wheat Barn is the Salisbury Cathedral.

Other Barns

Coggeshall Grange Barn

This will probably turn out to be very similar in its tree content to the Barley Barn. (For details of this barn, see Stenning in this volume).

The Third Barn at Cressing Temple

The rafters of the Granary at Cressing Temple are reused from some enormous medieval building, presumably a vanished barn. They were originally at least 25ft long. They had collars but no passing-braces and no sign of notched-lap joints. They had wind-braces pegged to their undersides, in the manner of the Wheat Barn. There were at least 30 full-length couples. If the building had aisles, it could well have been bigger than the surviving barns. Typologically, it would be later than the Wheat Barn; it could not be much later, since it ran through four cycles of tiling (including the original) before being recycled into the Granary in the 16th century.

The rafters measure 7 x 4 inches, each coming from a tree 9-9½ inches in diameter - bigger than in the Wheat Barn, but this was a wider roof. They illustrate the medieval preference for flat sections, even though this expended more labour and produced a weaker rafter than scappling the tree to a square section.

Rafters 25ft long imply tiebeams nearly 30ft long. It is clear that around 1300 barn design was not unduly limited by scarcity of long oaks, at least for clients like the Knights Templars.

Monks' Barn, Netteswellbury, Harlow

This is the most graceful of all - a Wells Cathedral among barns (Plate 17). It is not closely dated, but with its big aisles, long passing-braces, and widely-set timbers in the side-walls is perhaps of the early to mid-14th century. It is, however, very robust; it withstood two determined attempts to destroy it, by fire and by decay, in the 1970s.

This barn has about half the floor area of the Wheat Barn, and comprises about seven-eighths of the number of trees. The distribution of tree diameters is intermediate

Plate 16 Monks Barn, Netteswellbury, Harlow (before restoration) (photo: ECC Historic Buildings Section)

between the Wheat and Barley Barns. In terms of occupancy, it required about half the woodland of the Barley Barn, or two-thirds of that of the Wheat Barn.

Merton College barn, Gamlingay, Cambs

A new barn was built by the College in 1358-9, when they were about to lease their manor to a tenant. The accounts for the first year contain these items:

9s. 1½d. received for the bark of 175 oaks felled for the new building, as shown below.

New building

Paid to Galfrid' Siluestr' by contract for ... 1 new barn containing 160 feet in length, together with making 3 doors for the said barn ...£6. 13s. 4d. and one quarter of wheat and one quarter of brase ...

And for the expense of carting the timber of 1 old barn bought by the Warden ... 3s.

And for 2 men for 20 days' work in levelling the place where the new barn will stand, 10s. at 3d. a day.

And for 7000 latthenayl bought, 13s. 4d. at 20d. a thousand.

And for 900 spikyngnayl bought, 3s. 9d. at 5d. a hundred.

And paid to Symon Selkman in part-payment for 36,000 tiles bought from him; for 12 thousand he shall have 30 cartloads of firewood, and for the remainder 6s. a thousand; of these 7 thousand tiles have been received, and 40s. and 9 cartloads of fuel have been paid in all.

The second year's account has 2s received for 'lops of oaks felled for the new building', and the following:

New building

... expense of the carpenter and men ... raising the great timbers for the new barn ... 3s. 10d. Carriage 6d.

Given to the carpenter Wilfred Silvester 12d. and to his servant 4d. ...

And for 3850 latthenayl bought ... 5s. 2d. at 16d. a thousand.

And paid to Wilfred Silvester, carpenter, for supervision on visits 12d.

And for expenses and men brought to rear the end of the barn, 3s. 4d. in all.

And for digging 120 cartloads of mud for covering the walls, by piece-work, 4s. at 2d. for 5 cartloads

And for preparing rods for the walls 9d.

And for 2 men brought for making and daubing the walls of the said barn, by piece-work as per schedule 40s. and 4 bushels of wheat.

And for 10 quarters of lime bought for daubing ... the walls of the said barn, 15s. 10d. at 19d. the quarter.

And for 1 carpenter brought for 3 days to fell 2 oaks, 1 elm, and 1 ash in the wood, and for scappling and preparing the said timber for sawing, 18d. at 6d. a day.

And 1 servant of the same carpenter brought for the same time, 12d. at 4d. a day.

And in sawing boards of the said timber for making 2
   great doors and 9 little doors, 2 sawyers brought for
   the same for ... 28s.
And for 300 nails called spikying bought for the said
   barn, 16½d. at 5½d. a hundred.
And for 750 great nails called spikying bought for the
   doors, 10s. at 16d. a hundred.
And for 250 great nails bought for the same, 3s. 2d. at
   20d. a hundred.
And for 2200 latth bought for the said grange, 22s. at
   12d. a hundred.
And for 1000 latth bought for the said grange, 7s. 6d. at
   9d. a hundred.
And given to Wilfred Silvester, carpenter, for his gown
   13s. 4d.
And for 800 latth bought, 8s. per hundred as above.
And for 38 thousand tiles bought, £9. 9s. at 5s. 6d. a
   thousand.
And for the expense of carriage of the same tiles, viz.
   from Huthe to Gamlingay, 26s. 3d., that is 1 man
   brought at 13d. per day, and one servant at 1d. per
   day, and for 6 horses at 4d. per day, carrying 11
   hundred.
And for 5 bushels of tylpynnes bought 5s.
And 1 tiler for them 67s. 6d. getting 18d. a thousand ...
And for levelling the floor of the barn and taking out the
   earth ... 2s.
And for 20 quarters of lime bought for tiling the said
   barn, 31s. 8d. at 19d. a quarter.
To inquire in the next account about the remaining tiles,
   and the tiler's pay, and the laths and nails.[2]

The next year's account does not survive, but there was
a small amount of tiling still to be accounted for in the following year.

This barn would have been about the size of one of the
Cressing barns and like them had nearly 80,000 tiles.
Building such a barn took nearly two years. It cost about
£40, but if the timber had had to be bought it would have
been more like £70. (The annual revenue of the whole
manor was something like £50.) Of the £40 the tiles,
including transport, would have cost nearly half. Wilfred
Silvester, the carpenter - we might call him the architect -
got about one-fifth of the value of the contract. The
remaining £12 was divided between labour and other materials bought in.

The Gamlingay barn seems to have perished in the great
fire of 1600, but the wood survives to this day (Rackham
1992). It was of only about 40 acres. It provided about
190 oaks, which we would expect to have been one-third of
the total needed; some, at least, of the rest was apparently
second-hand timber. The wood also was expected to provide fuel in part-payment for the tiles (probably from the
branches of the felled oaks), and a modest amount of
underwood for the wattle and daub. It must not be supposed that felling 190 oaks in a 40-acre wood was in any
way exceptional. Twenty-five years previously, the
College had felled 390 oaks in the same wood, apparently

for an abortive project to build a great barn at Cambridge.
There had been several lesser fellings since. There was
evidently a rapid turnover of small oaks, and no difficulty
about replacement. By Essex standards, 40 acres is not a
large wood. The Knights Templars almost certainly had at
least 100 acres in Witham, Cressing and Rivenhall. They
could have built two, or even three, great barns in the
course of a century without using all the timber produced
by the woods.

We notice also that the barn had eleven doors; sawing
timber was much more expensive than scappling; the tile-
battens were bought in, not made; and some 15,000 nails
were needed. There was a major re-tiling in 1437, when
the barn was 78 years old.[3]

Priory Hall Barn, Widdington
This is another big aisled barn, attributed to William of
Wykeham, founder of New College, Oxford, in the 1390s.
It is built partly out of top-lengths of trees whose butt-
lengths cannot be accounted for in the barn itself, and presumably were used in some other building. It may seem
surprising that such a grand structure, on an estate which
possessed three sizeable woods, should have been built
from leftovers, but there is a parallel in Southchurch Hall,
the seat of an aristocratic family in south-east Essex, who
could afford a fine of £1000 for perjury (Rackham 1986b).

The Lordship Barn, Writtle
This is a barn supposedly of the 15th century and presumably built by the Dukes of Buckingham, who were near-
royalty. They had about 600 acres of woodland in Writtle
Forest and two parks. The barn is about half the size of the
Barley Barn. It has curiously narrow, almost vestigial,
aisles, and two original porches. The tree content is about
the same as that of the Wheat Barn, with a similar prepon-
derance of young trees.

Rookwood Hall Barn, Abbess Roding
This is an un-aisled building, one-quarter the area of the
Barley Barn, of imposingly massive appearance, and built
by an aristocratic owner. It has been tree-ring dated to
1539 (see Tyers in this volume).

Most of the rafters here are each a single tree, but this is
not true of the other timbers. The great posts, a foot square,
are each one-quarter of a big oak sawn lengthwise. The
tree must have been 3+ feet in diameter - not such an
exceptional oak now, but I know of only two medieval
buildings which contain bigger ones. The tiebeams,
although of greater depth than those of the Cressing barns,
are each one-half of a tree. Most of the other timbers are
halves, quarters, sixths, or eighths of logs.

This barn contains a rather small number of oaks, but
with a very wide range of sizes, including two classes bigger than any in the earlier barns. In terms of woodland
occupancy it is not far short of the Wheat Barn, although
only one-third the size.

General Conclusions
All these barns, from the Cressing Barley Barn to Writtle,
tell much the same story: of timbers grown mainly in cop-

pice-woods, perhaps with a few of the biggest coming from some other source. Each barn contains between 400 and 500 oaks, predominantly of small sizes which would be difficult to get today. Their construction avoids lengthwise sawing. In all this they conform to the pattern of most medieval secular buildings, and of colleges and the less grand churches.

It may seem somewhat surprising that the bigger barns should not contain proportionately more trees than the smaller ones. One reason is that the width, which is the decisive dimension, depends on the length of trees but not on their number. By making each rafter 2 feet longer, a barn could be made 10% bigger in area with almost no increase in the number of trees.

The transition to managed woodland had already occurred before the growing of the trees used in any of these barns - including, probably, even the Coggeshall Barn. There is no sign of the lengthwise sawing of great trees found in the Blackfriars Priory, Gloucester, for which the timber was brought from the Forest of Dean in the 1250s (Rackham *et al.* 1978).

By the standards of Essex, the building of great barns would have been well within local resources, and would not have involved special arrangements for bringing in timber.

However, it must not be supposed that such barns are confined to relatively well-wooded parts of England. At Milden Hall in Suffolk, which had not much woodland, I know of two immense barns at right angles, contemporary and evidently both by the same architect.

The latest barn, at Rockwood Hall, is transitional to the Tudor period, when oaks were bigger and lengthwise sawing was becoming fashionable. A good parallel is Queen Elizabeth's Hunting Lodge, in Epping Forest, built in 1543. The use of unnecessarily big oaks here is a reminder that the biggest timber in a medieval building is often a 16th-century addition. However, small oaks continued to be used for the rafters. Such oak poles were still used for the rafters of the late 16th-century Wheathampstead Barn, Herts; they continued to be available for other types of building well beyond 1600.

Notes

1. PRO DL/44/143. Report of Commissioners set up by Queen Elizabeth to survey defects in the manor of Epping Bury, 1566 2.
2. MCR no. 5409 and no. 5410.
3. MCR 5425 m.29.

A Brick and Tile Typology for Cressing Temple

by Pat Ryan and David Andrews

Introduction

The typology presented here has been set within the context of the development of bricks in Essex, being based upon observations made of dated buildings elsewhere in the county. The history of brickwork has attracted considerable interest over the years, and attempts to establish new typologies could be regarded as re-inventing the wheel. What is new to this study is the proposition that by considering not just dimensions but also the characteristics of a brick, it is possible to date it. Of course, there will always be exceptions, but in general terms an accuracy of 50-100 years is attainable.

This typology has been broken down into chronological divisions, within which there are numbered types. Where possible, common names, such as Garden Wall Tudors or London Stocks, are used for the bricks as being more readily comprehensible and memorable than a classification distinguished by numbers or letters alone. The scope of this paper has been extended to include flooring tile and brick, and roof tile, related categories of material which were produced in much the same way as brick.

Characteristics of brick

In dividing the bricks into types, the following criteria have been used: fabric, dimensions, regularity of shape and appearance, sharpness of arrises, smoothness of faces and bottom surface, and the presence or absence of such features as sunken margins, pressure marks and frogs.

The qualities of the clay or brickearth influence the characteristics of the finished product. The bricks described here, with the exception of the Coggeshall bricks, some if not many of the 19th-20th century bricks, and the flooring bricks, seem to have been made of unrefined brickearth which gives a sandy fabric containing occasional large pebble and angular flint inclusions. This impression is in agreement with the more scientifically reached conclusion of the Firmans (1967) that early bricks were made from superficial deposits of clay and brickearth without any significant addition of other materials.

Colour is very variable, depending not only on the constituents of the raw material but also on how a particular kiln or clamp was fired, and on the conditions obtaining in the different parts of a kiln. The final size of a brick also depends on how much shrinkage has taken place in the drying and firing, and this is also influenced by conditions in the kiln.

Size has also been determined by various regulations which attempted to standardize the manufacture of bricks. Amongst the more significant of these were the following (cf. Lloyd 1925, 12). The Tylers' and Brickmakers' Company charter of 1571 stipulated a size of 9 x $4^{1}/_{4}$ x $2^{1}/_{4}$ inches (230 x 110 x 60mm). A statute of 1725 fixed a size of 9 x $4^{1}/_{4}$ x $2^{1}/_{2}$ inches (230 x 110 x 65mm) for place bricks, and 9 x $4^{1}/_{4}$ x $2^{5}/_{8}$ inches (230 x 110 x 70) for stock bricks. During the 18th century, smaller bricks were allowed within a 15 mile radius of London, a statute of 1729 fixing a size of $8^{3}/_{4}$ x $4^{1}/_{8}$ x $2^{1}/_{2}$ inches (225 x 105 x 65mm), and one of 1769 a size of $8^{1}/_{2}$ x 4 x $2^{1}/_{2}$ inches (215 x 100 x 65mm). The latter dimensions were extended to the rest of the country in 1776. However, the Brick Tax of 1784 led to the manufacture of larger and thicker bricks, though the doubling of the duty on bricks in excess of 150 cubic inches in 1803 checked this tendency. The tax was repealed in 1850.

Other characteristics are the result of manufactory processes. Whilst slop moulding (i.e. wetting the mould before making the brick) has been typical of the brickmaking tradition in some parts of England, in Essex it has been the custom to sand the mould. The appearance of the bottom surface of a brick is an indication of where the freshly moulded brick was put to dry. In former parlance, bricks were known as 'place' and 'stock' bricks (Neve 1726, 42-44; Gunther 1928, 229). Stock bricks were made of stiffer clay, and were dried much more carefully than place bricks, which were laid on the ground after they were moulded and, being of a softer clay, acquired rough or pitted bases which may have straw or grass impressions. In contrast, stock bricks were laid between boards which were initially stacked three bricks high, hence their relatively smooth sandy bases. They were then set on their narrow edges to dry in open-sided shelters known as hacks. Rough bases are most common on medieval and 15th-16th century bricks. It seems that as the practice of drying bricks on the ground lapsed, the term stock became used for utilitarian bricks, whereas previously stock bricks had been superior to, and more expensive than, place bricks. (More recently, the name London Stock has been applied to a particular type of brick made for the London market, a usage so prevalent it has been retained as a common name in this typology).

Sunken margins and pressure marks are also effects created in the process of moulding and drying bricks. Sunken margins are slightly stepped down top edges. They were probably formed by the brickmaker using the edge of his strike to press the clay firmly down to completely fill the corners of the mould. Pressure marks are impressions occurring in a stretcher face of the brick, and are caused by stacking bricks on top of each other to dry when they are still rather soft. Another distinctive feature are frogs, the familiar concavities present in the base of many modern bricks. They may be made in a variety of ways.

Kiln-burnt bricks often have light and dark stripes or 'kiss' marks caused by the arrangement of the bricks in the kiln, the exposed parts being burnt to a light colour and the parts where the bricks rest against each other to a dark colour (Mitchell 1930, 136).

It has only proved possible to satisfactorily identify

types where large areas of brickwork are built uniformly with one type of brick. It is important in identifying a brick type to have a large statistical population which illustrates the full range of variability that might occur within one type. When examining small numbers of bricks, it may be possible only to distinguish them in broad terms such as Tudors or 19th century soft reds.

Brick development as illustrated by the types present at Cressing Temple

Apart from some fragments of Roman ones, the oldest bricks known at Cressing Temple are excavated examples of the Coggeshall type datable to the later 12th and 13th centuries (cf. Gardner 1955). They are unusually large, about one foot long, and are noticeably sandy textured, sand temper having been added to the clay. They are also, exceptionally for an early brick, accurately moulded with square arrises. Such bricks are increasingly being identified in the fabric of churches where previously they have been mistaken for reused Roman material. Drury and Rodwell have explored the possibility that the Cistercians found a market for their bricks within a ten mile radius of their abbey at Coggeshall (Drury 1981, 126). It is possible however that there were other manufacturing centres of these bricks. In view of their size, it is natural to compare these bricks with the Great Bricks which are known from 14th century and earlier contexts at Waltham Abbey (Huggins 1972, 111-14).

The other characteristic type of medieval brick, the predominantly yellowish bricks probably imported from the Low Countries (Drury 1977a, 84; Andrews *et al.* 1990, 89), have yet to be identified at Cressing. They are known to occur locally, having been excavated at Rivenhall (Rodwell 1986, 95-96) and being found in the fabric of St Nicholas church, Chipping Hill, Witham.

Bricks definitely attributable to the 15th century are also so far wanting at Cressing. In most cases, it is not easy to distinguish them from 16th century Tudors. They can be smaller and better fired, with more vitrified examples. They are generally 9 inches (230mm) or slightly less in length, about 4¼ inches (110mm) wide, and 2-2½ inches (50-65mm) thick. Early 15th century bricks can be less than 2 inches (50mm) thick (e.g. Writtle, Pleshey), whilst late 15th century bricks (Rochford church tower, Fryerning church) may be up to 9½ inches (240mm) long.

16th century Tudor bricks tend to be large and rough in appearance, often distorted with very creased faces and sides that are by no means parallel. They are at least 9 inches long, usually 9¼-9½ inches though some are up to 10 inches. The width ranges from approximately 4¼-4¾ inches (110-120mm), usually about 4½ inches, though exceptionally it might be as much as 5 inches or more. As might be expected, the thickness is less variable, though still in the range 2-2½ inches (50- 65mm).

The most plentiful Tudor bricks at Cressing are the Garden Wall Tudors, common to the garden wall and the Wheat Barn nogging (Plate 17A). These are a large rather crude Tudor, usually not very high fired and in the Wheat Barn nogging very soft and underfired. They are place bricks, having rough bases. It may be assumed (and this is no more than speculation) that similar bricks were used for the Great House. There are at least no other distinct types of Tudor brick present in quantity on the site, and those that are recognizably reused are mostly of this type. It is possible that that they were made in the clamps that apparently existed in the field across the road to the south of Cressing Temple .[1]

Other recognizable types of Tudor are few. The brickwork from the pond over the road includes bricks that are smaller than the Garden Wall Tudors, as well as Garden Wall Tudors. The other distinct group, the Granary Tudors, so-called because used in the nogging of that building, are not local to the site, having been used in a series of post-war repairs.

As the 17th century progressed, bricks became better made, with sharper arrises and a less distorted and irregular appearance, but retaining creased faces. In size, they became slightly smaller, though the limited number of reliably dated buildings for this period means that this tendency is difficult to assess accurately. They are generally not quite as thick as before, not being in excess of 60mm. They are more likely to be stock bricks with smooth bases. They may also have diagonal pressure marks on their stretcher faces (Plate 17C). Such pressure marks seem most characteristic of the 17th and 18th centuries, though they also occur on 19th century bricks. These improvements may reflect the increasing use of kilns rather than clamps, and possibly the use of stiffer clay. At Danbury and Stanway (Drury 1975; Fawn 1984, 1985), the only manufacturing sites in the county of this period which have been investigated, kilns were being used. Sir Roger Pratt, writing in the third quarter of the 17th century, observed that kiln bricks were the best (Gunther 1928, 48). The only bricks of this type recognized at Cressing are those from a wall found under the bullock shed in 1991. To judge from their relatively large size, they date from early in the 17th century, or even the end of the 16th century (Plate 17B).

By the end of the 17th century and in the early 18th century, bricks were becoming smaller and neater, more precisely made with smoother less creased surfaces (Plate 17D). They typically measure 8-9 x 4 x 2-2¼ inches (205-230 x 100 x 50-55mm). A large proportion of these bricks were fired to a higher temperature, with the result that they are darker in colour. Bricks in the plinth and nogging of the west wall of the Wheat Barn are of this type. Such bricks are not however common at Cressing, otherwise only having been identified in two of the buttresses on the east side of the garden.

These more accurately made bricks made it possible to obtain the precisely laid brickwork with neat, narrow joints that is a distinctive feature of the better quality houses of the period. The more roughly made Tudor bricks could only be laid with rather wide joints in less precise courses, and were often rendered. Render was often conceived as a means of disguising brickwork as stone (cf. Andrews,

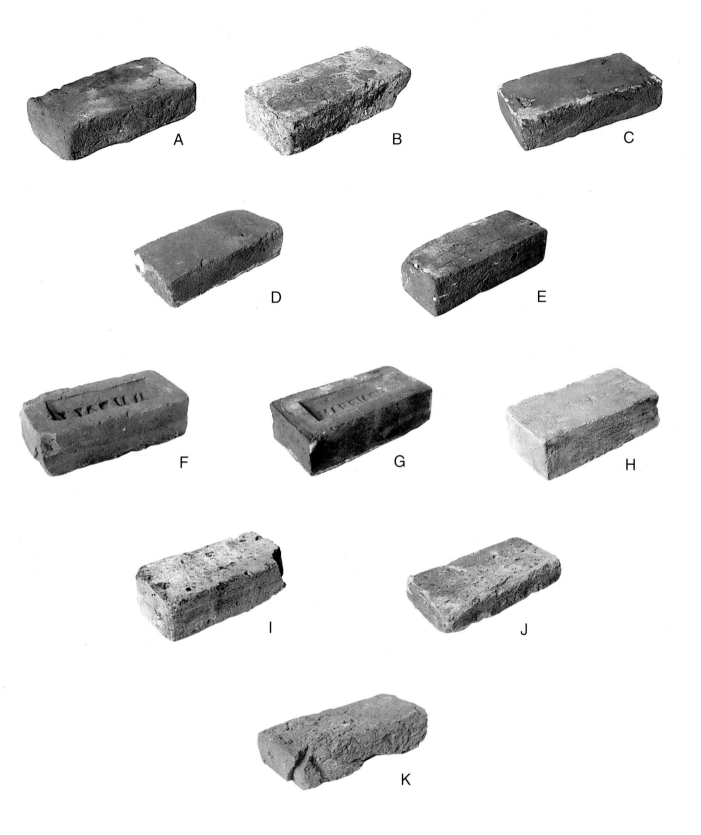

*Plate 17 Examples of Essex bricks: **A**.Cressing Garden Wall Tudor (248 x 115 x 60mm), **B**.Early 17th century brick from the bullock shed excavations (250 x 110 x 60mm), **C**.17th century brick from Bardfield Saling church (230 x 110 x 52mm, **D**.Late 17th century brick from a drain excavated in the walled garden (220 x 100 x 50mm), **E**.Early 19th century Soft Red from the dovecot at Berechurch Hall (220 x 100 x 65mm), **F**. Late 19th century Soft Red made by W. H. Bott of Hatfield Peverel (235 x 110 x 70mm), **G**.20th century Soft Red from the Cressing walled garden made by the Marriage brickworks (230 x 110 x 63mm), **H**.Suffolk White from Duke Street, Chelmsford (226 x 110 x 65mm), **I**.London Stock from Beeleigh Mill, Maldon (230 x 110 x 65mm), **J**.19th century flooring brick (225 x 115 x 43mm), **K**. Dutch clinker found at Cressing (154 x 65 x 35mm)*

95

Bedwin and Hall 1986). What is difficult to assess is whether the bricks were roughly made because they were intended to be plastered, or were plastered because of their rather crude appearance.

By the mid-18th century, bricks tended to be thicker and much more accurately made with sharp arrises, parallel sides, and smoother surfaces. Mid- to late 18th century bricks measure 8¹/₂-8³/₄ x 4-4/₄ x 2¹/₂ inches (220 x 105 x 65mm). These bricks tend to be consistent in colour (though this may be because they were sorted with greater care by the bricklayer).

This sets the pattern for 19th century bricks, which retain the same general characteristics, but vary slightly as to dimensions. Typically they measure 9 x 4¹/₄-4¹/₂ x 2¹/₂-2 ⁵/₈ inches (230 x 110-115 x 63mm), although in the earlier part of the century there is a tendency for bricks to be a little smaller (e.g. 8³/₄ x 4 x 2¹/₂ inches, 225 x 105 x 65mm). Later 19th century bricks are more uniform in size and appearance, with sharper, squarer arrises and smoother faces, though there are exceptions. This development is the result of the introduction of mechanical manufacturing processes from the first half of the century (Cox 1979, 36). Such bricks are often referred to by builders today as Soft Reds, and this is a useful general term to describe them.

Two features can be of assistance in the identification of 19th century bricks. One is horizontal pressure marks (Plate 17E), which seem to largely supersede diagonal ones from a little before 1800. They probably continue into the early 20th century (as do diagonal ones, though they are very much less common). The other is the frog. Frogs are known, it seems, from the 17th century (Harley 1974, 80), but in Essex do not become at all common until the 19th century. Early frogs tend to be crude and rudimentary; later ones are larger and more precisely made. After c.1875, the maker's name may be impressed in the frog (Plate 17F).

Of the new types of bricks that appear at this period, two occur at Cressing, the Suffolk Whites and London Stocks (Plate 17 H and I). 'White' or whitish bricks made from Gault or lime rich clays, or clays to which lime has been added, have been called Suffolk Whites because that is the principal area in which, locally, they were manufactured. They were made from the 18th century, but in Essex are most common from the end of that century until the middle of the 19th.

London Stocks, as already mentioned, are utilitarian bricks made for the London market. They are rough in appearance, and yellow to purple in colour with black patches. They were made from a clay which contained naturally occurring or added powdered chalk. Fuel, either breeze from gas works or decomposed town waste with a high proportion of partially burnt cinder, ash and coal dust, originally known as Spanish soil, was also mixed with the clay (Hartley 1939, 167-71). After moulding and drying, the bricks were burnt in clamps skilfully constructed from the unburnt bricks and fuel in the form of breeze, town waste and a small quantity of coal and wood faggots. They were originally manufactured in the environs of London

and larger towns, and at coastal sites where cheap transport by Thames barge was available for both fuel and the finished product. The advent of the railways also encouraged the use of this type of brick throughout the county. At Cressing, they seem to have become available about the middle of the 19th century. An early dated example of their use is to be found a few miles away at Bocking where there is a house in Woolpack Lane built of London Stocks with a plaque bearing the date 1846.

Floor tiles and paving bricks
Also needful of consideration are flooring bricks and tiles. Three main categories of material can be identified in Essex: floor tiles generally five to six inches square, large floor tiles nine or twelve inches square, though sometimes larger, and rectangular flooring bricks or pavers similar in size to a normal brick but invariably thinner.

The small floor tiles include the well-known slip-decorated examples found at churches and monastic sites. However, just as common and probably more so, are plain lead-glazed tiles of this size, and also those with a plain cream slip coating covering all or half of the tile (cf. Drury 1977b; Drury 1976; Drury and Pratt 1975, 112). Typically, these are 14th-15th century in date.

Nine-inch square tiles were found by Gardner (1955, 24) in the chapter house at Coggeshall where they seem to be late 12th century. It is not until the 15th century that glazed and slipped or partially slipped tiles of this size are found. Those with nail holes in their bases are considered to be of Flemish origin (Drury 1977b, 113). Those without, such as the partially slipped and glazed nine inch square floor tiles found in Great Sampford church in 1992, may be made locally.

Unglazed nine- or twelve- (or exceptionally fifteen-) inch square floor tiles are often known today as pammets, and this is a useful term for distinguishing them. It would seem logical that they derive from the large floor tiles discussed in the previous paragraph. However, the discovery in 1992 in a cellar of the former Tudor house adjacent to Hatfield Peverel church of a pammet which is essentially a double brick measuring 9¹/₂ inches (240mm) square by 2 inches (50mm) thick suggests another origin for them. Certainly early examples are usually in a brick-type fabric which tended to be too fragile for heavy wear unless the pammets were very thick. Later ones are often in a pinkish to cream fabric, with a marbled or streaky appearance when broken. Flooring bricks or pavers (Plate 17J) cannot as yet be taken back with certainty before the 18th century, though before then and indeed later ordinary red bricks were sometimes used for flooring but can never have proved very durable. Flooring bricks improve in quality with the passage of time like ordinary bricks, early ones being rougher in appearance and 19th century ones often being very precisely made. The fabric is usually pinkish to cream, streaky in fracture, and hard and durable. They were usually laid flat, but in areas of intensive use like threshing floors might be laid on edge.

Several small fragments of pammets or similar were

found in the 1978-80 excavations at Cressing, including a glazed example from the chapel floor. Flooring bricks occur reused in some walls and can be a useful dating indicator. (The flooring bricks in the north room of the Granary are second-hand and were laid in 1991).

A few Dutch 'clinkaerts' or clinkers have been found in the excavations (Plate 17K). These are small misshapen paving bricks which were designed to be laid on edge. In 1850, Dobson stated in his treatise on brick and tile manufacture that Dutch clinks, clinkers or paving bricks were made at Moor near Gouda, from slime from the river bed and sand (Celoria 1971). However he also referred to Dutch clinks made in England. Sir Roger Pratt advocated their use for stable floors in the 1660s (Gunther 1928, 128). They have been found during fieldwalking over the site of Old Thorndon Hall which was demolished in the 1760s.

Roof tile

An archaeological sequence excavated at Harwich indicates that at that town roof tile or pegtile was not used before *c*.1300 (Andrews *et al.* 1990, 89). In general, there can be little doubt that in Essex its use only became at all common in the 14th century. However large nibbed tiles have been found in 13th century contexts at a number of ecclesiastical and manorial sites throughout the county, including Waltham Abbey, Great Braxted church, Chelmsford Dominican priory, Pleshey and Great Easton. At the Grange Barn, Coggeshall, erected *c*.1180-1225, exceptionally large nibbed tiles measuring 13 ½ x 6 ¾-7 x ⅝ inches (342 x 170-180 x 15mm) were found in the 1984-85 restoration. Areas of large nibbed tiles (12 ½ x 8 x ⅝ inches; 320 x 200 x 16mm) were also found during the re-roofing of the Cressing Barley Barn, and there seems no reason to doubt that they were original and were made locally.[2] A patch of similarly large tiles exists on the roof of Barnston church, and is thought to have come from Tilty Abbey, which like Coggeshall was a Cistercian foundation.

It seems likely that the production of nibbed tiles declined in the second half of the 13th century and was replaced by pegtiles. Large flat pegtiles 13 x 7¾ x ⅝-¾ inches (330 x 198-203 x 15-18mm) have been found at Cressing. The similarity in size of these pegtiles and the nibbed tiles suggests they are early pegtiles produced in the latter part of the 13th century. The standard late medieval pegtile has remained basically unchanged in dimensions into modern times. Tiles from the medieval tile factory at Danbury (Drury and Pratt 1975, 111) measured 10⅝ x 6-6 ⅞ x ½ inches (270 x 150-175 x 12-15mm). Some of these tiles were glazed, and a few glazed fragments of pegtile have been found at Cressing. A tile used to raise the height of the chancel wall of Bradwell-iuxta-Coggeshall church in the 14th century measures 10¼ x 6¼ x ½ inches (262 x 160 x 14mm). A statute of 1477 fixed dimensions of 10½ x 6 ¼ x ⅝ inches (267 x 160 x 13mm) for roof tiles (Salzman 1952, 230). An intact pegtile from the 16th-17th century mansion at Copped Hall, Epping, measured 10½ x 6 x ½ inches (265 x 155 x 11mm).

The Cressing Temple Brick Typology
Medieval Bricks
1. Coggeshall bricks. Reddish brown with reduced core. 318 x 165 x 40-50mm. 12 ½ x 6 ½ x 1 ½-2 inches. Regular appearance, smooth faces, base and upper surface; granular fabric. Found in the excavation on the west side of the Barley Barn, and in the drain leading off the tank in north room of the Granary. Suggested date 1180-1220.

Tudor Bricks (Place Bricks)
1. Garden Wall Tudors (Plate 17A). Orange to purple, but predominantly light in colour. Very rarely with blue grey glaze. 240-247 x 115-120 x 60-65mm. 9½-9¾ x 4½-4¾ x 2¼-2⅝ inches. Irregular appearance; irregular, slightly rounded arrises; creased faces, pitted bases. Sandy fabric with pebble and angular flint inclusions. A large Tudor, exceptionally long and thick.
Found in J. Hope's excavations (types A1 and A2); the main build of the garden wall; the Wheat Barn nogging (which seems to be made of very underfired examples of the same bricks); and reused in the the cartlodge plinth.
2. Granary Tudors. A distinctively orangey brick, paler and softer than those in the garden wall. 230-240 x 115-120 x 55-60mm. 9-9½ x 4 ½-4¾ x 2⅛-2⅜ inches. Fairly regular appearance; fairly regular, rounded arrises;creased faces, pitted bases. Sandy fabric with conspicuous iron ore inclusions giving a somewhat speckly apearance, together with some pebbles and angular flints.
Found in Granary nogging; rounded south-east corner of the garden wall; ?buttress by north garden door; nogging panels at west end of south wall of Wheat Barn. Suggested date 16th to early 17th century.
The presence of this brick in repairs dating from the 1950s and 1960s suggests it may not be local to the site, but was acquired by Mr Cullen from elsewhere. It may also be significant that it has not been identified amongst excavated samples of bricks from Cressing.
3. Tudor brick from pond across the road. A small Tudor. Orange, sandy fabric with pebble and angular flint inclusions. 230 x 110 x 50-60mm. 9 x 4¼ x 2-2⅜ inches. Fairly regular appearance; fairly regular, fairly rounded arrises; creased faces, pitted base with groove running length of brick.
?15th-16th century.

Late 16th to Early 17th Century Bricks (Stock Bricks)
1. Wall under bullock shed (Plate 17B).Orange, sandy fabric with pebble and angular flint inclusions. 240-250 x 110 x 60mm. 9½-9⅞ x 4⅜ x 2⅜ inches. Fairly regular appearance; fairly regular, slightly rounded arrises; fairly smooth faces, fairly smooth base, oblique pressure marks. Similar bricks with perhaps more pebble inclusions occur in the northernmost buttress of the west wall of the garden.
c.1600-1650, but thickness suggests it is earlier rather than later, datable to the beginning of the 17th century.

17th Century Bricks

1. A small orange brick with a sandy fabric. 220 x 105 x 50mm. $8^3/_4$ x 4 x 2 inches. Fairly regular appearance; fairly regular, slightly rounded arrises; creased faces, fairly smooth base.

   Third buttress from south end of the east wall of the garden. ?same as type B from J. Hope's excavations.

2. Farmhouse chimneystack bricks (as seen in roof void). $8^3/_4$-9 x 4-$4/_2$ x 2-$2^1/_4$ inches. 225-230 x 110-115 x 50-55mm. Fairly regular, fairly smooth faces. A few examples are vitrified. Some have diagonal pressure marks.

Late 17th to Early 18th Century Bricks

1. Bricks from drain along south side of the garden, and drain along the south side of the Granary (thought to be one and the same drain). Dark red, well fired, some vitrification. $8^1/_4$-9 x 4-$4^1/_4$ x $1^3/_4$-2 inches. 210-230 x 100-110 x 45-50mm. Fairly smooth bases, slightly creased faces. Regular shape, somewhat rounded arrises.

2. Purplish, dense, well-fired, sandy fabric, pebble and angular flint inclusions. 220 x 105-110 x 55-57mm. 8 $^3/_4$ x $4^1/_8$-$4^1/_4$ x $2^1/_8$-$2^1/_4$ inches. Regular appearance; sharp, fairly regular arrises; smooth and slightly creased faces; kiss marks. J. Hope's excavations type D. A few examples also occur in the east plinth wall of the cartlodge, the upper courses of the west plinth of the Wheat Barn, whilst the nogging in the west wall of the Wheat Barn is entirely in this type of brick.

18th - 19th Century Bricks

1. Suffolk Whites. A distinctively pale brick. Rather variable in colour: may be white, cream, grey or pinkish. Sandy fabric, interior of brick sometimes marbled. 220 x 100 x 60mm. $8^5/_8$ x 4 x $2^1/_2$ inches. Regular appearance; regular sharp arrises; smooth and slightly creased faces, smooth base.

   Found in oblique south-west garden wall; east plinth of cartlodge; and south plinth of granary
   *c.*1750-1850

19th and 20th Century Bricks

1. London Stocks

   Yellow to purple with black patches. 230-235 x 110 x 65-70mm. 9-$9^1/_4$ x $4^1/_4$ x $2^5/_8$-$2^3/_4$ inches.

   Regular appearance; sharp, regular arrises; creased and cracked faces, smooth bases.

   Found in oblique south-west garden wall; patch in top courses of north garden wall near Wheat Barn corner; north wall of building next to Granary; west and north walls of wood shed next to Wheat Barn.
   *c.*1850-early 20th century

2. Orange to dark red, dependent on firing. Sandy fabric with pebble and angular flint inclusions. Rather distinctive sandy faces.

   215-235 x 115 x 65-70mm. $8^1/_2$-$9^1/_4$ x $4^1/_2$ x $2^1/_2$-$2^3/_4$ inches.

   Fairly regular appearance; sharp arrises; smooth and slightly creased faces, horizontal pressure marks; some sunken margins, small frogs 45mm wide and 15mm

deep. Found in central section of east garden wall; also in two buttresses against west wall.
?second half of the 19th century

3. Marriage bricks (Plate 17G).

   Dark red brown to purple, well fired.

   230 x 110 x 63mm. 9 x $4^1/_4$ x $2^1/_2$ inches.

   Regular appearance; sharp, regular arrises; smooth faces, smooth base; sometimes slightly distorted in shape. Frog with 'Marriage' impressed in it. Horizontal pressure marks. Found in paving of east terrace and boundary wall of terrace. Hugh Marriage is recorded in trade directories as making bricks at Hatfield Peverel between 1899 and 1922.

4. Rather soft reds, orange, red and purple in colour.

   230 x ? x 65mm. 9 x ? x $2^5/_8$ inches.

   Regular appearance; regular arrises; some horizontal and oblique pressure marks.

   Found in rounded south-east corner of the garden wall. This was built in the 1960s, but the bricks are presumed to be reused. Probably late 19th-early 20th century.

5. Dark orange to purple

   230 x 112 x 65mm. $9^1/_8$ x $4^1/_4$ x $2^5/_8$ inches.

   Regular appearance; sharp, regular arrises; smooth and slightly creased faces, smooth base; horizontal pressure marks, shallow frog (160 x 50 mm; $6^1/_4$ x 2 inches), possible impression of brickmaker's name but if so very worn. Found in cartlodge plinth.

6. Dark soft reds.

   220 x 110 x 65mm. $8^1/_2$ x $4^1/_4$ x $2^1/_2$ inches.

   Very regular appearance, sharp arrises. Horizontal pressure marks. No frogs.

   Plinth on west side of Wheat Barn midstrey. Bonded with 19th century gritty mortar.

7. An unusually thick brick.

   230-235 x 110 x 70mm. 9-$9^1/_4$ x $4^1/_4$ x $2^3/_4$ inches.

   Very square with very sharp arrises; smooth faces. Horizontal pressure marks and long shallow round-ended frogs.

   Plinth in the Barley Barn.

20th Century Bricks

1. Soft reds.

   215 x 105 x 63mm. $8^1/_2$ x $4^1/_8$ x $2^1/_2$ inches.

   Regular appearance, very smooth surfaces which have a slight tendency to spall. Occasional traces of pressure marks. Present in an extensive refacing on the south side of the Wheat Barn plinth, and dated by an inscription: BUILT 1967.

Flooring Bricks or Pavers

1. White flooring bricks

   Dense fabric. Regular appearance; sharp, fairly regular arrises; smooth faces; smooth base.

   225 x 110-115 x 47-50mm. $8^5/_8$ x $4^1/_4$ x 2 inches. Present in cartlodge east plinth; south wall of the Granary which includes at least six such bricks; ?south-west oblique garden wall. 18th-19th century.

2. Dutch clinkers. (Plate 17K).

   Cream, yellow and grey. Dense, fine textured fabric.

150 x 75 x 40mm. 6 x 3 x 1½ inches
Very misshapen; very irregular, rounded arrises; green-ish glaze on some bricks. Signs of wear on one stretcher face. J. Hope's excavation, type E.

NOTES

1. The site of a clamp in the field to the south of the road (Great Warren Field) has been identified by Mr. R. Martin. An area of scorched subsoil measuring about 17 x 12m is evident in this field after ploughing. In the absence of any brick associated with this feature, it may be doubted whether it represents the site of a clamp, but it is difficult to suggest other explanations for it.
2. A tile kiln in a field to the north of the site (Ten Acre Barn) was excavated in 1946 by the farm manager Mr. P. Bayliss and is indicated on the 1953 OS map. According to the OS Field Reports cited by the Essex Sites and Monuments Record (TL 81/4), the kiln was located at TL8041/1903, and was 'constructed of brick and clay, measuring 33ft long by 18ft wide, with exterior flues which were filled with charcoal and wood ash. The floor of the kiln was approximately 3ft to 3ft 6 inches below present ground level'. It was dated by M.R. Hull to the 16th century. Only one kiln was excavated but it seems there were probably two more. A cursory inspection of this field in January 1992 revealed a concentration of rather thick crude-looking tile comparable to the early tiles found on the Wheat and Barley Barns.

Table of Dated Brick from Essex

NOTE: The majority of Essex brick is orange, red or purple in colour according to the temperature reached during burning. In the descriptions colour is only mentioned when it is other than these. The descriptions are arranged in the following order - colour, where applicable, general shape and appearance, creasing or otherwise of stretcher and header faces, kiss marks, pressure marks, characteristics of base, any further observations, and type.

Date	Building	Dimensions	Description of Brick
late C12th	Coggeshall Abbey guest house	13 x 6¼ x 1½" (330 x 160 x 40)	Regular, smooth faces, smooth base and upper surface, added sand temper, reduced core. Coggeshall
late C13th/ early C14th	Maldon Friary excavation	8¼ x 4 x 1¾" (210 x 100 x 45)	Cream/pink, very irregular, creased rough base. Medieval
early C14th	Maldon All Saints aisle	10 x 4½ - 5 x 2½" (255 x 115 - 130 x 65)	Cream/pink/purple, very irregular, very creased, rough base, grass marks on base and sides. Medieval
early C14th	Dengie church	8½ - 9 x 4 x 1¾ - 2" (215 - 230 x 100 x 45 - 50)	Creamish to brown, green glaze, irregular, creased. Medieval
early C14th	Purleigh church tower	7¾ - 8½ x 4 x 2" (195 - 215 x 100 x 50)	Cream/buff, green glaze, irregular, used decoratively. Medieval.
c.1340	Witham church tower and north aisle	9½ - 10 x ? x 1¾ - 2" (240 - 255 x ? x 45 - 50) ? x 4½ - 5 x 1½" (? x 115 - 130 x 40)	Yellow/pink/red, very irregular, very creased, possibly slop moulded. Medieval
c.1340	Lawford church chancel	7½ x 3¼ - 3½ x 1¾" (190 x 85 - 90 x 45)	Cream/pink/brown, green glaze, irregular, creased, used decoratively. Medieval
1369 (? reused)	Waltham Abbey gatehouse	14½ - 15 x ? x 2 - 3" (370 - 380 x ? x 50 - 75)	Fairly regular, creased, reduced cores. Medieval Great Brick
early C15th	Writtle, Kings John's Hunting Lodge	9 x 4 x 1¾ - 2" (230 x 100 x 45 - 50)	Irregular, creased, rough base, blue/grey glaze, some straw impressions. C15th
early C15th	Maldon, Moot Hall (D'Arcy Tower)	9 - 9¼ x 4¼ x 2 - 2¼ " (230 - 235 x 110 x 50 - 60)	Irregular, creased, rough base, some sunken margins. C15th

Date	Building	Dimensions	Description of Brick	
C15th	Pleshey castle bridge	9 x 4 - 4¹/₄ x 1¹/₂ - 2" (230 x 100 - 110 x 40 - 50)	Irregular, creased.	C15th
*c.*1439	Faulkbourne Hall tower	8¹/₄ - 9 x 4 - 4¹/₄ x 2 - 2¹/₄" (210 - 230 x 100 - 115 x 50 - 55)	Fairly regular, creased.	C15th
1460s	Roydon, Nether Hall gatehouse	8 - 9 x 4¹/₄ x 2¹/₂" (220 - 230 x 110 x 65)	Fairly regular, fairly creased, rough bases, sunken margins.	C15th
late C15th	Dedham church tower	9 x 4 - 4¹/₄ x 2" (230 x 100 - 110 x 50)	Irregular, creased.	C15th
late C15th	Rochford church tower	9¹/₂ x 4¹/₂ x 2 - 2¹/₂" (240 x 115 x 50 - 65)	Irregular, creased, diaperwork.	Tudor
late C15th	Fryerning church tower	9 + x 4 - 4¹/₄ x 2" (230 x 100 - 110 x 50)	Irregular, creased, diaperwork.	Tudor
1489-90	Hadleigh deanery tower	9¹/₂ x 4¹/₄ - 4¹/₂ x 2¹/₄ - 2¹/₂" (240 x 110 - 115 x 55 - 60)	Irregular, creased, diaperwork.	Tudor
1496	Billericay church	9 - 9¹/₂ x 4¹/₄ x 2¹/₄ - 2¹/₂" (230 - 240 x 110 x 55 - 65)	Irregular, creased.	Tudor
1498	Gestingthorpe church tower	9¹/₂ x 4¹/₂ - 4³/₄ x 2¹/₄ - 2³/₄" (240 x 115 - 120 x 55 - 60)	Irregular, creased, diaperwork.	Tudor
early C16th	Thaxted, Horham Hall	9 - 10 x 4³/₄ x 2¹/₂ - 2³/₄" (250 - 255 x 120 x 65 - 70)	Irregular, creased.	Tudor
early C16th	Layer Marney church	9 - 9¹/₄ x 4¹/₄ - 4¹/₂ x 2 - 2¹/₄" (230 - 235 x 110 x 50 - 60)	Irregular, creased, blue-grey glaze diaperwork.	Tudor
early C16th	Woodham Walter Hall	9 - 9¹/₄ x 4¹/₄ - 4¹/₂ x 2¹/₄" (230 - 235 x 110 - 115 x 60)	Irregular, creased, sunken margins, rough base, diaperwork.	Tudor (place)
1543	Chingford, Queen Elizabeth's Hunting Lodge, plinth	8³/₄ x 4 - 4¹/₄ x 2¹/₄" (220 - 230 x 110 x 60)	Irregular, creased, rough base.	Tudor (place)
*c.*1540	Tolleshunt Major church	9¹/₂ x 4¹/₂ x 2¹/₄ - 2¹/₂" (240 x 115 x 60 - 65)	Irregular, creased, diaperwork.	Tudor
*c.*1540	Leighs Priory inner gatehouse	9¹/₂ x 4¹/₂ x 2" (240 x 115 x 55)	Irregular, creased, blue-grey glaze, diaperwork.	Tudor
*c.*1540	Ingatestone Hall	9¹/₂ - 10 x 4¹/₂ - 5 x 2¹/₂" (240 - 260 x 115 - 125 x 65)	Irregular, creased.	Tudor
mid 16th	High Roding, New Hall barn and moat	9¹/₄ x 4¹/₄ - 4¹/₂ x 2" (235 x 110 - 115 x 50)	Irregular, creased, rough base.	Tudor (place)
1556	Ingatestone church south chapel	9¹/₂ - 10 x 4¹/₂ - 4³/₄ x 2¹/₄ - 2¹/₂" (240 - 255 x 115 - 120 x 60 - 65)	Irregular, creased.	Tudor

Date	Building	Dimensions	Description of Brick
1563	Woodham Walter church	9½- 10 x 4½- 5 x 2 - 2½" (240 - 260 x 115 - 125 x 50- 65)	Irregular, creased, rough base. Tudor (place)
1586	Springfield church tower	9 - 9¼ x 4½- 4¾ x 2" (230 -235 x 115 - 120 x 50)	Fairly regular, creased. Tudor
1589	Chingford, Queen Elizabeth's Hunting Lodge chimney	9 x 4¼ x 2¼" (230 x 100 x 60)	Irregular, creased, rough base. Tudor (place)
1594	Rivenhall church, Wiseman monument	9¼ x 4¼ x 2¼" (235 x 110 x 55)	Fairly regular, creased, fairly smooth, diagonal pressure mark. Tudor (stock)
c.1600	Audley End, College of St Mark	8¼- 8¾ x 4 x 2¼- 2½" (210 - 220 x 100 x 55 - 65)	Irregular, creased, some yellowish to purple. C17th
1605-1609	Markshall, Marks Hall (demolished)	9½ x 4½- 5 x 2" (240 x 115 - 125 x 50)	Irregular, creased, rough base, some sunken margins. Tudor (place)
c.1625	Ingatestone church, north chapel, lower part of walls	9 x 4 x 2¼" (230 x 100 x 55)	Fairly regular, creased, kiss marks. C17th (kiln burnt)
1658-c.1700	Stanway, Olivers brick kiln	8¾- 9 x 3¾- 4¼ x 1¾- 2" (220 - 130 x 95 - 110 x 50)	Regular, fairly smooth base, diagonal pressure marks. Late C17th/early C18th (stock)
c.1665	Gt Maplestead, Hopwells, hall chimney	9 x 4½ x 2" (230 x 115 x 50)	Fairly regular, creased diagonal pressure marks. Late C17th/early C18th (stock)
1674	Stebbing, Quaker Meeting House	8 - 8¾ x 4 - 4¼ x 2" (205 - 220 x 100 - 110 x 50)	Fairly regular, slightly creased, diagonal pressure marks. Late C17th/early 18th (stock)
1680	London, St Anne Lutheran Church	8½ x 4 x 2¼" (220 x 100 x 55)	Regular, slightly creased. Late C17th/early 18th
1682	Black Notley church, buttress	8¾ x 4¼ x 2 - 2¼" (220 x 110 x 50 - 55)	Regular, creased, kiss marks. Late C17th/early C18th (kiln burnt)
late C17th	Maldon, Plume Library	8 - 8½ x 2 - 2½ x 4 - 4¼" (200 - 215 x 100 - 110 x 50 - 65)	Regular, creased and fairly smooth kiss marks, diagonal pressure marks, chequerwork. Late C17th/early C18th (stock, kiln burnt)
c.1693	Faulkbourne Hall (Bullock build)	8½ x 4 x 2½" (215 x 100 x 65)	Regular, smooth and creased, diagonal pressure marks, chequerwork. Late C17th/early C18th (stock)
1699	Great Saling, Saling Hall	8½ x 4 x 2¼" (215 x 100 x 60)	Regular, slightly creased, chequerwork. Late C17th/early C18th

Date	Building	Dimensions	Description of Brick
*c.*1700	Terling U R church	8$\frac{1}{4}$ - 8$\frac{1}{2}$ x 4 - 4$\frac{1}{4}$ x 2$\frac{1}{4}$" (210 - 215 x 100 - 110 x 60)	Regular, slightly creased and smooth, kiss marks, diagonal pressure marks, black headers used decoratively. Late C17th/early C18th (stock, kiln burnt)
1708	Little Baddow U R church	8 x 8$\frac{1}{4}$ x 3$\frac{3}{4}$ - 4 x 2$\frac{1}{4}$" (200 - 210 x 95 - 100 x 55)	Regular, smooth and slightly creased, diagonal pressure marks, chequerwork. Late C17th/early C18th (stock)
*c.*1718	Colchester, Hollytrees, east wall north & south walls	8 x 3$\frac{3}{4}$ x 2$\frac{1}{4}$ - 2$\frac{3}{8}$" (205 x 95 x 60) 8$\frac{1}{4}$ x 4 x 2$\frac{1}{2}$" (210 x 100 x 65)	Regular, smooth and slightly creased, kiss marks, diagonal pressure marks. Rubbed red brick dressings, dark headers, tuck pointing. Regular, smooth or slightly creased. Late C17th/early C18th
*c.*1720	Belchamp Walter Hall, garden wall and stables	8$\frac{3}{4}$ - 9 x 4$\frac{1}{4}$ - 4$\frac{1}{2}$ x *c.*2$\frac{1}{4}$" (225 - 230 x 110 - 115 x 60)	Regular, slightly creased, diagonal pressure marks, chequerwork. Late C17th/early C18th (stock)
1728	Maldon All Saints, north wall of nave	8$\frac{3}{4}$ - 9$\frac{1}{2}$ x 4 - 4$\frac{1}{4}$ x 2$\frac{1}{2}$" (220 - 235 x 100 - 110 x 65)	Fairly regular, fairly smooth, diagonal pressure marks, chequerwork C18th (stock)
*c.*1730	Ingatestone, 23 High Street	9 x 4$\frac{1}{4}$ x 2$\frac{1}{2}$" (230 x 110 x 65)	Fairly regular, slightly creased and smooth, diagonal pressure marks, chequerwork. C18th (stock)
1732	Terling church tower	8$\frac{3}{4}$ - 9 x 4 - 4$\frac{1}{4}$ x 2$\frac{1}{4}$" (220 - 230 x 100 - 110 x 50)	Regular, slightly creased and smooth, diagonal pressure marks, chequerwork. Late C17th/early C18th (stock)
1734	Ingrave church (230x110x65)	9 x 4$\frac{1}{4}$ x 2$\frac{1}{2}$"	Regular, slightly creased, diagonal pressure marks. C18th/early C19th (stock)
1757	Woodham Walter Lodge	8$\frac{1}{2}$ x 4 x 2$\frac{1}{4}$ - 2$\frac{1}{2}$" (215 x 100 x 55 - 60)	Regular, slightly creased. C18th/early C19th
1758	Chelmsford, Mildmay almshouses	8$\frac{3}{4}$ x 4$\frac{1}{4}$ x 2$\frac{1}{2}$" (220 x 110 x 65)	Regular, slightly creased and fairly smooth, kiss marks, diagonal pressure marks. C18th/early C19th (stock, kiln burnt)
c.1760	Markshall church	8$\frac{3}{4}$ x 4 x 2$\frac{1}{2}$" (220 x 100 x 65)	White, regular, smooth and very slightly creased, smooth base. Suffolk White
1779	Hutton church, T. Hills vault	8$\frac{3}{4}$ x 4 x 2$\frac{1}{2}$" (220 x 100 x 65)	Regular, smooth. C18th/early C19th
1789	Chelmsford, Shire Hall	9 x 4$\frac{1}{4}$ x 2$\frac{1}{2}$" (230 x 110 x 65)	White, very regular, fairly smooth, horizontal pressure marks. Purchased from Playford near Ipswich (Briggs 1991, 98). Suffolk White

Date	Building	Dimensions	Description of Brick
*c.*1805	Maldon Friary	9 x 4 x 2½" (230 x 100 x 65)	Regular, smooth and slightly creased, smooth base. C19th
early C19th	Maldon, Beeleigh Mill	8¾ x 4 x 2½" (220 x 100 x 65)	Regular, smooth and slightly creased, smooth base. Late C18th/early C19th
early C19th	Maldon, Beeleigh Mill	8¾ x 4¼ x 2½" (220 x 110 x 65)	Yellow and purple with voids and black patches, regular, smooth and slightly creased, horizontal pressure marks. London Stock
1827	Woodham Mortimer, Elm Farm barn	8¾ x 4¼ x 2½" (220 x 100 x 65)	Very regular, smooth, smooth base C19th
1832	Tillingham, Baptist manse	8¾ x 4 x 2½" (220 x 100 x 65)	Regular, smooth and slightly creased, smooth base, diagonal pressure mark. C18th/early C19th
1843	Chelmsford railway station	9 x 4¼ x 2½" (230 x 110 x 68)	Yellow and purple with voids and black patches, regular, creased. London Stock
*c.*1874-1890	Hatfield Peverel brickworks	9¼ x 4¼ x 2¾" (235 x 110 x 70)	Very regular, smooth, horizontal pressure marks, frog impressed W H BOTT. Late C19th/C20th
1878-1895	Boreham brickworks	9¼ x 4¼ x 2¾" (235 x 110 x 70)	Very regular, smooth, horizontal pressure marks, frog impressed W CLOVER BOREHAM. Late C19th/C20th
*c.*1894	Chelmsford, Old Court Nonconformist chapel	9 x 4¼ x 2¾" (230 x 110 x 70)	Very regular, smooth, frog impressed BEACH. Late C19th/C20th
*c.*1900	South Woodham Ferrers brickworks	8¾ x 4 x 2½" (220 x 100 x 65)	Yellow and purple with voids and black patches, irregular, shallow frog. London Stock

The Walled Garden at Cressing Temple

by Pat Ryan and David Andrews

Introduction

This study of the walled garden was prompted by the repointing of the wall by Rattee and Kett for ECC Property Services in spring and summer 1991. It was carried out on an occasional basis by the authors over a period of months, and proceeded by means of a careful and protracted examination of the wall, in the course of which types of brick, and less successfully mortar, have been identified. The brick typology for Cressing Temple is set out in another article in this volume. Building phases have been recognized by tracing the bond through each length of wall and noting where it is interrupted. This has been done reasonably thoroughly, but it is not excluded that others remain to be identified.

The garden is approximately rectangular with its long axis aligned north-south (Fig. 38). It measures about 60.0 x 42.5m, occupying an area of 2550 square metres or 0.63 of an acre. Its north wall scrapes the south-east corner of the Wheat Barn. Abutting its west wall are a former dairy and two buildings now used as garages. Immediately to the south of it, there was the Templar and Hospitaller chapel and other buildings which have been found by excavation (Hope 1986, 1987).

The wall, where original, is built of what we have called Garden Wall Tudors laid predominantly to English Bond. It is one and a half bricks thick above a plinth of somewhat variable height which is two bricks thick. Three small gates with modern wooden doors exist in the north, west and south sides of the garden. The description below proceeds clockwise round the garden considering each side separately.

Mortar

Being made of locally occurring materials, mortar tends not to change over long periods of time, and to be a poor guide to different phases of construction unless they are widely separated chronologically. At Cressing, no very serious attempt has been made to identify all the varieties of mortar present in the wall, but the following types can be readily recognized.

The main build in Tudor brickwork is bonded with a pale brownish mortar which, like most mortars of the period, is distinguished by the presence of small lumps of unburnt lime. Apart from a few small stones and a little grit, the quantity of sand in it seems to be relatively small, and seems to include as much silt as sand. This material could well be derived from a locally occurring brickearth. By modern standards, the proportion of it to lime seems to be low. It is interesting to note that the proportions for mortar mixes given by Neve (1726, 198-99) are of the order of one to two parts sand to one of lime.

A very conspicuous mortar is a gritty type which occurs

Plate 18 The north wall of the garden and the Wheat Barn (photo: D. A. Andrews)

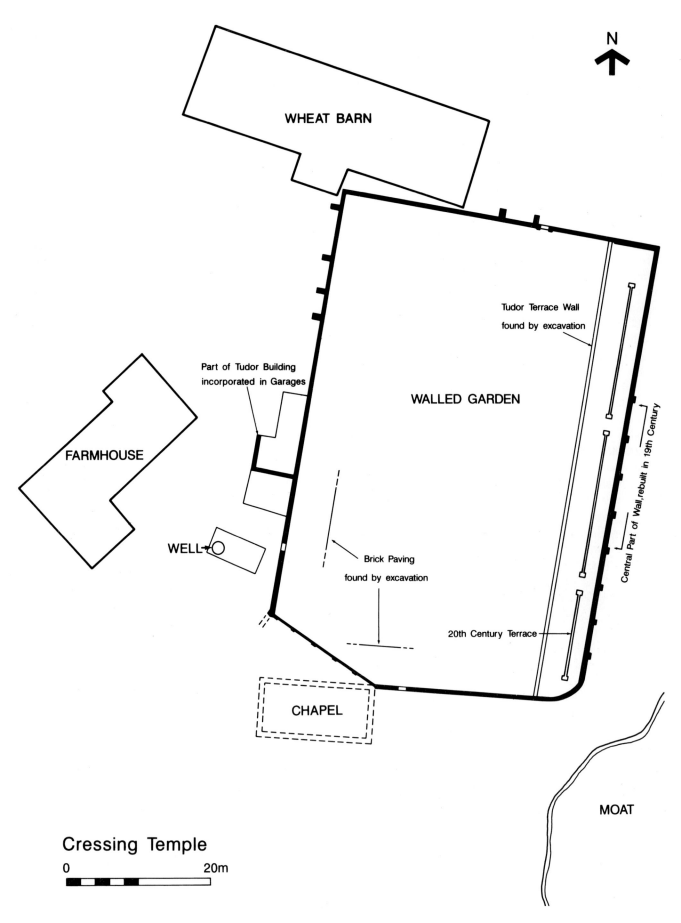

N

WHEAT BARN

Part of Tudor Building
incorporated in Garages

Tudor Terrace Wall
found by excavation

WALLED GARDEN

FARMHOUSE

Central Part of Wall, rebuilt in 19th Century

WELL

Brick Paving
found by excavation

20th Century Terrace

CHAPEL

MOAT

Cressing Temple

0   20m

Fig. 38 Plan of the walled garden. (N.B. The chapel is not precisely located)

in association with 19th century brickwork. It is sandier and darker than those in the Tudor brickwork, lacks lumps of lime, and has coarser better sorted aggregate. A brick in the nogging of the south wall of the Wheat Barn with 1829 scratched on it and set in this mortar, gives an indication of the date by which it was coming into use. 20th century mortars tend to be distinctly sandy, as a result no doubt of the availability of bulk produced washed sand.

Foundations

Excavation has shown that the west and south walls extend about seven courses below existing ground level inside the garden. However, this ground level has risen, and the brickwork of the walls in fact continues for only about two courses below the brick paving which has been found by excavation. The absence of foundations explains why the wall leans precariously in several places, though the possibility of this being caused by archaeological features such as ditches should not be excluded.

The north wall

This wall is about 43m long and belongs entirely to the main garden wall build, although much refaced and repointed (Plate 18). About 15m from the north-west corner, there is a gate. The top of the wall is finished with a soldier course for the most part in reused Tudors, though some 19th century bricks are also present. For much of its length, the wall has a very pronounced outward lean.

As elsewhere, the plinth is built in consistent English Bond. Above this, the first three courses are in the same bond, but thereafter the bond deteriorates in the header courses, there being a tendency to have a stretcher every two to three bricks.

Plate 19 The door in the north wall
(photo: D. A. Andrews)

The thicker base of the wall, two and a half bricks wide, which has also been identified in the east and south walls (see below), can be traced for 5.61m westwards from the north-east corner. This build is two courses higher than in the east wall, but the topmost course is in fact in modern bricks and seems to represent a tidying up operation.

The gate seems to be of one build with the wall, but much rebuilt above the level of the arch springing (Plate 19). This is not to be wondered at, in view of the crazy northward lean of the wall at this point. Inside, it is plain, but externally there is a hood mould made of bricks with plain chamfers on the upper and lower faces. This hood mould is interrupted at the two top corners, which suggests that the builders could not resolve this detail and therefore omitted it, an indication that the hood mould is not original in its present form. The surround in which the gate is set is the same thickness as the plinth like that of the other two gates, but, exceptionally, has a plinth on its inside face. This surround is the same width on both sides of the wall, but its edges are not opposite each other, suggesting that originally there was a rebate for a gate formed in the brickwork of the reveals. Traces of such a rebate can be recognized in the patching round the modern wooden frame of the existing door. When this door was hung, the arch on the inside was rebuilt. The eastern external jamb is also particularly rebuilt, with the use of London Stocks.

To the west of the gate, the plinth (the chamfered bricks of which have been totally renewed in this section) steps down by four courses. Curiously, this step does not correspond to the level of the plinth on the west wall where it is two courses lower. Presumably the step in the plinth is in part occasioned by a general drop in ground level from east to west, which is today more pronounced externally.

Just to the west of the step in the plinth, there has been a rebuild of the top seven courses of the wall, which are almost entirely in headers. There is an interruption in the bond above the plinth just to the east of the north-west corner. This may indicate a rebuild to the east; or else, that the corner had initially been built up to a certain height prior to the construction of the main part of the wall. A similar effect is observable in the west wall (see below).

Externally, the wall has been cut into to accommodate the south-east corner of the Wheat Barn roof. Presumably there was once a gap of a few inches but the structures have subsequently moved so that they touched each other. Since the barn would not originally have had guttering, there must have been an eaves drip ditch along this side of it in the very narrow space between it and the garden wall. In view of the likely presence of this ditch, it is surprising that the wall is more vertical in the area where it overlaps with the barn than to the east where it leans dangerously. Here it is reinforced with two buttresses, one built of 19th century bricks with horizontal pressure marks and measuring 9 x 2 $^1/_2$ x 4$^1/_2$ inches, and the other of reused Tudors resembling those used in the Granary nogging, and hence of recent construction. The latter can be seen to be built off a shallow concrete foundation. Just to the west of the recess made for the barn roof, the wall steps down three courses in height.

Apart from the features and repairs referred to above, no major rebuilds have been identified in this wall. The significance of the thicker base at its east end is discussed below.

The west wall

This wall runs north-south from the south-east corner of the Wheat Barn midstrey for a length of about 57m, at which point it turns and runs obliquely across the south-west corner of the garden. In its southern half, there is one of the three gates into the garden. To the north of this gate, the wall is adjoined externally by the former dairy and the two garages. The northern part of the wall, which is well preserved, has a conspicuous outward lean and has been buttressed. The southern half is much rebuilt above the plinth.

Below the plinth, the wall is built in English bond. Above this level, however, the bond is much less consistent: the stretcher courses include occasional shorter part bricks, whilst the header courses are very irregular with the second, third, fourth or fifth brick a stretcher or part brick.

Internally, the wall face is in places very eroded and is surprisingly unrepointed. The large number of nail holes and surviving nails, which are present right at the very top of the wall and are more numerous than on the other walls,

show that the wall has had plants trained up it. Externally, the wall is very patched, refaced and repointed. Inside, it is possible to recognize repairs done in a 19th century gritty mortar.

There are four buttresses externally at the northern end of the wall, which are described from north to south:-

1) built in tumbled brickwork, predominantly in Tudors like those in the Granary, except that these are thicker (60-65mm) with more numerous inclusions, and some on the northern side have diagonal pressure marks. The bottom of the buttress and its corners are in 19th century bricks. The buttress has been repointed in cement and it is difficult to assess the date of the original build.

2) mainly of Garden Wall Tudors, except for the western face which has been repaired and reinforced in 19th century bricks like those in the central part of the east wall. It has been much repointed and it is difficult to assess its date.

3 & 4) both clearly contemporary, built in tumbled brickwork with 19th century bricks set in gritty mortar. The bricks resemble those in the central part of the east wall.

In the area of the dairy, and for 6m to the north of it, the top of the wall, which is here 9ft 5in (2.9m) high, is finished with a coping comprising a saw-tooth course, above

Plate 20 The inside face of the west wall of the garden with the surviving portion of original coping (photo: D. A. Andrews)

which there is a stretcher course covered with pegtiles (Plate 20). This is largely built in Tudors, and in places there is in the course above the saw-tooth bricks mortar that looks original. Also present is a harder whiter mortar that must be associated with an old rebuild which might date from the 17th-18th centuries. Several modern repairs to the saw-tooth course and the course above it can be identified: 1) at the northern end, it has been remade externally in purplish frogged bricks; 2) in places, cement mortar can be detected beneath the tiles; 3) quite extensive repairs in 19th century bricks set in gritty mortar. By the northern garage, the coping has a curved profile above the saw-tooth and overlying course, whilst on the outer face the top of the wall has been raised in Tudor and 19th century bricks to serve as the end wall of the garage. It is very probable that the saw-tooth course and curved coping above it represent the original way the top of the wall was built. In support of this belief may be cited the extensive use of Tudor bricks in the coping, the original-looking mortar present in places, and the existence of early repairs. The pegtiles must be a replacement of the curved coping, which would have been finished with a single course of stretchers. Contemporary examples of brick copings with saw-tooth courses and curved sides can be seen at Beckingham Hall (Tolleshunt Major, c.1546), Leez Priory, Writtle Vicarage, Spains Hall

Plate 21 The door in the west wall of the garden showing the evidence at the base of it for it having been inserted (photo: D. A. Andrews)

(Finchingfield), and Little Braxted Hall.

It is no coincidence that this coping has survived in the vicinity of the adjacent buildings, as these must have had the effect of preserving the top of the wall from being rebuilt with soldier courses as elsewhere. Externally, where the coping begins, there is a vertical black line indicating the position of a weatherboarded structure which had been painted with pitch. This is slightly in advance of the dairy, and must mark the extent of the buildings shown on the 1794 map (Plate 8). The north garage is in origin a much older building: its south wall has a plinth and though it is rendered, it is apparent that for much of its height it is built of Tudor bricks. It can be seen that this wall returned to the north just inside the line of the existing west wall of the garage. This structure, presumably an outbuilding of some kind, was added to the garden wall, being built over its plinth, probably not long after its construction. This is no doubt the rather long narrow building depicted on the 1794 plan. It must have been rebuilt in its present form after that date. The reused 17th century timber in the north garage, which includes a spine beam with lamb's tongue chamfers and a queen-post roof, may come from the original building.

Between the north and the south garage, the wall steps down and has a Tudor soldier course flush with the inside face and covered with lead for the width of the garage. This difference in the way the top of the wall is built reflects the differing ages of the two garages.

The gate located in the southern part of the wall is 38 inches (960mm) wide. Internally the voussoirs and the top half of the jambs have a quarter round moulding like the inside surround of the south gate. This seems to be an original feature, but otherwise the gate shows much evidence of both having been inserted into the wall and of having been rebuilt. That it is an insertion has been shown by excavation at the base of it which has revealed a ragged joint between it and the wall to the north (Plate 21). Above the plinth, the wall on each side makes a straight joint against it. When the modern wooden frame was inserted, the outer face of the gate was rebuilt in 19th-20th century bricks.

The exterior of the southern part of the wall has been much refaced in 19th-20th century bricks. At the southwest corner, the wall terminates in what seems to be an angle buttress (Plate 22). In fact, the wall originally changed direction here and ran off towards the south-west. This is shown by the splay visible on the inside of the corner which is reflected externally in the presence of bricks rubbed to span this change of direction, and by the existence of a plinth on both sides of the 'buttress'. This change in direction would presumably have linked the wall with the buildings located to the south of the garden and associated with the Tudor Great House. It probably joined the brick cellar excavated by Hope (1987). The west wall of this lay outside the 1978-81 excavations, but its apparent position has been revealed by a parchmark and lines up well with the changed orientation of the garden wall at this corner (T. Robey pers. comm.).

The following features or building phases may be iden-

Plate 22 The south-west corner of the garden wall (photo: D. A. Andrews)

tified in this length of wall:

1) in the north-west corner, there is a header course above the plinth. After about 4m, this changes to stretchers and in fact the bond changes throughout the wall, apparently indicative of a rebuild to the south of it or else that the corner had been built before the rest of the wall.

2) at the north-west corner, the wall has been cut back to create circulation space between it and the Wheat Barn midstrey, being reinforced on the inside with a buttress built of reused Tudors and 19th century bricks. This alteration was presumably made necessary by movement and settlement bringing the garden wall and the midstrey into contact with each other.

3) just south of the junction between the two garages, there is an irregularity in the brickwork represented by the presence of many part bricks and a shorter plinth brick. This irregularity continues into the plinth. It corresponds with, and is presumably associated with, a slight reduction in the thickness of the upper part of the wall so that this no longer coincides with the chamfered edge of the plinth. Instead, at the top of the plinth there is a flat shelf of variable width. This suggests that the top of the wall has been rebuilt from a point just south of the garage to the south-west corner of the garden. This rebuild is bonded with an old whitish mortar which has lumps of unburnt lime and is harder than the mortar in the Tudor brickwork. A 17th-

18th century date might be suggested for it. Further evidence that this must be an old rebuild is the fact that at its southern end it preserves the change in orientation where it joined the buildings to the south which were dismantled probably in the 18th century. Internally, the face of this part of the wall has been patched with London Stocks.

4) about 3m from the south-west corner, there are what seem to be four vertical joints in the plinth brickwork about 1m apart.

The oblique wall at the south-west corner of the garden

This stretch of wall runs obliquely to the orientation of the other sides of the garden across the south-east corner of the garden, a distance of about 18m (Plate 23). Where excavations have been carried out adjacent to it inside the garden, the wall can be seen to have a shallow foundation with two slight offsets. Traces of limewash on the exterior of the wall mark the position of a former row of lean-to privies.

The main body of the wall is built of reused Tudors, including many part bricks, some with mortar adhering to their faces. On the inside face of the wall, the bricks have been laid in a fairly regular Monk bond, a variation of Flemish bond with two stretchers coming between the headers. This bond is not so regular in the lower part of the wall. The effect of this bond is that the wall consists of two brick skins with a combined thickness of 230mm tied together relatively infrequently. Externally, the bond is really only detectable in the upper four courses of the reused Tudors. This may be because the exterior face, with its southern exposure, has been more extensively repaired than the inside one.

The top seven courses, including the soldier course, are in London Stock bricks. Since a few of these Stocks occur in the lower part of the wall together with some Suffolk Whites and a possible flooring brick, it is concluded that the top and bottom of the wall are all one build. This conclusion is also supported by the the fact that the Stocks are also laid predominantly in Monk bond, and that, so far as it is possible to tell, the same type of mortar seems to have been used throughout the wall.

It has been seen that the west wall of the garden continued southwards and must have been linked with the Tudor buildings situated in area. The gap at the south-west corner of the garden was partly occupied by the chapel. This is known to have been still in existence in the mid-17th century, and is presumed to have been demolished later in that century or early in the succeeding one at the same time as the Great House. The 1794 estate map (Plate 8) shows a wall in approximately the same position as the existing one at the south-west corner. The 1842 tithe map represents the garden as rectangular, without a chamfered corner. The 1st edition OS map of 1875 shows the garden wall as it is today. This evidence is difficult to reconcile with the date

in the first half of the 19th century indicated by the brickwork of the oblique wall. The tithe map may be inaccurate, as it depicts a group of trees at the south-west corner which may have concealed the wall's alignment. The situation on the 1794 map may be explained by there having been a fence or an earlier wall on the position of the existing one, or by the top of the wall being a rebuild, or by London Stocks having been used earlier at Cressing than is thought.

The south wall

This is a wall of one build running from the curved southeast corner to the oblique stretch at the south-west angle of the garden. There is a gate located in the west end of it.

The wall is built of Garden Wall Tudors, laid consistently in English bond in the plinth. Typically, in the few courses of the wall that survive above the plinth, the bond is much less regular. Externally, the wall is very repointed. Both internally and externally, there are numerous replacement bricks, often conspicuous because of the tile slips and part bricks adjacent to them, the modern bricks being shorter than the Tudors.

At its west end externally, the wall is butt-ended, terminating in alternating headers and stretchers, the headers being preceded by closers (Plate 24). Something of the same effect can be seen on the inside face, though here it is not so clear, partly because on this side the oblique wall has been built up to and over it. Both inside and outside, this end of the wall looks rebuilt. It will be argued below that

Plate 23 View of the south side of the walled garden (photo: D. A. Andrews)

Plate 24 The south door, with to the left of it the joint with the 19th century build (photo: D. A. Andrews)

this end of the wall originally adjoined the chapel. If this was indeed the case, it is very likely that it was butt-ended from the first and that its altered appearance results from repairs and refacing.

There are three drain holes at the base of the wall, one to the west of the gate and two to the east of it. Because these are capped with stretchers which occur in header courses, they must be original. That to the west of the gate is two courses deep and at the same level as the brick paving; those to the west of it are three courses deep. The easternmost drain hole is visible in the hole created when the medlar tree fell in the 1987 gale. This also exposed a Tudor brick wall running northwards which is interpreted as forming one side of a terrace running the full length of the east side of the garden. This terrace wall is butt-ended and would seem to have made a straight joint against the plinth at the base of the garden wall. The gap of 3-4 inches between the terrace wall and the garden wall is probably to be explained by the outward lean of the latter.

The gate (Plate 24) seems to be integral with the wall. Externally, however, the presence of closers in three courses in the plinth to the east of it may be evidence to the contrary. To the west the wall is very patched and there are no closers to be seen. The gate has been rebuilt above the arch springing, the arch today being slightly too wide for the jambs on the inside. Furthermore, the square hood mould

on the inside, which is made of rubbed bricks with an ogee profile, has gaps at its corners, evidence that it has been reset. There is however no reason to think the hood mould is not original; indeed, some of the hood mould bricks have traces of plaster adhering, as do some of the moulded jamb bricks, indicating that on the inside at least the gateway was originally plastered in imitation of stone. The jambs and voussoirs on the inside are shaped to a quarter-round moulding, which on the jambs stops somewhat above ground level. Externally, a piece of oak can be seen in the east jamb. It doubtless served as a fixing for a pintle or a door-frame. The modern oak door hangs on a frame set in the outside of the gateway arch, which was rebuilt when it was inserted. The urn in a greyish synthetic stone on top of the gate would seem to be an interesting and important instance of the survival of a piece of garden furniture, but it is of uncertain age and provenance.

At the base of the east end of the wall, the plinth is two and a half bricks wide, instead of two bricks wide, for a distance of or at least 5.33m. This thicker plinth exists for the full length of the east wall, and also at the east end of the north wall. As on the east wall, the top three courses of this original build have been hacked off. It seems probable that this was done to make the plinth coincide with the new ground level formed when the existing terrace in the Marriage bricks was created. Measuring from the top of

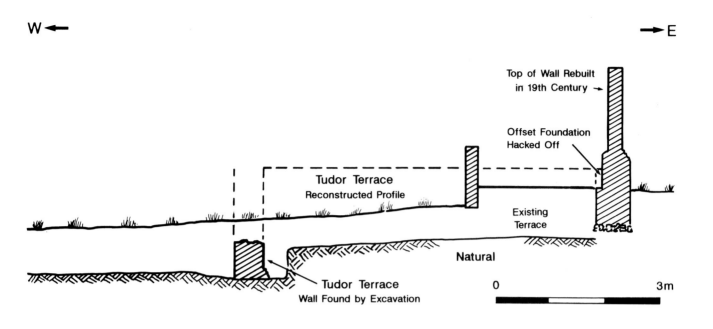

W ←   → E

Top of Wall Rebuilt
in 19th Century →

Offset Foundation
Hacked Off

Tudor Terrace
Reconstructed Profile

Existing
Terrace

Natural

0   3m

Tudor Terrace
Wall Found by Excavation

Fig 39 Sketch section through the east side of the garden to show the former and existing terraces

Plate 25 View of the east side of the walled garden (photo: D. A. Andrews)

the original build to the level of the nearby drain hole, which coincides with the level of the brick paving found in the excavations, gives an estimated height of about 1.3m for the original terrace (Fig. 39). The reduction of the level for the modern terrace presumably provided spoil to create a gentle slope down from this terrace to the ground level in the rest of the garden. The west end of the thicker plinth has been tidied up and squared off in modern bricks.

The east wall

This is a very obviously much rebuilt stretch of wall 60m long (Plate 25). The base of it has a dramatic outwards lean. Several buttresses have been built in the pious hope of controlling this instability.

The wall can be divided into three main builds (north, central, and south). Its building history is however more complicated than this, and may be divided into the following building sequence:

1) as already mentioned, the entire length of the wall has a plinth two and a half bricks thick, half a brick thicker than elsewhere. This is evident at the base of its central and southern sections where there are three apparent courses of headers which are the result of the wall having cut

Plate 26 The east wall of the garden, showing the contrast between the Tudor brickwork of the northern part of the wall and the thinner 19th century build of the central section (photo: D. A. Andrews)

back and reduced in thickness by half a brick. The original wall thickness is discernible at ground level where the brick facing survives at the same level as the modern terrace paving. This wall two and a half bricks thick could be interpreted as representing either an earlier phase of garden wall or else the remains of some other building entirely. There is however nothing to indicate convincingly that it is of a different build to the rest of the wall. In particular, there is no evidence of a rebuild externally. It seems reasonable to conclude therefore that the thicker plinth was an original feature of the garden wall. The northern third of the east wall is constructed of Garden Wall Tudors (apart from extensive 19th century refacing) and seems to be of one build with the plinth. This part of the wall, and the plinth for its entire length, are therefore interpreted as what survives of the original wall on this side of the garden.

2) the three small buttresses on the exterior of the southern section of the wall are built with rather distinctive well made bricks that look late 17th to early 18th century.

3) the central part of the wall was rebuilt above the plinth to a thickness of only one brick in Flemish bond with 19th century frogged bricks (19th-20th century type 2 bricks, Plate 26). The mortar is gritty, as is typical of the 19th century mortars at Cressing. Externally, this build has four buttresses, the bottoms of which are in reused Tudors and cut into the plinth. They could originate with an earlier build, but there is no obvious reason to think that this was so. At the base of this central portion of wall, there are three courses of Tudors which are part of the 19th century rebuild, because they belong to a wall only one brick thick and are bonded with gritty mortar. These bottom courses are overlapped by the stretch of wall to the south, indicating that this middle part of the east wall is earlier than the build at its southern end.

4) the top of the plinth in the southern third of the wall is capped with a tile course, which served not just to level off the plinth but also to protect the joint that is exposed because of the reduction of the wall thickness to 9 inches above the plinth. Above the tile course, the wall is made with reused Tudor bricks, including part bricks, laid to stretcher bond with the occasional header. The mortar is sandy and yellow. At two points, possible building phases are evident in this section where headers appear one above the other in alternate courses. It may or may not be of significance that 19th century bricks occur in the north and south parts of this section, but not the central one.

5) the terrace that flanks the wall here is built with rather dark red bricks, the frogs having 'Marriage' stamped on them. They are datable to the early 20th century.

6) the south-east corner of the garden is rounded. That it was rectangular can be seen from the original footings apparent at the base of it on the inside. The plinth is largely of reused Tudors, including Granary Tudors. Otherwise the wall is built of soft red bricks bonded with a sandy mortar. One of the bricks has the date '1965' scratched on it, apparently recording the reconstruction of this corner after it had been damaged in an accident (R. Martin pers. comm.).

Discussion

The garden wall was built originally with a large somewhat rough Tudor brick datable to the 16th century. Since it would make best sense for the garden to have been laid out after Cressing Temple passed to the Smyth family in 1539, its construction may be assigned to the second half of that century.

The wall lacks true foundations. On its west side, there survives a length of curved brick coping above a stretcher course overlying a sawtooth course which represents the way the top of the wall was originally built. If correct, then the wall was 9-10 ft (2.7-3.0m) high. It is one and a half bricks thick (380mm), increasing at the base below a chamfered plinth to two bricks thick (500mm). On its east side, however, the plinth is two and a half bricks thick, and the base of the adjoining 6-7m of the north and south walls is of a similar thickness.

Initially, it was thought that this thicker portion of the wall represented an earlier structure, but it is more likely to be associated with a terrace wall which is one of the few original features of the garden that has been identified. This has been found by excavation. It runs north-south the full length of the garden, its south end terminating by the fallen medlar tree. This terrace was about 6m wide, and can be estimated to have been about 51 inches (1.3m) high. It is suggested that the walls on the east side of the garden were thicker because they had to revet this extra depth of earth, which would have put a significantly increased load on them in view of the absence of good foundations. Against this interpretation, it should be noted that the terrace wall only butts, and is not bonded with, the garden wall, and is only one and a half bricks thick.

The terrace reveals the garden to have been ornamental in character, not simply a kitchen garden, though in the manner of Tudor gardens it would have served for the cultivation of useful herbs and vegetables as well as being a place of resort for the occupants of the Great House. The terraces of Tudor gardens generally had features such as pavilions, viewing platforms, and summer houses. There is only circumstantial evidence that such things may have existed at Cressing. The very rebuilt state of the east wall could be because it was once adjoined by buildings or because its pronounced outward lean has caused it to collapse on several occasions. The southern two-thirds of it date from the 19th century. Any structures that may have existed had disappeared long before then as none are depicted on the 1794 plan.

The only other possibly original feature of the garden has also been found by excavation. This is an area of brick paving just over 5m wide which has been found flanking parts of the south and west walls. It is in similar bricks to those of which the wall is built, but now very badly weathered, patched and repaired. Three drain holes exist in the south wall at the level of this paving. These too seem to be original, and indicate that the pavement is at original ground level, which is about 200mm below the existing one.

The garden, which occupies an area of 0.6 of an acre,

was fitted into the space between the Wheat Barn to the north, and the chapel to the south. There were other buildings by the chapel, including the Tudor Great House which had superseded the medieval hall and preceptory. By analogy with other Tudor mansions and their gardens, the garden ought to have adjoined the Great House and to have been at approximately right angles to it. But at Cressing, it is difficult to reconcile such theory and practice. Today, all the surviving buildings have slightly differing alignments, for reasons that are elusive. The south wall of the garden is itself not at right angles to the west and east walls. It is possible that it took its orientation from the medieval chapel which must have been incorporated into this side of the garden. The exact position of the chapel in relation to the surviving above ground structures cannot be plotted with great precision, but the excavation plan (Hope 1987) shows it as being practically on a line with the south wall, and its presence may be related to the gap at the south-west corner of the garden now filled with the modern obliquely orientated blocking wall. That the south side of the garden continued on the line of the south wall in the area of this gap is demonstrated by the fact that the edge of the brick paving here is parallel to the south wall.

The south wall may simply have butted against the east end of the chapel. The west end of this wall looks butt-ended today, but it is not impossible that it has been rebuilt, in which case it may have turned southwards and formed the east side of the chapel. This is consistent with the excavator's plan which represents this end of the building with a different convention suggesting that it was in brick rather than stone. This implies that the chapel had a chancel which had been demolished either before or at the time of the construction of the garden wall. In contrast, the south end of the west wall of the garden originally changed direction slightly to the south-west. It may have been linked to other buildings than the chapel, or there may have been an entrance at this point.

The garden could not be laid out at right angles to the alignment of the chapel because this would have caused its north end to obstruct the Wheat Barn midstrey. What is not clear is why, given this inability to plan the garden as a true rectangle, its other three sides did not take their alignment from the Wheat Barn, and so avoid the very awkward junction between the two which with subsequent movement and settlement has brought them into physical contact. It might be that there were constraints in the form of other buildings. On the west side of the garden, there are the remains of a Tudor building incorporated into the northernmost of the existing garages. This probably corresponds with a long narrow building shown on the 1794 estate plan. There is however no evidence to show it pre-exists the garden. Rather it seems to be later than it, having been built up against the garden wall.

The gates into the garden are very rebuilt, and an analysis of their fabric is not an easy matter. Originally the surrounds in which they are set, corresponding to the plinth in thickness, were two bricks or 500mm wide, consisting of alternating courses of two stretchers, and one stretcher and two headers. One of the more significant alterations which has taken place to the gates is the fitting of the modern oak doors. These are hung in frames fixed in rebates which, in the case of the west and south gates at least, have been cut into the gateway reveals. The brick arches have also had to be partially rebuilt to accommodate the segmental-arched lintels of the frames. The south and west gates have the doors hung on the outside, whereas the north one has it on the inside.

The north gate differs from the other two in other ways. The brick surrounds flanking it are of equal width, but do not have their edges in opposed positions on either side of the wall. This implies that the reveals were originally rebated, and that new rebates were not cut to hang the existing door. The reveals are extensively patched, but it is possible to detect traces of such an original rebate. The gate seems to be of one build with the wall, the coursing of the brickwork to either side of it apparently not being disrupted. Otherwise the gate has chamfered jambs, and a rather crudely reconstructed hood-mould made of chamfered bricks over the external arch. At the back, but curiously not at the front, the plinth continues on to the gateway surround. At 43 inches, the gate is also wider than the other two.

The other two gates are basically similar. They are of comparable width (36 inches and 38 inches), and both have quarter-round mouldings on the inside jambs and voussoirs. The brick surrounds are no longer of equal width internally and externally, as they have been cut into to receive the oak doors, but their edges are opposite each other on either side of the wall, suggesting that originally there was not a rebate formed in the brickwork. If they originally had doors, which is presumably the case, and if these observations are correct, the doors must have been hung on wooden frames as today. An old oak baton visible in the wall thickness on the east side of the south gate might be a fixing for such a frame.

The contrast between the north and the other two gates makes it seem probable that they are of different dates, though at present it is not possible to do more than speculate as to why this might be. Excavation has, however, shown that the west gate has been inserted into the wall. It may be that, with the construction of the farmhouse which assumed its present form in the 17th century, it became useful to have an entrance on this side of the garden.

The garden wall is thus a more complicated and interesting structure than it might at first seem. It is all that remains of the Great House and its adjacent buildings, and it sheds some light on those structures. Sufficient of its original features have been identified to reveal its original ornamental character, and the many reconstructions that have taken place can be traced in some detail.

Epilogue: Future Directions

The past five years have seen a significant increase in our knowledge about Cressing Temple, as the papers in this volume show. A secure foundation has been laid for using the site as an educational resource, for presenting it to the public, and for longer term research. The work already done has made it possible to plan for the laying-out of the historic garden in the walled garden, and for the setting up in the Wheat Barn of an exhibition about the site, its buildings, and the Templars and the Hospitallers. Research will be an on-going process which will continue to inform these initiatives by assisting in our understanding of the site.

With regard to historical research, a thorough trawl has been made of the archives that obviously hold material related to the site to reconstruct the descent of the manor and the most salient facts of its history. There is however considerably more scope for work on the documentary sources, especially those relating to life on the manor. Much may also be learnt from putting the history of Cressing Temple in the context of that of other such estates, and from looking more closely at the sources for Witham and the Templar/Hospitaller property there.

From an archaeological viewpoint, the approaching completion of the restoration and upgrading of the site means that rescue work will substantially diminish. In many ways this will be no loss, as we are at a point where we need to do research work orientated to shed light on particular problems. There is immense scope for research excavation but there will always be a question mark over the resources available for such work. Since the site is a Scheduled Ancient Monument, the presumption is also that its archaeology is to be conserved rather than excavated. Non-destructive investigation such as geophysical surveying may be one way forward. A further limitation is that in Essex centuries of intensive farming and the active development of the farmyards from which this was conducted means that manorial sites often have their archaeological deposits very badly damaged whilst their surrounding landscapes are, in historic terms, degraded. The contrast with other parts of England where such sites are conspicuously advertised by the presence of various types of earthwork is striking.

Archaeology in the sense of fieldwalking and survey as much as excavation does have great potential for adding to our knowledge of the site. At present, evidence for prehistoric settlement at Cressing and its environs is minimal. But evidence for prehistoric exploitation of the Boulder Clay lands in Essex is growing. In particular, the identification of a pattern of long linear fields of apparently prehistoric date, a totally new discovery in Essex, suggests that the area was being opened up early for agriculture and that there are a number of settlement centres yet to be identified.

The Roman settlement, which was clearly of some significance, remains to be investigated, and its main focus has yet to be located. In the past, it has been regarded as possibly a villa, but the available evidence is more cautiously interpreted here as indicating a farmstead.

Whatever the case, no argument for continuity of settlement of the sort that has been put forward for Rivenhall (Rodwell and Rodwell 1986) can be proposed here, because for the moment the Anglo-Saxon period is a total blank apart from a few late Saxon sherds. There is as yet no clear archaeological evidence of occupation between the 4th century and the arrival of the Templars in 1137. Whether this is an accurate reflection of the site's settlement history, or the result of the notorious difficulty of finding traces of Anglo-Saxon occupation in Essex, is something that perhaps only large scale excavation could demonstrate.

However, although not mentioned by name, Cressing is thought to be identifiable as part of the main Witham holding described in Domesday Book. In theory, therefore, there is a Late Saxon farmstead that remains to be discovered. It is uncertain in the present state of knowledge where this is likely to be, for there is a question mark over the settlement and ecclesiastical geography of Cressing. The problem is the relative importance of Cressing Temple and the village site. Why did the Templars opt for Cressing Temple rather than the existing village centre? The problem has been discussed by Ryan above (p. 19). In brief, both places have produced Roman finds and might be regarded as centres of some antiquity. The parish church has been partially excavated, and evidence has been found for a pre-existing timber structure of uncertain function together with a little Saxon as well as medieval pottery (Hope 1984b). Matilda's grant of 1137 included 'the church of the vill', though this might be a standard phrase rather than an accurate description of the situation on the ground. The wording was certainly incorrect in detail, as Cressing parish church was not officially recognized as such until the 15th century. Previously it was a chapel dependent on Witham church. A 14th century document records the foundation by Elphelinus and his wife of a chapel at Cressing, presumably the existing parish church, at some unknown earlier date but probably in the 12th century. Stephen's grant of the manor of Witham excluded Witham church, and thus the chapel at Cressing, as it had previously been granted to St. Martin le Grand. This implies that the chapel was in existence at the time of the gift of the Witham church to St. Martin le Grand.

There can be no doubt that Cressing was originally part of a larger estate based on Witham, even if in the time of the Templars and the Hospitallers it was a more valuable manor than Witham. Of the development of Cressing itself, it can be speculated that:

1) it was a polyfocal settlement, with farms or hamlets at Cressing Temple and Cressing village, both places which had been, or were close to, settlement centres in Roman and earlier times.

2) that the Templars took over the main estate and set-

tlement centre at Cressing Temple, moving the local inhabitants out to the existing village where Elphelinus and his wife founded a new chapel.

3) that the Templars established a new estate centre at Cressing Temple, either coincidentally occupying a Roman site or bringing new importance to an ancient but now decayed settlement site. Progressive reclamation of the land, reflected in the building of the two barns, could be interpreted as supporting this view.

These hypotheses raise wider questions about the local topography and settlement pattern. It is uncertain whether this settlement pattern was in place before the Norman Conquest, or whether the Normans made radical alterations to it in the 71 years before the Templars were granted Cressing. The Templars very probably carried out some reorganization of the settlement pattern, but whether this was small or large scale has yet to be established.

In an exceptional piece of detective work, Ryan and Hunter have reconstructed the extent of the Templar demesne farm and woodland. It is proposed that the Cressing Temple estate was reclaimed from the extensive woodland which had recolonized the area in post-Roman times. If so, then this would best fit the parameters of the third model suggested above. By examining the timber conversion required for the construction of the two great barns, Rackham has shown that they were built of material from systematically managed woodlands. It is clear therefore that the Templars began to manage their woodland in this way immediately upon their acquisition of the estate, or else that the woods were already being so managed. These are issues on which a parish-wide fieldwalking programme and hedgerow survey would undoubtedly shed much light, and ideally such work needs to be carried out.

It is not only the wider landscape but also the microtopography of the site of Cressing Temple itself which presents problems. Apart from the surviving buildings, little is known about the layout of the Templar manor. Only the chapel and a stone building, a hall or more likely a detached chamber with an upstairs room over an undercroft, have been located. It is predictable that the buildings on the site comprised the usual suite of structures typical of any manorial centre, and indeed there is documentary evidence that this was so. The ground plan of a manor is however less predictable, and if the excavated Templar site of South Witham (Current Archaeology 1968) is anything to go by, it could be quite irregular. Equally it is predictable that the site was divided into courtyards or wards by boundary ditches, but exactly where these were is uncertain. It may be speculated that the existing moats, which do not define a normal moated site but instead a rather extensive and, because they are incomplete, undetermined area, began life as substantial boundary ditches enclosing the manorial site. Their original course, and the alterations effected to them, have yet to be understood. The pond to the south on the other side of the Braintree to Witham road may have been part of them, or else a fishpond or a millpond.

The best understood features of the Templar manor are the two great barns. The study of these is nearing completion though there are still problems over the original size and structural details of the Barley Barn, and there is still more to do on the the investigation and survey of the Wheat Barn. Their carpentry had already been fully investigated by Hewett (1967, 1969, 1980). The successive alterations to them have now been largely unravelled and, with the aid of dendrochronolgy, dated. By skilfully reconstructing contemporary barns from fragments of timber which have been incorporated in later buildings, Stenning has succeeded in putting the Cressing barns in context. What emerges is that they were much larger than those erected at many other manors, and the superior quality of their carpentry and design has been confirmed.

By the 16th century, if not before, the Hospitallers were leasing out the manor house at Cressing. This may well have led to alterations at the site, with the residential accommodation being improved. The dissolution of the Hospitallers in England and the transfer of the estate to the Smyth family certainly saw changes to the topography of the manorial centre. The only surviving buildings of this period are the walled garden, the north wing of the farmhouse, and the Granary. The Great House, the brewhouse and dairy, the dovehouse and the coach house with a granary above have all vanished, and in most cases their location can only be guessed at. There can be no doubt that much could be discovered about them by further excavation. The changing fortunes of the farm once it became tenanted in the 18th century are reflected in its buildings. The Great House and many of its outbuildings were pulled down and the walled garden became a kitchen garden. The Granary, the ground floor of which had functioned as a malthouse, was converted into stabling in the late 18th century. Stockyards were created in the 19th century round the two great barns which had lean-to structures added to them. With the increased importance of cereal growing in the 20th century, these have since been almost all pulled down.

Cressing Temple has proved a valuable laboratory for dendrochronolgy and for the study of local brickwork. The majority of attempts to obtain tree-ring dates for Essex timbers had hitherto been unsuccessful. Cressing has provided timbers with suffcent rings and covering a sufficiently wide time span to make it possible to construct an Essex tree-ring sequence from the 12th to the the 18th century, albeit with two significant gaps. Further work planned on the Granary should help to reduce the size of those gaps, and this sequence should prove invaluable for dating buildings elsewhere in the county and the region. By looking simultaneously at the full range of characteristics of the brickwork, it has been possible to create a dated typology and to show that bricks can be dated with greater precision than was previously thought, often to within fifty years. This typology should prove very useful to those interested in or working with old buildings.

In the light of what has already been learnt about the site, the following research objectives can be indicated:-

Buildings	- completion of the study of the barns - full study of the Granary and farmhouse, including tree-ring dating	
Excavation	- investigation of the Roman and earlier deposits on Dovehouse Field, to define their extent and character - investigation of the central area of the site, to check for Anglo-Saxon settlement, to unravel the changing pattern of moats and boundaries, to establish the ground-plan of the Templar/Hospitaller manor, and to discover the site of the Tudor Great House - investigation of the area of the pond to the	

south of the site

Field and parish survey - completion of the documentary study of the parish and of Witham
- completion of the hedgerow survey for the parish
- study of medieval buildings in the parish
- fieldwalking throughout the parish
- trial excavation at selected sites in the parish.

Just as Cressing has become a type-site for barns, dendrochronology and brickwork, so it is to be hoped that it will come to have similar importance in the study of Essex settlement patterns and manorial centres.

Bibliography and References

Andrews, D D and Boutwood, J 1983-84 Grange Barn, Coggeshall. Notes on discoveries made during the 1983-84 restoration, *Essex Archaeology and History*, 16, 150-53

Andrews, D, Bedwin, O and Hall, R 1986 Plaster or stone? Some observations on Layer Marney church and tower, *Essex Archaeology and History*, 17, 172-75

Andrews, D D, Milton, B M, and Walker, H 1990 Harwich: its archaeological potential as revealed in excavations at George Street and Church Street, *Essex Archaeology and History*, 21, 57-91

BL British Library

Bray, W ed 1907 *The diary and correspondence of John Evelyn*, London: Routledge & Sons

Briggs, N 1992 *John Johnson. Georgian architect and County Surveyor of Essex*, Chelmsford: Essex Record Office

Britnell, R H 1968 The making of Witham, in *History Studies* 1, Oxford: Pergamon Press, 13-21

Britnell, R H 1983 Agriculture in a Region of Ancient Enclosure, 1185-1500, in *Nottingham Medieval Studies*, 27, 37-55

Broughton, H E ed 1985 *Nevill Holt: studies of a Leicestershire estate*, Leicester: Leicestershire Record Office

Brown, N 1988 A late Bronze Age settlement on the Boulder Clay plateau: excavations at Broads Green 1986, *Essex Archaeology and History*, 19, 1-14

Brown, N 1989 Great Waltham, Broads Green, in A Bennett, and P Gilman, The work of the County Council Archaeology Section, 1988, *Essex Archaeology and History*, 20, 147-56

Brown, N and Bartlett, R 1992 A tanged chisel/leatherworking knife from Sheering: and prehistoric finds from the valley of the Pincey Brook, *Essex Archaeology and History*, 23, 114-65

Brown, N and Flook, R 1990 Archaeology at Cressing Temple, 1988-90, *Essex Journal*, 25, 39-41

Butler, L and Given-Wilson, C 1979 *Medieval monasteries of Great Britain*, London: Michael Joseph

Cal Inq Post Mortem *Calendar of Inquisitions Post Mortem and other analogous documents preserved in the Public Record Office. Edward I*, vol. II, London: HMSO, 1906

Cal State Papers, Committee for Compounding 1643-46 *Calendar of the proceedings of the Committee for Compounding &c., 1643-1660, preserved in the State Paper Department of Her Majesty's Public Record Office. Cases 1643-1646*, London: HMSO, 1890

Cal State Papers, Committee for Compounding 1654-59 *Calendar of the proceedings of the Committee for Compounding &c. 1643-1660 preserved in Her Majesty's Public Record Office. Cases Jan. 1654-Dec. 1659*, London: HMSO, 1892

Cantor, L 1987 *The changing English countryside 1400-1700*, London: Routledge and Kegan Paul

Caulfield, S 1978 Neolithic Fields: the Irish Evidence, in H C Bowen and P J Fowler, *Early land allotment*, Oxford: British Archaeological Reports 48.

Celoria, F ed 1971 Edward Dobson's "A rudimentary treatise on the manufacture of brick and tiles" (1850), *Journal of Ceramic History*, 5

Clarke, C P Forthcoming *Excavations to the south of Chignall Roman villa, Essex, 1977-81*, East Anglian Archaeology

Cox, A 1979 *Survey of Bedfordshire. Brickmaking. A history and gazetteer*, Bedfordshire County Council

Current Archaeology 1968 South Witham, *Current Archaeology*, 9, 232-37

Dobson, L B ed, 1970 *The Peasants' Revolt of 1381*, Macmillan

Drury, P J 1975 Post-medieval brick and tile kilns at Runsell Green, Danbury, Essex, *Post-Medieval Archaeology*, 9, 203-11

Drury, P J 1976 Observations at Bardfield Saling church, *Essex Archaeology and History*, 8, 275

Drury, P J 1977a Brick and tile, in F Williams, *Excavations at Pleshey Castle*, Oxford: British Archaeological Reports 42, 82-86

Drury, P J 1977b Floor tiles, in F Williams, *Excavations at Pleshey Castle*, Oxford: British Archaeological Reports 42, 92-123

Drury, P J 1981 The production of brick and tile in medieval England, in D W Crossley ed *Medieval industry*, London: CBA Research Report 40, 126-42

Drury, P J and Pratt, G D 1975 A late 13th and early 14th-century tile factory at Danbury, Essex, *Medieval Archaeology*, 19, 92-164

Dyer, C 1986 English Peasant building in the later Middle Ages, *Medieval Archaeology*, 30, 19-45

Emmison, F G 1978 *Elizabethan life - Essex gentry's wills*, Chelmsford: Essex Record Office

ERO Essex Record Office

Fawn, A J 1984 A kiln at Olivers, Stanway, *Colchester Archaeological Group Annual Bulletin*, 27, 19-24

Fawn, A J 1985 A kiln at Olivers, 1985; second report, *Colchester Archaeological Group Annual Bulletin*, 28, 7-20

Fergusson, P 1984 *Architecture of solitude. Cistercian abbeys in twelfth-century England*, Princeton University Press

Firman, R J and P E 1967 A geological approach to the study of medieval bricks, *Mercian Geologist*, 299-318

Gardner, J S 1955 Coggeshall Abbey and its early brickwork, *Journal of the British Archaeological Association*, 3rd ser, 18, 19-32

Gervers, M 1982 *The Cartulary of the Knights of St John of Jerusalem in England - Secunda Camera*, Oxford: British Academy

Gibson, A V B 1974-76 The medieval aisled barn at Parkbury Farm, Radlett: thirteenth-century rafters re-used, *Hertfordshire Archaeology*, 4, 158-63

GLRO Greater London Record Office

Gunther, R T ed 1928 *The architecture of Sir Roger Pratt*, London (reprinted 1972)

Hall, D 1988 The Late Saxon countryside: villages and their fields, in D. Hooke ed., *Anglo-Saxon settlements*, Oxford: Blackwell, 99-122

Hale, W 1858 *The Domesday of St Paul's of the year MCCXXII*, London: Camden Society Old Series no. 69

Harley, L S 1974 A typology of brick: with numerical coding of brick characteristics, *Journal of the British Archaeological Association*, 3rd ser, 37, 63-87

Hartley, D 1939 *Made in England*, London: Eyre Methuen (1977 reprint)

Harvey, P D A 1991 The documents of landscape history: snares and delusions, *Landscape History*, 13, 47-52

Henderson, T 1986 *The parish church of Saint Nicholas, Witham, Essex*, Witham

Hewett, C A 1967 The barns at Cressing Temple, Essex, and their significance in the history of English carpentry, *Journal of the Society of Architectural Historians*, 26, 48-68

Hewett, C A 1969 *The development of English carpentry 1200-1700. An Essex study*, Newton Abbot: David and Charles

Hewett, C A 1980 *English historic carpentry*, Chichester: Phillimore

Hope, J H 1976 Preliminary Excavations at a Belgic Site at Cressing, *Essex Journal*, 11, 50-60

Hope, J H 1978 A cropmark at Cressing, *Essex Journal*, 13, 27-31

Hope, J H 1984a Excavations in Cressing churchyard, 1979, *Essex Journal*, 18, 72-95

Hope, J H 1984b Excavations at All Saints church, Cressing, Essex, 1979, in *Four church excavations in Essex*, Chelmsford: Essex County Council Occasional Paper no 4

Hope, J 1986. The Knights Templar and the excavations at the Cressing Temple, 1978-81, part 1, *Essex Journal*, 21, 31-34

Hope, J 1987 The Knights Templar and the excavations at the Cressing Temple, 1978-81, part 2, *Essex Journal*, 22, 67-71

Hope, J. In prep. *Excavations at Cressing Temple, Essex, with a a survey of the parish of Cressing*

Hunter, J M, Hedges, J D, Roberts, G C S, and Ranson, C E 1974 *Essex Landscape no.1: Historic features*, Essex County Council .

Huggins, P 1972 Monastic grange and outer close excavations, Waltham Abbey, 1970-72, *Essex Archaeology and History*, 4, 30-127

Larking, B L and Kemble, J M 1857 *The Knights Hospitallers in England, being the Report of Prior Philip de Thame to the Grand Master Elyan de Villanova for AD1338*, London: Camden Society Old Series no. 65 (reprinted 1968)

Lees, B A ed 1935 *Records of the Templars in England in the twelfth century - The inquest of 1185*, London: British Academy

Lloyd, N 1925 *A history of English brickwork*, London: H. Greville Montgomery (reprinted 1982, Antique Collectors' Club)

LRO Leicestershire Record Office

Jones, S 1980 Whiston Hall Barn, Whiston, *Archaeological Journal*, 137, 431-32

MCR Records of Merton College, Oxford

Mitchell, C F 1930 *Building construction. Part 2. Advanced course*, London: Batsford

Morant, P 1768 *The history and Antiquities of Essex*

Neve, R 1726. *The city and country purchaser, and builder's dictionary: or the compleat builder's guide*, London (reprinted Newton Abbot: David and Charles 1969)

Newton, K C 1960 *The manor of Thaxted in the fourteenth century*, Chelmsford: Essex County Council

Newton, K C 1970 *The manor of Writtle*, London

Ollard, S L and Crosse, G 1912 *A Dictionary of English Church History*, London and Oxford: Mowbray & Co.

Perkins, C 1910a The Knights Templars in the British Isles, *English Historical Review*, 98, 209-30

Perkins, C 1910b The wealth of the Knights Templars in England and the disposition of it after their dissolution, *American History Review*, 15, 252-63

Poos, L R 1991 *A rural society after the Black Death: Essex 1350-1525*, Cambridge University Press

PRO Public Record Office

Rackham, O 1972 Grundle House: on the quantities of timber in certain East Anglian buildings in relation to local supplies, *Vernacular Architecture*, 3, 3-10

Rackham, O 1976 *Trees and woodlands in the British landscape*, London: Dent

Rackham, O 1980 *Ancient woodland: its history, vegetation, and uses in England*, London: Edward Arnold

Rackham, O 1986 *The ancient woodland of England: the woods of south-east Essex*, Rochford: Rochford District Council

Rackham, O 1992 Gamlingay Wood, *Nature in Cambridgeshire*, 34, 3-14

Rackham, O 1993 The Rivenhall woods, in W J and K A Rodwell, *Rivenhall: investigations of a villa, church and village, 1950-1977*, London: CBA Research Report 80, 120-25

Rackham, O, Blair, W J, and Munby, J T 1978 The thirteenth-century roofs and floor of the Blackfriars monastery at Gloucester, *Medieval Archaeology*, 22, 105-22

RCHM 1921 *Royal Commission on Historical Monuments (England). An inventory of the historical monuments in Essex*, vol. II, London: HMSO

Rigold, S E 1966 Some major Kentish timber barns, *Archaeologia Cantiana*, 81, 1-30

Rodwell, W J, and Rodwell, K A 1986 *Rivenhall: Investigations of a villa, church and village, 1950-1977*, London: CBA Research Report 55

Salzman, L F 1952 *Building in England down to 1540. A documentary history*, Oxford: Clarendon Press

Tittensor, A M and Tittensor, R M 1986 *The rabbit warren at West Dean near Chichester*, Arundel: Tittensor

Tyers, I 1992a *Cressing Temple Barley Barn*, Museum of London Archaeological Service Dendrochronology Report DEN01/92 (unpublished report)

Tyers, I 1992b *Cressing Temple Wheat Barn*, Museum of London Archaeological Service Dendrochronology Report DEN05/92 (unpublished report)

Upton-Ward, J M 1992 *The Rule of the Templars*, The Boydell Press

Weller, J 1986 *Grangia et orreum*, Bildeston Booklets

Wymer, J and Brown, N Forthcoming *Excavations at North Shoebury, Essex: Settlement and economy in south-east Essex 1500 BC-AD1500*, East Anglian Archaeology